Unexpected

The sequel to *The Silver Poplar*

Edmond Smith

Ark House Press
arkhousepress.com

© 2022 Edmond Smith

All rights reserved. Apart from any fair dealing for the purpose of study, research, criticism, or review, as permitted under the Copyright Act, no part may be reproduced by any process without written permission.

Unless otherwise stated, all Scriptures are taken from the New International Translation (Holy Bible. Copyright© 1996, 2004, 2007, 2013 by Tyndale House Foundation. Used by permission of Tyndale House Publishers Inc., Carol Stream, Illinois 60188. All rights reserved.)

Some names and identifying details have been changed to protect the privacy of individuals.

Cataloguing in Publication Data:
Title: Unexpected
ISBN: 978-0-6455397-8-3 (pbk)
Subjects: Biography;

Design by initiateagency.com

The Call

"Come, my Way, my Truth, My Life:
Such a Way, as gives us breath:
Such a Truth, as ends all strife:
And such a Life, as Killeth death"

(George Herbert, 1593 – 1633)

Contents

Acknowledgements vii

Introduction ix

The Unexpected Teacher (Part One) 1

The Unexpected Teacher (Part 2) 22

By and Beyond the Pentridge Walls 45

Is That a Place? 91

Wal Wal 103

To the Satellite Town 115

Watsonia 135

Meeting the Queen 146

Fanning into Flame God's Gift 191

The Broken Spirit, a Mending Heart 210

The Unexpected Teacher Again 229

Restoring the Years of the Locusts 263

Waterloo Bay 287

Anyone Can Know 304

Abdul Abul Abul Amir 329

Aradale 352

Aradale Revisited 367

Acknowledgements

To the one I have loved "more today than yesterday, but not as much as tomorrow." I speak of Kerryn, who has been a soulmate for more than fifty years, and who has greatly contributed to this book *"Unexpected."* She has been a typist, assisted a friend to edit, an arranger of all the material that went towards submitting the manuscript. It would not have been possible to have this book published without her.

To James and Nicole of *Ark House* for their patience and the encouragement to "press on" (excuse the pun!)

To two wonderful friends in the Lord – Bill and Tony, who, despite their busyness, made time to read the manuscript and were able to reach the heart of *"Unexpected"* in their own individual ways.

To my family who are not only close geographically to Kerryn and me, but have given close support and inspiration in my life as an author. Of particular thanks to Brent and Belinda who helped with preparation of the photos.

Introduction

When I was contemplating on writing a sequel to *The Silver Poplar*, I decided to title it *Unexpected*, for it begins with my life once I left the Sutherland Homes for neglected children in early 1960, weighed down by anxiety in attending Coburg Teachers' College with a view merely to become a primary schoolteacher.

I left the institution at the age of eighteen to live with Christians who had been guardians at the institution some years before, and who lived down in the valley of the village-like Diamond Creek, only two miles east of the institution.

I had become a Christian at aged 17 in a staggering way. *The Silver Poplar* tells of how it happened. For any reader unacquainted with the book, *Unexpected* will draw some attention to it again, as it was to form my future, though not in the way I expected.

Unexpected, I trust, is a true and honest story of fighting real odds of a disadvantaged start in life, but it tells also of fighting the imagined odds that dogged my days and haunted me for years once I left the institution. Anxieties clung leech-like to me, despite having a good degree of assurance from the start that all is well if one is in God's hands.

One friend said upon reading *The Silver Poplar* that I have possessed "an incredibly strong spirit to all that life had presented" to me. Admittedly, I left the Sutherland Homes with little spirit in a sense, but any strong spirit that I acquired thereafter stemmed over time from being groomed by God, Who both overcomes what weaknesses there are in all of us and Who allowed some to remain in order to remind me I shall never be as perfect as I wish until Christ comes again.

As far as possible, unlike *The Silver Poplar*, *Unexpected* has sought far more to use people's true names. Two important names no longer remain fictitious : those of the Churchmans, and that of my sister, whose Christian name is Joyce. This has a bearing on the way this book begins. At the point of leaving the institution, a certain name led to the nightmarish imagined odds that I thought I faced in the world beyond the institution's pale. It would not be a troubling matter of a true surname, but, as the story unfolds it is one I sought to hide behind in public and with no suspicion.

Still, God often brings about the unexpected – not only for His glory but as a triumph over what appeared to be a disabled mind.

The Unexpected Teacher (Part One)

"Was your mum home?" David asked as I climbed in the back seat of his baby Austin.

"Er..er,…, yes," I feebly answered.

"Let's go! To get back in time for the first afternoon lecture!" he called out.

We three teacher college students roared off down the gravel road from home in the direction of Coburg Teachers' College.

It was a day when, to my dismay on arriving at the college, I had forgotten to bring my assignment that had to be handed in that day. It was crucial to hand it in on time, otherwise one could fail the subject in mind, which could lead to failing the whole course. It was said also that the better a student's score upon completing the two years of college training, the greater the chances of being placed at a primary school in a location that you preferred to start your career. Did anybody want to be forced to teach in the dry, dusty Mallee, for instance?

Diamond Creek was not exactly next door to Coburg. I had no car. Only two students in the 30 of my college group had one – John Storey and David Smith. Both of them were full of self-confidence, could be quite risqué with raised voices, and I felt far too timid to ask them to take me home to collect the assignment. Yet, when David learnt of my plight, to my surprise he offered to drive me home to collect it. At lunchtime? Was there time? He was confident there was. Hurriedly we sped off to Bell Street, whizzed up the hill to a service station in Preston where David pulled in to fill the tank of his car. Yet, instead of going in to pay for the fuel, he leapt from the pump and jumped in the driver's seat and tore away laughing! I squirmed uncomfortably as David and the other student kept laughing well along the way.

I shrank to think David had stolen the fuel, and yet by way of dismay did not say anything to rebuke him out of a Christian conviction, for wasn't he being good in helping collect the assignment?

We barely made it to college before the afternoon lectures began.

I was grateful that David helped me out, but remained uneasy about not being seen as a consistent Christian in allowing his wrong to pass by.

Yet, I was more uneasy in a way about the question "Was your mum home?" My mum?

Cyril and Beryl Smith had been guardians at the Sutherland Homes from 1949 to 1954. It is said that Beryl was originally hired as a sewing mistress and only later was she appointed matron of the institution. Cyril retained his full-time position with the State Electricity Commission after Beryl's appointment, but played a leading role in general maintenance of the 40 acre institution. He and his wife were fervent Christians, and Cyril in particular saw himself as a spiritual guide and tutor for the boys and girls, who had been neglected by their parents for one reason or another, though 'neglected' should be seen as a loose term, since there were those urchins whose parents simply could not financially afford to keep their children in tough times, shortly after World War 2. Sutherland, strictly speaking, was not an orphanage but with children coming from homes of either wilful or unwilful neglect. Cyril and Beryl as guardians appeared to be an ideal couple to show concern for our welfare. They had two young boys; therefore they seemed to understand how many of us had known little or no family life.

However, the Committee of Sutherland became discontented with Cyril and Beryl, asking for their resignation. In a book put out with Berry Street's blessing it is stated that 'the move (of the Smiths) was of more religious or Christian nature.' It is further suggested that Sutherland's children felt relief at their resignation, for there was 'no longer any jumping out of bed and kneeling down on cold, hard floors to pray every morning.' Perhaps my memory has faded on that score, for my only memory of rising in the morning out of our dormitory beds in the Smith's days as guardians was of music blaring out of the loud speaker system (which Cyril with his skill in electrical engineering had installed), of music such as *'On Top of Old Smokey,' 'In a Persian Market Place,' 'Mockingbird Hill.'*

It was ironic for the Smiths that the Sutherland Homes in Melbourne was founded by an indomitable Scottish lady named Miss Selina Sutherland, who was also of strong Christian convictions. It is said that around 1894 she was probably the best-known woman in Melbourne. It is claimed that 'she was probably the only woman of her day who had sufficient courage to be seen in certain parts of the city,' and that 'she was the only woman of her day who was safe in such parts.' In a close-fitting two-piece dark costume and an alpine hat that carried a prominent feather she rescued thousands of children from slums in Melbourne, from gutters, from neglected homes, from starvation and desertion. After her death in 1909 a professor claimed that even though some said Miss Sutherland made blunders, he did not care. He only cared that it be known that the brave woman saw what was 'the main secret of the mission of early Christianity – to save the lost – to save the tempted – to save the wronged and the shamed – and above all, to keep them from being lost.' Cyril and Beryl merely carried out Miss Sutherland's work in the same spirit and with the same Christian conviction, only to be forced to resign!

I was at Sutherland at tender years between 8 and 13 when Cyril and Beryl were guardians.

In 1954 they left, and not long after that, they settled in Diamond Creek, a mere two miles from Sutherland. Because I attended St. John's Anglican Church quite regularly for Sunday School and the worship services each Sunday, I continued to see them. Under the new matron 'the Homes seemed more relaxed, less rigid.' The new matron was not religious, so that it made Sutherland go on record as 'more relaxed, less rigid.' It may have accounted for me feeling less concerned about spiritual matters. As a teenager, I was revelling under Matron Roscholler in a rebellion reputed to be embodied in James Dean, the young, handsome American actor, whose looks sent out the signal of discontent and broodiness. In one of James Dean's movies 'Chicken' was played. I got to playing 'Chicken' with other teenage boys on the two mile walk to church on a Sunday – lying down on the road until the oncoming cars sped towards us, jumping up and leaping from the road at the last second. I took to swearing at one of the Sunday School teachers. Cyril learnt of it, rang the new matron, and she in great anger scolded me.

Imagine Cyril's surprise, when a year on perhaps, he discovered I had become a Christian! His joy was such that, even at the risk of annoying the new matron, he began to visit me after dinner one or two times a week. We would sit in his black Dodge Brothers 1938 car as night fell – through study and prayer, talking of walking with the Lord. They were precious times for me when I was so young in the faith and Cyril was so mature in it.

Such a change had come over me that I found a love for anyone who loved Christ as I did, especially a love for him whom I called at the time 'Mr Smith.' He could have been my father, as he had a son who was only 20 days younger than me.

It would not have been the occasion perhaps to tell the fellow teachers' college student in David about my true background at the time of collecting my assignment, and at the point of racing back to college before afternoon lectures, but, even when there was sufficient time to tell the truth in those days about my upbringing, and let people such as David know that the folk of Haley Street of Diamond Creek were not my true parents, I held back. The problem lay not so much in Cyril and Beryl carrying the same surname as me, but in my sense of shame about having been raised in an institution without knowing my parents – being an orphan. Less than three years before, I would never have dreamed about living with them, nor would anyone else had thought it possible.

Not long after entering the Sutherland Homes at the age of six, an older boy tormented me for being an orphan. "Orphan, orphan!" rang on in my ears, and for all I knew it was true. Unknown to me, I was not one but that did not count: I did not then know if I were one or not, but I could not entertain the possibility I was not. It appeared my parents were dead, but with no living proof that they were not. An older boy than my tormentor countered the taunt of 'Orphan' by threatening to pummel him. It cheered me to have a stronger boy come quick to my defence, but the taunt lingered on well after that day. Even the occasional and covert slipping into my hand of a little confectionery by a certain elderly lady among the staff, seemed to single me out as someone different from the other inmates – someone to be especially pitied and to my hurt.

The fact that my tormentor labelled me an orphan suggested I may well have been an oddity among so many. Came Visiting Day – held weekly on a Sunday – and some parents would pay a visit to their children. Some never received such visits, but they knew of their parents. Some saw their fathers, or mothers, or both, only at Christmastime, but they knew their parents were at hand should they care. All I recall of Visiting Day was the strange longing for my mother to appear, even though I had no proof that I had a living mother. Such a kind of hope springs up eternal in a child. The hope was gossamer but no wild wind could break it.

The early Matrons, and the other staff, never took me aside to talk of what led to me being placed in the institution. Then again, they took no other little beggar aside either. Some knew of where they had drifted in from, but even for many of them they had emerged from a haze too thick to penetrate.

All of us were drifting to none knew where. Still, each day spun out a hope though of gossamer.

Then came the day, at age nine, when I was introduced to 'Uncle Charlie,' a man of retirement who, with his ageing wife, lived at Preston. They wanted a little boy to give him a Christmas holiday. It puzzled me that I had been selected from the other children for this, as some, who despite having parents, did not spend any time at Christmas away from the institution. I had been spending the Christmas break for a couple of years with a generous couple on a sheep farm down near Bairnsdale. This event of having two Christmas holidays to fill up the whole six weeks in the absence of the Homes impressed on me that perhaps there was something different about my past that singled me out for a special privilege, untwisting it to mean that I was not an object of pity but perhaps one worth heaping some unusual happiness on.

THE UNEXPECTED TEACHER (PART ONE)

During the first holiday with 'Uncle Charlie' and 'Auntie Lil' at Preston, 'Auntie Lil' and I walked down Dundas Street, turned the corner opposite Huttons Meat factory and into High Street, where we entered a shoe shop.

"I'd like to buy you some sandshoes, Edwin," she said.

"May I help you?" asked the retailer.

"Oh," said 'Auntie Lil,' "I wish to buy some sandshoes for the little boy."

"What size are we looking at?" asked the man.

"Do you know what size would be best, Edwin?" said 'Auntie Lil' in her rasping voice.

"I don't know," I quietly answered.

"You see," said 'Auntie Lil,' Edwin is a little orphan boy of the Sutherland Homes and he is holidaying with us; he may not know his size."

A chill ran through me.

That was just the beginning of a number of embarrassing encounters with people in public – with many neighbours in Sussex Street, with 'Auntie Lil's' family, tram conductors on the High Street run, having me labelled albeit innocently as 'the little boy from the Sutherland Homes.' It went on for several years until I became a teenager. To be branded an orphan by a tormented inmate at Sutherland was a cut with the cruel intention to shame, but then the shame carried over, despite Auntie's kind intentions. It was perhaps more like a chill than a cut. The cut made in the institution stung with no relief, but the cut did not gift me sandshoes and other good things. It was more of a chill somewhat tempered by the warmth of the old folks' kindness. All the same, I came to fear being in public with Auntie. Uncle would simply introduce me as a little boy named Edwin, a friend of the family. I suppose the dear old lady was seeking to solicit pity for sympathy's sake. It was with total relief that the second half of the Christmas holidays saw me board the train with its hissing steam bound for Bairnsdale, and arrive at Meerlieu where self-consciousness of being a supposed orphan was dulled by a welcomed silence about my origins.

Even if I had understood I was an orphan, should it have mattered? Yet a young child is sensitive to a name shot forward out of malice. I could not forgive that boy at Sutherland. An ugly silence hung over the name 'orphan'. In silence it spoke of shame or pity. It spoke of certain backwardness. No staff thought there might be a sinister silence that had to be broken.

At age 12 came high school, fronting a vast sea of unknown students, with an onrush of nightmares and fitful sleep for a month or more. That was until Matt, who regarded me as his best friend at Sutherland, unwittingly drew away from me any imagined uneasy attention with his antics. I hid behind his persona. He was a rascal but highly intelligent. Yet, at the end of his only year, and my second year at Eltham High, the time came too soon for him to leave Sutherland. Because Matt had turned 14 and Matron Roscholler found herself at the mercy of Matt's mother, who surprised even Matt in wanting to take him out of the institution and get him off to work, he left and it left me marooned, wondering about my own future. I had turned 14 that year as well. Would my father and/or my mother suddenly turn up to take me out of Sutherland and school as well? Yet did I have a father or mother? The sound of sinister silence grew louder.

I still had dreams of my mother suddenly appearing at Sutherland on Visitors' Day, and pinned my hopes on that. Yet I was too shy to ask of my origins and too afraid to do so, lest the past had truth that would be crushing.

With Matt leaving Sutherland and school, the gap between those of my year, who studied French and those who did Art and Craft instead, seemed to widen even more in terms of intellectual ability. Matt and I had been placed in the Art and Craft form from our first days at Eltham High but it did not faze me all that much until Matt left. Then it seemed that those of us at Sutherland were bound to leave school early because we lacked the nous to progress all that far scholastically. I had taken short-lived pride in becoming dux of Sutherland's primary school, which school, though little, had in my sixth year also a boy who was bound for secondary schooling at Scotch College. Why was I therefore deemed incapable of learning French at Eltham High?

On the other hand, I took solace in having done well enough at school in the year Matt left to inspire the inspector of the Children's Welfare Department of Melbourne to report that 'further schooling recommended.' In the inspector's report it was stated that my ambition was to become 'a commercial artist' or do 'clerical work in a bank.' At that time the inspector stated 'parents or relatives not known.'

Fast forward to April of 1956, Form 3 at Eltham High, when the inspector of the Children's Welfare Department visited me again. He cottoned on at last that I was commonly called 'Eddie,' said I was 'tall for (my) age.' It was before the era of teenagers thriving on chicken hormones, so perhaps I was tall for my age! He noted that I aspired to be a draughtsman upon leaving school, but went on to say: 'He is at present undergoing a phase where he feels a grudge against society which he believes owes him more than he has received from life.' His solution to bitterness lay in the 'ideal for the boy if an interested family could take him on probation, particularly with a view to furthering his education,' for 'Edwin has never been visited by any relatives.'

'Had any investigation been made concerning the possibility of relatives?' I brooded.

As Providence would have it, Providence stretched out the hand when I was sinking under the sound of silence. Four months after the inspector wrote of my "grudge against society", Matron called me to the institution's office, where she stunned me with the news that I had a sister! I had to wait three weeks for Visiting Day to come around before I could see her, and I longed for the weeks to turn into days. The discovery of a sister came about through a great-aunt of ours in Canada making enquiries through Melbourne's Children's Welfare Department.

Excitedly I wrote a letter to 'Auntie Lil.' When I woke up next morning to catch the bus for school, I could hardly contain myself through joy. Yet I told no one at school, though elated in my soul. I kept repeating to myself 'Joyce! Joyce!,' and dreaming of what she may look like. Bursting to tell everyone at Sutherland, but holding back at Eltham.

It was odd that Matron had asked me, when breaking the news to me of Joyce, if I remembered having a sister. I had been on this planet for fifteen years, and did no one know how I got here? Little if anything was learnt through meeting Joyce in those early days, as we were ever in the presence of her foster-parents whenever I spent a weekend in their terrace house in Brunswick. We would look at each other and wonder, until we discovered that the Welfare Department had made a mistake in the past by which we, as brother and sister, had been separated at the Royal Park Depot – Joyce dispatched one way, I another. We were considered too young to know its reason. But we were old enough to sense something was amiss.

The Children's Welfare Department thought they had found the answer to their prayer through the securing of a place for me with an interested family to further my education. Now that I had found my sister, would it not be more ideal for the Fordes – Joyce's foster-parents – to take me in and give me a private home at last? Over the years the Department had been exasperated at not finding interested people, finding it 'hard to understand why he had not been placed on a private basis earlier in his life, as he seems to have been quite suitable for such a placement.' In the mist of memory I recall a family once taking me out for Christmas Day but I did not warm to them, and at another time it appears that a family that had a boy around my age at Bentleigh had me stay on one weekend but they did not warm to me. Perhaps those two visits coincided with early days when the Matron of the time said 'she is afraid he is backward' and is 'very slow at learning.' The same Matron said 'he speaks very little,' perhaps would 'make better progress in a private home.' At the time that I met my sister, the inspector of the Department relished the prospect of Joyce and I living together in Brunswick. Miss Richardson reported that Mrs Forde appeared to be 'a co-operative type of woman who might possibly be able to give Eddie accommodation and home life.'

Was leaving Sutherland and living with Joyce at Brunswick to work out at the end of year Three at Eltham High? I was not initially privy to the Department's hopes but, as the weeks went by, I sensed a move on their part was afoot. For several weekends Matron dropped me off in Victoria Street, Brunswick, in front of several narrow terrace houses. We found the right place quickly after the first two or three Friday nights. Whenever we knocked on the front door, Mr and Mrs Forde were there to greet us. Mr Forde once or twice was in his fireman's uniform. He was of medium height, with greying hair brushed back, and he possessed a gravelly voice. Mrs Forde was somewhat short, quite thin and spoke quietly. Joyce came behind them, quite shy understandably, standing midway in height between both of her foster-parents. Mr and Mrs Forde saw the likeness between my sister and me, though Joyce was quite short and had dark hair above her high forehead.

Those first few weekends were spent in becoming familiar with all three of them, though the Fordes sought to focus only on the future. The sound of silence pervaded in that tiny terrace house about Joyce's past – indeed, she had the surname of Forde, and it then appeared she had been adopted into the family, for Joyce would speak warmly of 'relatives,' relatives of both Fordes.

Joyce was a ward of the Welfare Department at that time and was listed as 'Joyce Smith, No. 71527' in their records. My number was '70840.' The Department, as well as Matron, seemed surprised that we had not known of each other's existence in earlier days.

What were my own feelings about Brunswick and living with the Fordes, even though I knew nothing at first of the Department's hopes? Mr and Mrs Forde were civil but there were no signs of interest in taking me in – indeed I sensed that Mrs Forde saw the discovery of Joyce's brother as an intrusion into their life. Perhaps Mrs Forde saw some foreboding arising from her habit of reading the tea leaves in her cup, and now and then Mr Forde would look leerfully at me. Joyce sensed some tension, though she seemed glad we had found each other.

As for the house, it was frightfully small. You could hear the neighbours talking through the common walls on either side. I could hardly sleep at night for the cars zooming up and down not many yards from the claustrophobic front lounge where I lay on the small sofa. If it was a sunny day and we had returned from Sydney Road, one had to feel the way down the hallway with fingertips touching the walls in the dark until we arrived at the little kitchen where we came across an electric light switch to light up our whereabouts.

THE UNEXPECTED TEACHER (PART ONE)

The Fordes were quite poor. Only Mr Forde worked and as a fireman. Their only extravagance was attending the picture theatre on Sydney Road each Saturday night. Hitting the back-brick wall of a house in the lane way behind their place with a tennis racquet and ball, was all there was to pass the time of day. It would have relieved the Welfare Department of the burden of providing what they did for my existence if I had have lived with Joyce. However, despite the Welfare Department's hopes, Matron Roscholler's desire was for me to continue living in the institution, with the Home's committee prepared to subsidise the cost of my schooling at Eltham High for the following year so that I could fulfil the ambition to be a draughtsman.

Yet, there was some yearning to live with Joyce. Mr Forde sensed it, and thought that if he and his wife could afford larger accommodation and moved out of their tiny, rented terrace house, I could live with them. He at least appeared somewhat keen to take me in.

As it was, a battle ensued between the Welfare Department, the Matron and the Superintendent of Sutherland. Number 70840 was going on to 16 years of age – beyond 14 – and so the Department was anxious to be relieved of the expenses of having me remain a ward of the state. Mrs Wenborn, Sutherland's superintendent, stated at the beginning of 1957 in a report required by the Department that her aim and that of Matron was for me to remain at Sutherland with Sutherland's committee subsidising the cost for my year of schooling, so I could obtain my Intermediate Certificate.

The Department appeared grudging to allow me to continue at Sutherland and Eltham High, and stated by way of a footnote on the same report that Mrs Wenborn submitted to them: 'However, the Fordes could be again contacted re possible probation – they may now have better accommodation.'

UNEXPECTED

At age 16 of that year the Inspector of the Welfare Department reported that I was managing schoolwork 'well.' The very next month, at the end of first term, found my school report showing the contrary. My maths marks slumped from 87%, 89% and 90% in Form (Year) Three to 37% and 49% in Form (Year) Four. In Commercial Principles and Practice I scored 23%, with an Examination Class Average overall of a bare 41.7%! There was little evidence for Sutherland to convince the Inspector of any prospects had he assessed me only a month later!

Moreover, I had decided against becoming a draughtsman, with 'future plans (being) rather nebulous,' as the Welfare Inspector detected. I gave him the impression that I was 'a little inclined towards being a teacher.' Matron told him that I could do well in the teaching field (perhaps primary school age) 'if he could develop a little confidence in himself.'

By April 1957, the Department at last appeared resigned to the fact that the Fordes could not afford to move from their little place in East Brunswick and have me live with them and my sister.

I became quite content to remain at Sutherland, and although scholastically there was little improvement as the year went on, High School was a ball. I lived for football, enjoying eluding the school prefects at recess so that my friends and I could dash off to the school's hawthorn hedge to smoke cigarettes and dabble in drinking stout; dodge school assemblies as well as carrying out any number of other escapades. All a good lead up to becoming a schoolteacher!

It was quite accurate to say my ambitions were 'nebulous'. I would mumble 'school teaching' if someone sought to extract my feelings about the future. I am not sure why Matron thought I could do well as a teacher – I seemed to have no aptitude for it. She had to preface such a thought with the conviction that I lacked confidence in myself. My antics at school (and beyond school when others and I should have been at school during

THE UNEXPECTED TEACHER (PART ONE)

school!), and becoming besotted with Elvis whose singing gave me thrills, served as a substitute for self-confidence.

Matron's husband, Mr Roscholler, may have planted seeds of thought about becoming a teacher – I am not sure. The length of holidays that teachers had was appealing. As for confidence before groups of people, no matter their age, it did not appear promising. Mr Roscholler was a fine teacher, moved quickly up the ranks of the Education Department and had become a lecturer at the Burwood Teachers' College. However, to my dismay I discovered that I began to stutter whenever I was in his presence. Consequently, I sought to avoid his presence as far as possible. He never said anything about my stuttering but I grew most conscious of it so that it began to haunt me every time I saw him. It could be unnerving even to be in his wife's presence, therefore as much as I could muster any confidence I became resolved to pause for as long as possible before I needed to answer Mr Roscholler or his wife, taking a deep breath to speak without stumbling, It may have been that Matron sensed my stumbling over words that led her to report to the Welfare people that I could do well as a teacher so long as I had more confidence.

Mr Roscholler took me more seriously than I did myself. He was even prepared to take me to Burwood Teachers' College to give me a feel for what it meant to be a primary school teacher. Ever since I knew him as my grade six teacher at Sutherland's school, he was proud of my progress and was hopeful that I could be a teacher.

Mrs Wenborn described my appearance at that time as 'fragile but *wiry*,' yet it seemed I was only *wired* to the sound of rock and roll! Mr Roscholler sought to put me right, of course, so that I could proceed to Fifth Year and gain a Leaving Certificate in order to qualify for primary teaching.

Would the Child Welfare Department see fit to enable me to do a Fifth year at Eltham High? The Inspector of the Department himself still toyed with the vague possibility of me living with my sister, whom he described only as a boarder with the Fordes! My sister would have been horrified to learn that the Department saw her that way. Then again, at that time Joyce was still number 71527 and so still officially a ward of the state. The Inspector feared that I would not pass Year Four at school and would be forced to start work, yet Matron pinned her hopes on me attaining a Leaving Certificate, declaring Sutherland would subsidise me for yet another year.

Towards the end of Year Four the Department told Mrs Wenborn that they would have the final say about my destiny. I was a ward of the state – not that of Sutherland. Boarding payments from the Department were not likely to continue beyond the end of the year.

What a laugh! My Form Teacher stated that because I had only scraped through Year 4, in order to do Year 5, I 'had to do some study during the Christmas vacation'. For study I went to the West Melbourne Stadium, for instance, to see in action rock singers Chuck Berry, Johnnie O'Keefe and Bobby Darin!

Come 1958 and I was leaning heavily on only doing the bare minimum of four subjects required for a Leaving Certificate. Other students were doing five or six to secure more definitely a pass.

I was in one of two wards (large bedrooms) for Sutherland's boys of various ages. As boys are, they could become quite noisy at night while I pursued the homework that the school set. Curiously, in a report that appeared to have been written in haste, I was assessed as being above average at school, even though in May in Year 5 I had scored a mere first examination average in the second term of 58%! The scant school report had me as a 'tall, quiet lad, dark'. Perhaps it had been written in the dark, as I had always been previously described as 'fair'.

THE UNEXPECTED TEACHER (PART ONE)

Matron Roscholler and Mrs Wenborn became engaged one day in a conversation to assist the Department in planning for my future, and not only to assist it but persuade it.

> Matron Roscholler began, "I need to submit a report about Eddie for the Department in the next few days."
>
> Mrs Wenborn said, "We need to convince them that Eddie is doing all right, even though his May marks were not exactly outstanding."
>
> Matron had given Mrs Wenborn a run-down on my results.
>
> Said Mrs Wenborn, "Well, he has passed the First Test, hasn't he?"
>
> "Just," replied Matron tersely.
>
> "May I compare his marks with the form averages?"
>
> "Yes".
>
> "Mmm, well… 'He finds the work difficult' says his Form Teacher. I am surprised that he does not fare better in English. What can we do?"
>
> Said Matron, "He improved somewhat last year when we sent him for some Saturday mornings to the Taylor's School in the city".
>
> "Could we do that again?" asked Mrs Wenborn.

"Maybe John (Mr Roscholler) could help him. He believed Eddie showed a lot of promise in language work when *he* taught him."

"The form average for English was nothing startling – only 58%," Mrs Wenborn commented.

"Still," Matron re-joined, "he must get 50% to get his Leaving by the State's standards. Well, where the Department asks the question 'Does the ward show any aptitude or express a wish for a particular avocation (sic)?' we will write 'Teaching', even though Eddie does not seem definite about it, judging on his lack of application thus far."

In the rest of the report where the question was asked 'Is there any reason why the ward shall not be returned to relatives or be placed in employment?' My two Sutherland guardians simply replied that my schooling was incomplete.

I have told in full about the most momentous event in my life in the book *The Silver Poplar*, which occurred midway through that year of 1958. 'Auntie Lil' gave me a Bible for my birthday in memory of 'Uncle Charlie' who died about a year before. I was hostile about receiving it in the mail, as I had expressly told her before my birthday that I did not want a Bible – any book but that! On the point of setting a lighted match to it at Sutherland's incinerator, I heard the Lord say: 'Take it and read it.' The Voice was irresistible. As I read the Gospel of John, the Holy Spirit convicted me of the urgency to be saved. I was given assurance that I had eternal life to look forward to because Jesus had died for me and spared me of condemnation. I was unbelievably happy. William Barclay once said: 'There are two great days in a person's life – the day we are born and the day we discover why.' To my joy I had discovered why.

> 'O happy day that fixed my choice
> On Thee my Saviour and my God'…

Although I was not entirely certain of what awaited me in the future, I knew my future lay not at the mercy of the Welfare Department, or even on Matron's determination to see me succeed at school.

Still, my results for the Second Test in early September were scarcely better than in the First. The average for all exams was worse, though it was a pass. Disconcertingly, I failed in two subjects.

We came to the final term, and those of us doing Leaving sat for the State exams. They were to be conducted in an unfamiliar place – a church hall in Eltham. This heightened my anxiety.

As it was, I failed to obtain the Leaving Certificate for that year. I sank in misery at first, for the future looked gloomy.

When the Welfare Department was contacted in the new year of 1959 about my failure, they pointed out that the 'boarding out' payments had been discontinued at the end of the previous year so that 'Edwin would cease to be a ward on 9/6/41' (sic), on the day I came into the world! Well, the true meaning was clear: 31/12/1958. When one recalls that Sutherland ran on charity and received nothing from the government, it was no mean thing for Matron and her husband, and Mrs Wenborn, to gun for me so that I would get a second chance to obtain my Leaving Certificate. They were prepared to rely on whatever funding could be rallied by Sutherland alone. Even so, Mrs Wenborn appealed to the Welfare Department to consider making further 'boarding out' payments until I was 18. The Department surprisingly and graciously agreed to making me a ward of the state until February 1960, when hopefully I would gain a place at training college.

Yet, in order to enter a training college a surety of seven hundred and fifty pounds had to be met. *(1960 equivalent currently $23,416).* Mrs Wenborn became distressed about the bond that was needed to assure the Ministry of Education I would go through the two-year training course of a teachers' college with success. She was sure that Sutherland's committee alone could not come forward with the required money. She told the Department that Sutherland was willing to forgo the boarding out payments provided by the Department – and be prepared to meet the cost themselves for 1959 – if they 'could overcome the obstacle of the bond.'

It turned out that another ward of the state had been in a similar position to mine and that upon an appeal to the Minister of Education, the ward was allowed to enter a teachers' training college without a surety. The Welfare Department felt confident that 'Edwin's case' would be balanced to his favour. If so, my guardianship by the Welfare Department would be extended to June 9, 1960, (my nineteenth birthday) in order to be accepted for teacher training on the grounds of being still a ward of the state, when application was made.

According to Welfare, Mrs Wenborn had a false impression: The Department had not even considered withholding boarding out payments for 1959 – it being only willing to provide such support until I was 18 – so as to remove me from Sutherland and send me out to work.

Quite a number of instruments were at work to ensure I could enter a teachers' training college, but there was One who was the most effective means of making certain of it all. Yes, there was Mr Roscholler and his wife, the matron, desiring that I should be given a second chance at Leaving; there had been high school teachers in Year 4 who said it was 'well worth sending him back to school;' there was Mrs Wenborn claiming I was 'a desirable type of lad, anxious to complete his Leaving Certificate;' plus the backing of Sutherland's committee behind Mrs Wenborn, and even the

Director of Welfare giving the approval of further schooling. Despite all these people, what would make their desires or dreams certain? The hand of God.

It reminds one of the times when Israel had returned to their homeland after exile, only to find opposition to their re-establishment of the city of Jerusalem. An appeal by Israel was made to Darius the Persian King for an ancient document that had initially decreed Jerusalem could be rebuilt. The document was discovered. Darius had various officials do what he ordered.

The people of Israel began to build. Two prophets, Haggai and Zechariah, inspired them to build. It is said that the building was finished by *decree of the God of Israel* and also by the decree of Cyrus and Darius and Artaxerxes King of Persia. It is first said that the building was accomplished by God's decree for, without His decree, the project was not possible. Yes, most of all, the hand of God would have to play the greatest part in me entering college.

Of course, the Leaving Certificate still had to be obtained through diligence and much study.

The Unexpected Teacher (Part Two)

At the beginning of the year of my 'second chance' there were 60 children in the institution, though around 20 of them were now living in two cottages on the land lying between the gravel playground and a poultry farm. The farm was owned by a Mr Thomas next door, and was where I worked during the summer holidays to help defray the cost of me remaining at the Homes for 1959.

Matron allowed me to have what once had been 'the Sewing Room' at the boys' end of the extensive brick building of the Homes. This was in the hope that there would be no distraction or hardship from being in a boy's dormitory with others while attempting to study.

The large windows to the north enabled me to view the scintillating star-studded sky at night. Now I had both books – one initially of my choosing for my 17th birthday ('Stars') and one initially not (the Bible). Yet it was the Bible and the enlightenment I received by the Spirit of God about God the Father that caused me to marvel at the beauty of the stars, for God the Father created them. Moreover, the Bible, in proving to be the greater book of stars, illuminated my mind about what will be a sweet destiny through Christ having become my Saviour.

> 'Stars are poor books, & oftentimes do misse:
> This book of starres lights to eternal blisse'
>
> (George Herbert)

Nights often found me gazing at the stars, while singing a hymn I had memorized –

> 'Sun of my soul, Thou Saviour dear,
> It is not night if Thou be near;
> O may no earth-born cloud arise
> To hide Thee from Thy servant's eyes.'

> 'When the soft dews of kindly sleep
> My wearied eyelids gently steep,
> Be my last thought, how sweet to rest
> For ever o my Saviour's breast.

> 'Abide with me from morn to eve,
> For without Thee I cannot live;
> Aide with me when night is nigh
> For without Thee I did not die.'

Nights also found me groaning over the sins of the day. On my knees I was aghast at sinning against Him Who loved me so much to die for me. It disturbed me greatly to love Him so dearly and yet to sin against Him. I longingly sang 'Let (me) no more lie down in sin.' This is the joyous, troubled lot of a newborn believer.

Days made for another kind of anxiety. To begin with, there was the new year at school, where much time was to be taken up with four subjects of British History, Geography (no, not Geography again!), Economics and Art. I had passed English and Modern History in the previous year but Mr Roscholler urged me to tackle four subjects to ensure I get at least the two needed to gain my Leaving Certificate. Two years before that saw me failing with 23% and 33% in Commercial Principles and Practice exams, and I was apprehensive about doing well in Economics, yet the choice of subjects was restrictive. Geography? – both times in the first year of Fifth Year scoring 44%. British History had to be done by correspondence. I became conscious of my age – I would be eighteen in June, sitting for Leaving again, while others of the same age had moved on to Sixth Year.

Being in a weak school house in school competition was frustrating to a degree, but that was to be fortunate for me. There were four houses. Andrew was the most formidable when it came to sport, which was the chief means by which the trophy for the best house was won at the year's end. Andrew had the best 'stud farm' – outstanding athletes who had brothers and sisters of equal, if not greater ability. Andrew was to go on and win the school football seven years in a row in that year of '59. Yet, being in Everard was fortunate for, when all the Everard boys voted for the house captain, I was elected on the grounds of being uniquely good in the house of a few talents at sport.

Oh, there were the nights of still wondering why I could sin against the One I loved so much! But Mr Smith continued to be like a father in the faith. He would still come up for a night each week and we would sit in his large black 1938 Buick, where in the dark we talked about what it means to be a follower of Jesus.

THE UNEXPECTED TEACHER (PART TWO)

Mr Smith was rather short in stature, had receding grey hair, twinkling brown eyes, and was sprightly in his movements and constantly smiling. Matron may have been reluctant to have him pay me visits – being suspicious of our time spent talking of Christian things – but Mr Smith and I revelled in fellowship with our common Lord. It was in those ongoing visits in 1959 that I began to fear less about sinning against our Lord, all in the knowledge that He would forgive me upon confession of my sins of the day, whenever I dropped down on my knees in my room and looked up at the stars through the windows. My grief at sinning was no less, but my relief of being forgiven was more.

> 'When thou hast done, thou hast not done,
> For, I have more' (John Donne).

Forgiveness is an ongoing thing God grants, even though we who are in Christ 'have more.' Is it possible He will keep on forgiving? Yet He does. Yes, He did when I had an anxious young heart.

In early 1959 the Billy Graham organization gathered people who aspired to be counsellors for the forthcoming crusade that the world famous evangelist intended to conduct around Melbourne. Mr Smith registered for counselling. He received permission from Matron to take me one night to a counsellors' class – there was no thought of being considered to counsel, but to get the feel for evangelism and learn of the bible texts that were viewed as vital for witnessing. One text was 1 John 9: 'If we confess our sins, he is faithful and just to forgive our sins, and to cleanse us from all unrighteousness.' It would be one to underline in the little black-covered bible, the book that opened my eyes to know that Christ keeps forgiving. While sitting among those of the large counsellors' class under Professor Basil Brown in the City of Melbourne that night, there were discovered any number of texts from 1 John to be well memorized and all that had the pivotal word of 'know.'

The method at the Billy Graham crusade meetings was for Billy to preach for an appeal. For the thousands who listened to his message there was the offer to come forward and be counselled by those trained to bring assurance to those who responded, so they would know that they were saved. The meetings would be charged with emotion, but Billy had declared in advance that a word of warning needed to be issued: '...do not mistake emotion in itself for faith'... 'faith first, and then if emotion ceases, very well.' Much hinged on the counsellors employing the texts from 1 John with the common word 'know.' If the counselees said they believed the texts, then that was the assurance needed that they had received Christ.

With Matron's permission I went one night and first heard the handsome, forty-year-old evangelist at the Agricultural Showgrounds. It was an awkward place for many people to travel to, and at the venue 'many in the audience were hundreds of yards from the preacher.' Billy spoke movingly on Samson, and we sang from the Billy Graham Songbook, purchased if desired for four shillings. By the end of the Showgrounds meetings, attendances for all twenty-three meetings in Melbourne at that point of the Crusade had reached half a million, with enquiries about salvation tallying twenty-two thousand.

Then came Billy Graham's final meeting in Melbourne. It was scheduled to be held at the Melbourne Cricket Ground as a brave venture, many scoffing at Billy Graham for claiming he would fill the whole stadium. Only twice in the ground's history had a crowd exceeded the seating capacity of 105,000. In 1956 there had been a crowd of 115,802 for a football final. On a warm autumn day, a group of we oldest inmates from Sutherland joined the thousands that swarmed into the stadium. All seats were filled early so that many people climbed over the steel pickets of the

THE UNEXPECTED TEACHER (PART TWO)

boundary, spilled onto the oval and sat down in a vast horseshoe around the central rostrum to hear the world-renowned evangelist. It is said that 143,750 attended that final meeting.

One staff-member said five of Sutherland's children made decisions for Christ on that occasion. I only know that the French boy Victor, to whom I had witnessed as best I could before Billy Graham came to Melbourne, showed later little sign of genuine faith, though he had gone forward at the MCG. Perhaps some had come to faith, but it was fallow ground under Matron Roscholler so that, humanly speaking, faith found it hard to grow.

While Mr Smith still proved to be a guiding light with his weekly visits at Sutherland, my admiration for Billy Graham knew no bounds and found me getting away from the other inmates and, ensuring I was on my own, imagine myself as a great preacher too, bending a Bible back in one hand as Billy did, and gesticulating with the other, punctuating the air with an audible authoritative 'The Bible says'... I eagerly procured books about his life. I seemed to be fluent, articulate when on my own. So caught up was I in imitation of the famous evangelist that I became oblivious in my dreams to the reality that I would never have the nerve to be so bold even before the smallest number of listeners – even in a classroom as a teacher?

Did I have the aspiration to be a preacher? It was only a dream. Reality would strike quite hard when I 'came to', when it dawned on me that as a nonentity I was a struggling school student, striving to obtain my Leaving.

At aged seventeen still dreaming audibly. Yet even though the dreams over the years had metamorphosed from the fantastic, for instance, in riding alongside Hopalong Cassidy and his horse Topper to partnering Lew Hoad in doubles to win the Davis Cup against the Americans, to singing songs of my own compositions to 'wide acclaim,' the dream of actually being a Billy Graham-like evangelist when acting audibly out of earshot somewhere in seclusion around Sutherland whenever I could, also was remote from reality.

Aged seventeen, and still acting out 'loud' dreams? It was commonly said 'Talking to yourself is the first sign of madness.' Over the years I had found great comfort in talking to myself, even though it had been embarrassing at times. Growing in age had not diminished my constant dreaming. I found friendship in always clinging to that dreamlike state, ever charmed more by fantasy, though at times by a fear that I had been overheard and was considered mad.

Unbeknown, was there method in the madness? Hamlet feigned madness and Polonius, in an aside while in Hamlet's presence, said, 'Though this be madness, yet there is method in it.' What Hamlet was saying appeared to be mad, but there was a sense to it. Polonius further said to this effect : 'Hamlet's words possessed a skill that madness often possesses.' Talking to myself out loud may well have been madness at seventeen, with a madness becoming heightened by dreaming of being an acclaimed evangelist, but unknowingly was there a promising method in what were soliloquies that were indulged in at the time?

At such a time Dr John Court of the Royal Children's Hospital publicly stated that childcare was more than feeding and clothing children – that mental health and emotional disturbances were important to consider in deprived children. The Education Department became the legal owners of the Sutherland primary school buildings, and we inmates' general growth and medical status became the subject of a study. With the Department taking over the school buildings, it was claimed that 'the high retardation level at the school was steadily declining,' perhaps arising from the progressive thinking of Dr Court at the time.

Many like me belonged to the age of welfare limited to 'feed and clothe.' My mental state had doubtlessly been assessed and coloured early on by

THE UNEXPECTED TEACHER (PART TWO)

the fact that my mother was a chronic schizophrenic, with the belief that 'any improvement in her health was unlikely.' Like mother, like son? I was at the school age of six but still stuck in the Presbyterian Babies' Home before the Welfare Department made me a ward of the state and sent me to Sutherland, after passing through 'the Depot' at Royal Park.

The Matron of the Babies' Home wrote of me that 'Edwin is a nice little boy but he is backward.' It was also said that 'his being with babies so long he is babyish in his ways.' The Matron at Sutherland was to take me in on condition that if I proved to be subnormal, I'd return to the 'Receiving Depot.' 'A good home' was a prospect for adoption after only a few months at Sutherland but, in three considerations put forward when contemplating adoption, the consideration of my mother being an inmate of a mental institution carried the day and left me still at Sutherland. Better progress was viewed as possible in a private home, but it was said that I was a slow learner and spoke extraordinarily little. It was not until I was in Grade three that the teacher at the school informed the Welfare inspector that "he is not backward" (underlining the words). Of course, 'Ward' (as I was known) was not privy to all the assessments being made – still, 'Ward' was regarded regularly by the authorities as quite happy. Yet 'Ward' was happy to day dream, most of all.

When Easter Sunday in 1959 came, there was no dream as to what I 'saw.' The morning service at the Greensborough Anglican Church perhaps stirred me a little, but it was in the afternoon in my room when I encountered one of the sweetest times I have ever known. I spent several hours engaged in prayer on my knees while the presence of Jesus as my risen Lord had me rapt at the wonder of it all.

Then, He further blessed me around that time with a vision of His anointed face – it was no dream – while I was waylaid with a fever in Sutherland's surgical room in isolation. I think this was the reason why

I only sat for one exam at the "First Test," scraping through in dreaded Geography. Still, early days were full of bliss in Christ –

'My dayes were straw'd with flow'rs and happinesse;
There was no moneth but May.'

My 'First Test' report in my second attempt at Leaving stated that I was doing 'very good work as house captain,' though I had to force myself into denying my natural shyness in order to get students of the house of Everard to do yard duty for points, or get them to volunteer to play in house sport if they were not inclined to do so. I had never had to command anybody before, so it embarrassed me to cajole fellow students to play their part so that we might win the house shield at the end of year on Speech Night. Persuasion seemed like coercion, particularly with seeking to win co-operation from senior students. Mine was not a forceful personality, nor a winning one – or so it seemed to me. You can be soft-voiced and still be winning in your ways, but I appeared a failure, more so when Everard fared poorly in house competition.

Then again, for me to excel in sport inter-school was a winning way, particularly when it came to football. In late July various teams of our high school made a trip to Albury to play against Albury High School in return to their visit to our school the year before. After a tumultuous farewell from all the students at the school gate, sixty of us set off by bus for Melbourne, then on to what was seen as an uneventful long train trip for most students; the only out-of-ordinary thing that happened on the train according to accounts was a suitcase falling off one compartment's rack, crashing down on the head of a boy who reportedly lost consciousness for four stations. Yet to me it was a most eventful trip, for a certain paperback that I took to reading on the rail so enthralled me that I could have burst with bliss. The

THE UNEXPECTED TEACHER (PART TWO)

paperback which hopefully appeared to be mistaken for a secular novel. It was called *Letters to the Young Churches*, a fresh translation of Paul's letters by J.B. Phillips.

On the back of the book was a photo of J.B. Phillips with his hand grasping a pipe sticking out of his mouth; it spoke of a free spirit for an Anglican. It was a paperback illuminating the ancient language of the Authorised Version that I was accustomed to. It was hard to hide my happiness as I was caught up with what appeared to make Paul more one of our generation in a way. For instance, in Romans 5 and 6 I read –

> 'Yet, though sin is shown to be wide and deep,
> thank God his grace is wider and deeper still!
> Now what is our response to be? Shall we sin
> to our heart's content and see how far we can
> exploit the grace of God? What a ghastly thought!'

Mr Smith had given me the paperback, as he too had been taken in by the vividness of the new translation. Apparently all Christians everywhere were talking in particular about J.B. Phillips' translation of Romans 8 where he had Paul saying 'The whole creation is on tiptoe to see the wonderful sight of the sons of God coming into their own,' and Romans 12 with 'Don't let the world around you squeeze you into its own mould.'

I would not have openly read my black Bible on heading to Albury because it would have been spotted to be a Bible. Quintessentially happy but ashamed?

In our school football team was a notable student among others who seemed intellectually much cleverer than me. Geoff Heard undoubtedly was destined to impose himself on the oncoming game against the border city high school. Against metropolitan schools he had already starred, from the centre bullocking his way through packs and bursting out with long-range punts towards goal. He was the only one to wear a sleeveless jumper. He was of solid build with rippling muscles, olive skin, thick lips and a broad grin. Yes, his talents were not limited to physical prowess.

He was among the most intelligent of our school. Talkative, somewhat argumentative, loud-mouthed but rarely caught out in debate. He shone in Written Expression, shone in Mathematics. It seemed that there was not anything he could not do. I cannot recall him having many friends, but he was not fazed; he struck up company by drawing anyone who thought they could match him in controversy and that made him happy.

One with a melancholic nature can be dogged easily by doubt. What if I had sought to witness for Christ to Geoff? Would he shake my confidence with an unexpected question for which I had no answer? When 'Bandy' Fallon had come back to the Homes for a visit, once he began to work, he mocked our guardians the Smiths for teaching we inmates about God. I could not contain myself within the circle of boys around 'Bandy,' boldly telling him how I found happiness in believing in Jesus. Yet, in the eyes of Geoff, happiness may not have been what it's all about. Many people find happiness without Christ. Besides, 'Bandy' seemed easier to convince possibly, as he proved himself backward at Sutherland's school.

Well, the joy of knowing Christ was unparalleled, and I learned that it was a joy founded on a firm foundation to do the part with right and wrong being a clue to the meaning of the universe. A bright boy of Year 6 at high school was also a Christian, and he gave me a slim paperback that helped me to be more confident than ever about 'the logic' of believing. And so, to be more courageous about Jesus. It was a copy of C.S. Lewis's *Mere Christianity*. C.S. Lewis argues that we all have a sense of right and wrong. People try to deny the reality of the universal moral law, and he counters the denial of this by showing what the moral law is and how it is independent of cultural differences, of personal taste, of mere instinct, of mere education or indoctrination. Nature is not all there is; there must be Someone giving us direction; that Someone is God. 'If the whole universe has no meaning, we should never have found out that it has no meaning.'

I could not get enough of *Mere Christianity*. Not only was C.S. Lewis's logic hard to refute, but he had a way of writing that hooked me page after page.

To read *Mere Christianity* did not make me quite bold enough to speak to the likes of Geoff, but it began gradually to boost more confidence in what I believed, if only I was to gain sufficient poise to speak without faltering in the presence of anyone among those beyond the boundary of Sutherland.

Mr Roscholler had become a lecturer at Burwood Teachers' College, and one day he finally took me to the college to get a sense of what training there was to be a teacher, and what being a teacher was all about. A recruiting officer was present and rather informally he interviewed me. I felt uneasy about it, and unbeknown to me he formed an opinion then and there that I was not suitable for a teaching career.

Still, I pressed on in ignorance of the recruiting officer's opinion, Mr Roscholler giving the impression that entering a teachers' college was ensured if only I could obtain my Leaving.

The Second Test in August showed me still struggling with school – a failure in Economics, and although doing well in British History, barely scraping through in Geography and Art. Yet, when the Welfare Department asked "Is there any reason why 'ward' should not now be returned to relatives (sic) or be placed in employment?", Sutherland's superintendent Mrs Wenborn doggedly said, "We would like the lad to remain with us until he is through his schooling." I knew it was vital to study harder and take in what I was being taught about secular knowledge, but I found myself taken away in spirit and made captive by books and periodicals that satisfied a longing to be more learned and acquainted with the things of God. *Mere Christianity* had set the pace. Sundays were also spent listening to one radio Christian program after another. When I moved to a new room on my own in what was called the Middle Building, set apart from the main building, – Lindsay (one of Sutherland's boys and who had become Sutherland's farmhand) gave me an Astor Bakelite radio.

I was exposed to several of Sunday's religious programs. The 'Back to God Hour' had the mellifluous voice of Peter Eldersveld on 3XY at 6.30pm, with the Aaronic blessing in song at the end of the half hour –

> "The Lord bless you and keep you,
> The Lord make His face to shine upon you,
> And be gracious unto you.
> The Lord lift His countenance upon you
> And give you peace."

The 'Back to God Hour' was put on air by the Reformed Churches of Australia, but that meant nothing to me. I eagerly heard on the 'Back to God Hour' about Jesus, and in fact any program that referred to Him lured me.

Two presenters known as Frank and Ernest lured me as well. I sent in for their material but when I showed it to Mr Smith upon one of his visits, he warned me against believing what it promoted.

> "What is wrong with it?" I asked.

He told me, "It has to do with British Israelism."

> "What's that?"

THE UNEXPECTED TEACHER (PART TWO)

"It is heresy."

"What is meant by 'heresy'?"

On the next visit he lent me a book called *Against Heresies*. In it all kinds of false teachings were exposed besides British Israelism: Seventh Day Adventism, Christadelphanism, Christian Science, Roman Catholicism, Swedenborgism.

Anything to do with Jesus had me listening, the Seventh Day Adventist hour had also been siren like with its opening of sweet harmony –

> "There is a place of quiet rest
> Near to the heart of God
> A place where sin cannot molest
> Near to the heart of God."

I began to learn about the 'sirens' and the treacherous rocks that could make shipwreck of my faith. Through a large bible dictionary Mr Smith had lent me, I became intrigued with what the bible said about Israel being God's ancient and special people, and so I, on first reading the material sent out by the British Israelites, had become bewitched into believing that we people of British stock are of the lost ten tribes of Israel. The Kingdom of David failed to survive in Israel. Where is it now? It is in England. King Zedekiah's daughters (Jeremiah 41) escaped death in Egypt and fled to Ireland in a ship with Jeremiah. From Ireland, with their children, they reached England, where they formed the English royal house that we know. Consequently, the British Empire was prospering. England was impregnable, so too we in Australia and the United States, for we are sons of Manasseh, as Joseph's branches were predicted to run over the wall as a vine

(Genesis 49). For one who had always loved stories, upon coming into faith in Jesus I had to learn to resist the 'sirens' in Frank and Ernest.

As a newborn believer in Christ, settling down by learning more and more about what it is to progress in the Faith, together with what to avoid lest I made shipwreck of my faith, I nevertheless had to keep steady on the high seas of secular study for success at the end of the year.

The new room deprived me of seeing the stars at night. I sorely missed both gazing at them and singing simultaneously "Sun of my soul" out of a deep love for Jesus.

Soon the Albury sports trip with the school faded in memory, so too the intrigue with mimicking Billy Graham once he had returned to the United States, as I sought to concentrate on acquiring success in at least two subjects at the end. I had less to do with everyone at Sutherland, being the only one who had a room in the large Middle Building. I was more alone than I had ever been in the institution. Over the years I had been accustomed to the constant presence of fifty to sixty boys and girls of varying ages, of mixing with the boys in the dormitories, and with the boys and girls in the dining room. However, the isolation suited my intense study, of both the spiritual reading and secular reading, pursuing the twin ambition of being a true Christian and an acceptable trainee for a teachers' college.

I saw to some degree a link between being a house sports captain in the large high school and any future as a schoolteacher, for similarity did lie in developing or cultivating the leadership ability to inspire others to follow commands. The athletic sports in Spring were a torment to me, as I was expected to align students of our house of Everard with events such as long and high jump, hurdles, javelin, shot put, and the running races and relays. An introverted person is not gifted to command. Some students such as Peter Brock and Chris Jarvis, did not have to be persuaded to compete, but it was hard to persuade others of less talent to champion the cause of

Everard. Besides, Everard had never fared well in athletics. We did not have as good a stable of thoroughbreds for athletics as the other three houses.

Among the events of the day, I put myself in the 440-yard race, in a generation when the 440 was not a sprint nor a long distance run. However, all the way the 440 proved to me long distance all right, with me coming last! Still breathing heavily, and with the carnival nearing the end, I threw myself down near our yellow house banner on the oval, lay on my back, looked up at the clouds in the sky, grieving at my failure to create the enthusiasm required to do our best for the house.

As it was, Everard came last. Andrew won the athletics for the seventh year in a row. Yes, Geoff Heard was the boys' Open Champion. At least Peter Brock was ranked a champion with a ribbon for Everard.

There was one group before whom I spoke and inspired. It was 'ISCF,' the Christian fellowship of students at the school. Self-consciously I joined them. It was a small group, largely of nonentities at the school. Mrs Smith, husband of him who was my tutor for the Lord's sake at Sutherland, whenever he could still give a night, invited me to give my testimony. Many years later a fellow student said he recalls that in my testimony I spoke about the opening words of Isaiah 55 –

> "Ho, everyone that thirseth,
> Come ye to the waters"…..

He remembered more about my testimony than I did, although I recall at least speaking about the satisfaction I had found in Jesus, and had composed a song based on the prophet Isaiah's words.

Quite a number of songs were composed and sung to myself at that time, when I would slip away and stroll down the paddocks of Sutherland unnoticed. I was eighteen but I still felt guilty that I was going 'out of bounds,' as for years we had been forbidden from going beyond the line of the cowshed and into the paddocks. Yet my heart yearned to be alone, panting to praise God. A friend at school, Ian, believed I had talent for song writing, though at that time he was not a believer. He saw potential in my secular songs as well as my spiritual songs, strange to say. I composed 'Everyone That Thirsteth,' 'Lost in His Love,' 'The Lord is Thy Keeper,' 'From the Prince of the Air's Kingdom,' but had no way of setting down on paper the melodies for them.

Mr Smith was not familiar with my desire for creating music, but such a thing did not need to 'carry the day' when we got together at nights in Sutherland in his 1938 Buick. When I was with him, my concern was for my spiritual growth through the Word, while I also expressed concern for my future. One night he enquired as to where I would be living the following year.

> "I know it perhaps depends on how well you do with your final exams," he said, "but have Matron and you talked about where you'll live next year?"
>
> I told him wonderingly, "No, we have not".
>
> "If you go to teacher's college, is there accommodation for the students?"
>
> "Yes, I believe there is a hostel".
>
> "Or, would you live with your sister?"
>
> "No, there's no room in her house".
>
> "We don't like to think about it, *son*, but what do you think you'd like to do if you can't get into teaching?"

"Gee whiz, I don't know," I moaned.

"Don't say that Eddie".

"Well, I *don't* know" I insisted.

"I mean that you should not say 'Gee Whiz', because it is a substitute for 'Jesus'. It is too close to blasphemy".

There was a kneejerk reaction to his advice about the circumlocution, but then I quickly realised that what he said was true. I was to wonder later how Pat Boone, the famous crooner and supposedly a Christian, could sing a song that was shot through with circumlocutions such as 'Holy smoke,' 'Suffering catfish,' in a song bearing the title of 'Gee Whittakers.'

"Still," continued Mr Smith, "we pray that God will give you the desire of your heart and you can do teaching. God's word says, 'Commit thy way unto the Lord; trust also in him; and he shall also bring it to pass'."

When we had prayed, and he started up the Buick and reversed it out of Sutherland's driveway, he headed back to his home at Diamond Creek. I went to my little room in the dark, took my bible and underlined with ink the verse he had quoted.

The year was drawing to a close.

I still searched the stars at night, slipping away in the dark to the paddocks for a break from the increasing tension of studying for the final exams that were to be held once again at Eltham's Methodist hall. As I gazed at the stars – being reminded of the new eyes I had for the glittering constellations above – I wondered about writing a poem to do with the stars for the school magazine *The Mercury*.

Yet I hesitated. Would the editorial committee of the magazine be prepared to publish what was religious and Christian? Did I have the nerve to write it, and thereby have it known – if it were published – by all the students that I believed in God? I had performed the year before in a concert in front of a 'huge audience,' miming Elvis, and singing a solo with a small group of us called 'Starlight.' I also had sung at a school social the year before. With the new year I had tried to live down the 'Eddie Elvis' image but even on the Albury trip they insisted that I sing at the inter-school social, so I sang Col Joye's 'Bye, Bye, Baby, Goodbye.' My God was the Maker of heaven and earth, and there ought to have been no shame in owning Him.

I wrote a long poem called *The Seeking World*. With apprehension I approached John, who had introduced me to C.S. Lewis's Christian apologetic *Mere Christianity*. John was on the editorial committee for *The Mercury*. The committee decided to include it in *The Mercury*, which was distributed to all of Eltham's students in the final days of the year. It pleased me to have it published – a twenty-two-line poem born out of a struggle to make known that the glory of the stars in the night sky lay in the creation of 'a wond'rous God.' Still, I was worried by the attention it may give me, even though I was beckoning readers to not 'give up the chase', but to acknowledge the glory of God as I had done.

The final week gave we, who were doing external exams, 'swat back.' I would sit in the sun on a green embankment at 'the boys' end' of Sutherland to study and gaze at the Silver Poplar with its green and silver leaves spinning in the summer wind, knowing that whatever was my future I was soon to leave Sutherland after eleven years.

The four final exams were met with quiet confidence. Even if I failed Geography, I hoped to gain success in the other three, whilst only needing two for Leaving.

THE UNEXPECTED TEACHER (PART TWO)

Before the external exams began, Mr Smith invited me to his house in Diamond Creek one Sunday afternoon. I walked the two miles from Sutherland in time to share an evening meal with his family. He and his wife, with their two boys and I, sat around the table and ate, while Mr Smith asked if I would like to live with them upon leaving Sutherland. After knowing them as my guardians at the Homes before they were forced to resign from there, I was glad to think I could live with them the following year. There lived with the Smiths a single lady called Nancy. She was a fine Christian, and worked in the city for a Christian man who distributed Fact and Faith films.

Once the exams were sat, there was a wait of almost a month before the results came out in the daily press. In the meantime, Mr Smith invited me to attend the Belgrave Heights Christian Convention with him, his wife, and their youngest boy David. The Smiths belonged to a parachurch group called the Diamond Valley Interdenominational Christian Fellowship. Several thousand people of all denominations from all over Melbourne attended the annual Convention for three to four days shortly after Christmas. The girls lived in rooms of an extended hut, while the boys slept in tents down on the slope from the hut.

The number of people frequenting large-scale meetings on canvas seats on a sawdust floor, singing joyfully and solemnly some hymns I knew, then listening reverently to arresting speakers at one meeting after another, was novel but exhilarating. Love among such brethren is another sign that we have passed from death to life.

I fell asleep one particular night in a tent with others full of wonderment – not only because we all seem to be secret agents in this strange world of ours as we read the Scriptures before torches were turned off in the late night, but because of the words of Mr Graham, the DVI camp leader, had spoken to me. (He had known before Mr Smith ever did that I was a believer, as he gave me a ride in his car when I had walked home to Sutherland in the dark from Greensborough after I had been to hear Billy Graham at the Showgrounds early that year). After telling us in the tent to stop talking when lights were to go out, he said to me, 'Your voice is very clear. I could hear every word you were saying from up at the hut. I believe God is going to use your voice one day.' The words took me by surprise. What did they mean?

I returned to Sutherland with a full heart, a heart that yearned to yield more of myself to my Saviour. A Convention hymn was memorized and sung over and over as I went alone before the sun grew too hot to daily water the pumpkin patch on the northern side of the lane, down beyond the hayshed –

> "Oh, the bitter shame and sorrow,
> That a time could ever be
> When I let the Saviour's pity
> Plead in vain, and proudly answered,
> 'All of self, and none of Thee'."

The hymn progresses and has a singer pondering about giving 'Some of self, some of Thee,' to 'Less of self, more of Thee,' and finally to 'None of self, and all of Thee.'

Where was I? At the point of giving only 'some,' or 'more,' or 'all?' At the convention, messages were given progressively through Romans, with emphasis thrown on all of us to examine ourselves regarding sanctification and full surrender. It was said that we have a tendency to sin, which cannot be completely conquered in ourselves but which can be countered by victorious yielding to the Holy Spirit. A call would be made at the conclusion of meetings for people to go forward and stand below the platform festooned with flowers as a sign that they wanted to give themselves in full surrender to Jesus. Had we all backslidden since becoming a believer? Was there not some sin that was holding us all back from giving our 'all?'

Many would move forward while a final hymn was being sung by the vast congregation.

I held back from going forward each time. I was a young Christian but somehow it did not seem the right thing to do. There crept into my mind that perhaps everyone ought to go forward, for did we not all desire to be fully surrendered to Jesus? I felt no pangs of guilt for not heeding the pleading of any of the preachers, and was just left in mere puzzlement.

Among the many sprawling Queensland Blue pumpkins at Sutherland – some of them delightful even hanging from the enclosing fence – I spent quite some time watering them under the warmth of the morning summer sun while meditating on that one hymn with a yearning, to have none of self, as far as it was possible, despite not going forward at the end of any of the Convention's meetings. I wanted to think 'Lord, Thy love at last hath conquered,' as it seemed I was actually more devoted to Him after an unforgettable convention, and after bathing in the bliss of becoming acquainted with believers who loved Jesus as I did.

The convention certainly increased my longing to begin living with the Smiths even more. Leaving Sutherland, my home for eleven years? As a young man, somehow there was no looking back with any bitter sweet memories of what had transpired at Sutherland, only the joyful prospect of living with Mr Smith, my father in the faith, filled up my mind.

Memories grow and germinate though they may well be dormant in a young mind. Memories will grow. Broad green leaves and yellow trumpet flowers like those of emerging pumpkins bursting from the soil, come with time. Age warms the soil and the years accumulate as subject to the seasons of life. Memories will follow as footfalls down the long hallway of time and open a wide door to a large garden that may have weeds but certainly beautiful flowers. Yet I was young, merely bent on what lay immediately ahead at first – moving out of Sutherland and waiting yet to get all Leaving results.

Come January 11, in the new year, and Ward No. 70840 moved out of the institution and into the town nestling in the valley down the road, where the Smiths lived.

I was to live with a family, as I had never done before. To live with Christians gave me even more security, but with such a happiness that failed to anticipate or visualize some anxiety that may lie ahead.

By and Beyond the Pentridge Walls

Two days after I moved in with the Smiths, the final exam results at long last came out in the newspapers. Mrs Wenborn, Sutherland's secretary, notified the Children's Welfare Department that I had obtained my Leaving Certificate.

Yet, it was another matter to be accepted as a trainee teacher at a teacher's college. The Welfare Department had been informed by the recruitment officer of the Education Department that I had been 'wrongly advised' about school teaching, since in his opinion I was not suitable for a teaching career. I was unaware of his opinion, as I previously mentioned.

As to how I obtained a primary school studentship for the Coburg Teachers' College, I shall never know. It can only be said that within the providence of God, it came about.

All I know is that the Welfare Department agreed to keep me as a ward of the state to overlap the period when I could possibly increase my chances of entering a teachers' college through the exceptional circumstances of being a ward of the state. Once I gained entry into Coburg's College, it was deemed no longer necessary to have me as a ward of the state until I was nineteen. Remaining a ward of the state until I was accepted for college may have given rise to making a special plea, but one would think that *pity* was not the sole name of the game. Yes, somehow the providence of God played its part.

I felt considerable relief after two seemingly long years of striving to obtain the gateway certificate for teachers' college, and yet it was with considerable apprehension I made ready for the first day of college after living for eleven years in the institution, and adjusting to living in a private home only recently.

The Smiths' house sat on a gentle slope, in sight of the railway station and the railway crossing on Diamond Creek's main road. You will recall, their family consisted of two boys, and a spinster lady who, in her thirties, boarded with them. Their eldest son lived in what they called a bungalow, a weather-board place on a slight slope behind the house. Actually, it was a bungalow joined to a garage. I moved into the bungalow with the eldest son.

Curiously, the house faced Brookes Crescent, but the address was Haley Street, the street situated up beyond the bungalow. There was quite a sizeable backyard that had a few gum trees which stood on what was mainly grass.

How sweet it was to conclude our evening meal with a bible study and prayer! Mr Smith was a chirpy man and his devotion to Christ was most evident. Straight after dining together and after devotions, their eldest son Peter would stand up from the table – blonde, with brown eyes and pixie-nose like that of his father – and excuse himself from the table. Soon he could be heard driving down the concrete driveway in his grey Austin A30, bound for the road towards Eltham to see his close friend, Graeme Collins.

Peter had disliked school and left Eltham High without completing Fifth Year. He was now serving an apprenticeship in carpentry and also loved farming. His friend Graeme had lived on a dairy farm.

Whenever he returned home from visiting Graeme, I found it difficult to strike up a flowing conversation with him. Mrs Smith hoped that I would be able to witness to their indifferent son about spiritual things and I sensed there was a blockage that prevented him from being interested in the things of God at that time.

Regarding Peter and me, there was a greater difficulty still.

It came when Mr Smith drew me in as it were to call him Dad. He was my father in the faith and in a way the thing bore a resemblance to the apostle Paul calling Timothy 'my own son in the faith,' when actually he was not a son by blood, so that there seemed to me some justification in Mr Smith looking on me as a 'son'. After all, ties of a spiritual nature are greater than blood ties, particularly when blood ties are not spiritual. I had noticed from time to time that Mr Smith in the course of everyday conversation would call me 'son' in what seemed at first a throwaway word. In quick time I could see it was not a throwaway name. Yet, although I was tempted at times within the home circle to call him 'Dad,' there were some reservations. I was only older than Peter by twenty days! How could I explain that fact, if I hoped to hide my background outside the home circle? So I drew back at calling him 'Dad,' even within the home circle. I loved the man, but I was now eighteen, and still sensitive about having lived in institutions nearly all my life.

Perhaps our bonds were stronger than they were between he and Peter at the time – Christ holding us fast together – but there were everyday things and instances that pointed to blood being thicker than water. I satisfied myself just to know he was my spiritual father but he could not be my blood father, of course.

At Sutherland Mr Smith came closest to being a father than any other man we inmates encountered, and we all knew few men in our time there. Many knew only a father or a mother – sometimes both. I knew neither. I had only known Mr Smith as a guardian before I became a believer. Now he seemed more like a father, but I mused that I may still have a blood father who may suddenly appear, though I shrank at wishing to see him.

There were things Mr Smith said in his good intentions to make up for what I lacked in certain knowledge – everyday things – and I noticed they were matters that he never raised with Peter. I concluded *he never had to*; Peter was his blood son. This engraved on my mind that I was not worldly-wise, that I was less streetwise than those who appeared to be normal people.

Yet I decided to play the game of pretence and give the impression, to many strangers who I would meet upon having left Sutherland, that Mr Smith was my blood father. Having the same surname was a haven. Otherwise, if I were open and were to disabuse any that Mr Smith was my biological father, there was much explaining to do, such explanation that in my mind meant humiliation and a sense of inferiority.

I still recoiled at the memory of 'Auntie Lil' of Preston singling me among strangers as 'the little orphan boy of the Sutherland Homes.'

Fellow students at high school who excelled in sport and who appeared scholarly had been envied, even though we of the Homes never found anyone among the hundreds of students asking us about our origins. They seemed to accept us as equals, though I suspected they did not entirely. Late afternoons they all *went home*, we travelled back to *the institution*.

Among people that the Smiths knew, no questions were asked. Was it assumed that I had left Sutherland and, with no place to go, the Smiths simply took me in? As one fostered? There was the spinster lady, Nancy, living with them in the house, but she was beyond the age of being invited to call the Smiths 'Dad' and 'Mum.' To her they were 'Cyril' and 'Beryl.' As for me I was a son of a kind. Among people that Smiths knew, no embarrassment was acutely felt, though they were initially strangers to me. It was assumed that they more than likely knew about me and, being Christians, or they were simply of St John's Anglican Church, they 'took me in.' Came a week or two of settling in, I prepared for my first day at Coburg Teachers' College. Some comfort was found in being accompanied by Mr Graham's daughter, Irene, as she was attending the college too. Mr Graham's words could not but leave me mystified: 'I believe that God is going to use your voice one day.' Would it be a voice for teaching? Even so, if it were a prophecy, it did little to ease my mind. And even if I was travelling with someone not a stranger in Irene, it did little to dispel the nervousness of that first day. Irene and I caught the train from Diamond Creek for Heidelberg, where we caught a bus to Coburg. There was a rail and bus concession as students: at 18 years of age and over the fare for me as a male was two-thirds the normal cost, and for Irene half.

The college was new, having been built only the year before. We new students of that year were just the second lot to enter it. Along with three other colleges around Melbourne, it had been formed around the same time because there was a demand for an increased number of teachers to be trained quickly in order to teach the rapidly increasing number of primary school enrolments on the heels of the post-war baby boom.

At first all freshers assembled on the oval in front of the college. It was February. We congregated eventually in the assembly hall, with its tapestry walls and the soft glow from a few chandeliers. The principal was Miss Ida Lowndes, a stately woman in her forties, tall and wearing a gown. Her words of welcome were carefully chosen, though the atmosphere of the occasion began to lend itself to a considerable extension of what we trainees knew in the regimen of high school – we trainees were to be placed in groups; college blazers and college ties were optional dress, but ties of any kind were to be worn by all males at all times; lecture times were to be observed strictly; permission was needed for males to remove their coats on days of prickly heat; females were to dress discreetly and wear dresses below the knees; and sport was to be held every Wednesday afternoon with a roll call to ensure that all students were present at their chosen sport.

A college anthem had been composed. We were to sing that we were 'all branches of one vast outspreading tree,' and there was I shaking like a *leaf!* As the tall stately woman waxed eloquently about the great need for us young teachers to be well prepared to serve our generation with dignity and drive, we sat below her stage in rows of seats dreaming or perhaps dreading the future in some cases.

We newcomers followed those in their second year by being grouped alphabetically according to our surnames, so that many in my group had surnames beginning with 'R' or 'S.' There were seven young fellows, and 22 girls in our group. It seemed a rather feminine profession to follow, but we were bound by a bond to teach for three years after graduating. The Education Department wanted to get their money back, as it were, for during training we were to be paid though not a handsome sum fortnightly - roughly sixteen pounds (or equivalent to $499.56 a fortnight currently.)

It was a two-year course, unless one desired to be an infant mistress and do another year. No fellow wanted to be one! A number of lecturers were quite young and were using the position of lecturing as a stepping stone for further promotion with the Education Department. All lecturers wore academic gowns while lecturing. After two years, unless one was of a few who did exceedingly well in their training, many students would be given a country placement, this to ensure that city slickers who despised the country may, all the same, be sent to cover remote rural schools. It seemed that several of our group did not look forward to going up country, if I could gauge it correctly by the ribbing that one of our groups quite often got – the distinctive girl came from Nar Nar Goon! Who would want to go there?

We were to attend lectures on Social Science, Art, Music, Speech Training, Education, Principles and Practice, Classroom Management and Handwriting. We were to do Blackboard for four weeks. There were electives as well. I do not remember doing the electives, though I do not think I did Needlework!

I still had a desire to play football, but not at college. When I discovered at home that Peter intended to attend training of the Hurstbridge team, I saw I would not be training or playing with total strangers. Spurred on by knowing Peter well, I trained and began playing regularly for Hurstbridge.

At college I kept to myself for the main part, particularly at lunch break, when I was glad to wander off to a nearby park, where in among the trees and in sight of the bluestone walls of Pentridge I would meditate on the things of God, or read a book or two that 'Dad' gave me from his library. Or, there was the municipal library close by, which housed the whole collection of the Interpreter's Bible, and I eagerly made notes from the commentary of 1 John. Gradually I got to know two girls who also sat in the back row of the lectures, laughing and commenting on the lecturers who often bored us. As for the fellows, I found their humour far too risqué for my liking.

Of course, there were things that stood out and ever remained with me to advantage once college was over. Mr White in Art taught us about the way children's art work develops from the 'haptic,' so that children will perhaps draw oversized hands (big sticks, as it were) because it will be a stage where they are impressed by people's hands. Colouring books are to be frowned on, children getting an inferiority complex through them. Let children tell you what they are drawing – never judge them by your thinking. Mr White impressed on us the ludicrousness of painting a garage door as if it is a house's primary feature. He was a more senior lecturer than most, with strong opinions but easy to listen to. From more than one lecturer it was drummed into us that as a teacher one must never repeat a child's correct answer and so detract from the pleasure they had in saying what proved to be correct.

We were constantly assessed through assignments. As already stated, such was the rigidity of getting them in by the set date that led David Smith of the college coming to my rescue, when I forgot to take a particular assignment with me one day, the day when David asked, "Was your Mum home?"

It was the first time I had been tested about the issue of my upbringing, and the real beginning of the game of pretence. The game gathered more momentum as one trainee called Michael grew acquainted with me through our weekly Christian group at college. To my relief he was not in Group E as I was. We had Christ in common, but I felt uncomfortable with him. Outside of lectures he would seek me out quite constantly. Outside of Christ we had little in common. He spoke much of Christ but in a way that was pedantic concerning the way to live for our Lord. To add to that: he kept asking me questions to do with home life, so I sought to avoid his presence without making it too obvious. It was a relief to retreat to the park nearby, and to head for the library when lunch hours seemed so long.

I attended the Belgrave Christian Convention again at Easter. It was better being in a youth camp with fellow-believers who did not ask 'questions.' What they knew of me I did not know, but solace was in them not asking. Some in the camp had glowing testimonies. I held back from giving my testimony before them all of how I was saved, but it was mainly because of self-consciousness about speaking in public, as well as the difficulty in testifying in a general way without speaking of the circumstances leading to me being saved. Besides, I observed that one young person followed another in giving their testimonies, each appeared to be a worse sinner than the one before them. Was my experience impressive enough? Still, I returned home after the convention stronger spiritually for being among such fervent fellow-believers.

After the convention 'Mum' spoke to me about a Christian man called Ken, who had been at the convention for one day. He was on the council of the Diamond Valley Interdenominational Christian Fellowship and had lunched at the DVI campsite with us.

> " 'Dad' said that Ken was interested to hear how you are training to be a teacher," she said.
>
> "Yes, he said he could help me with a music assignment that I'm to do soon."
>
> "What's the assignment about?"
>
> "I want to do it on music in Negro spirituals. It is hard to find material on it. He says that he has a book with the words and music of many of the spirituals."
>
> Continued 'Mum,' "It's good that he wants to help you."

Ken came around one evening with the book, The *Treasury of Negro Spirituals*. It was his own book but he said that I could keep it, sensing my love for music. His generosity was appreciated, so too his warmth and affection as we talked of spiritual things at the front of our house. His smile was most engaging.

A few weeks later I received a letter in the mail. It was from Ken. He said that it is heart-warming to have fellowship with me, but his letter was soured by the hint that I should not be playing football with Hurstbridge, the hint arising from Ken quoting from 1 Timothy 4:7 and 8 as couched in the KJV –

> '…and exercise thyself rather unto godliness.
> For bodily exercise profiteth little: but godliness is
> profitable unto all things….'

My immediate reaction was to defend myself by noticing that the apostle is not saying bodily exercise is of no value at all, that the apostle claims bodily exercise has some value. Admittedly, it was difficult to be a Christian among fellows whose blasphemy and vulgarity could reach a high pitch when they came together for Thursday training and Saturday's matches, with its barrel of beer. Ken was concerned for my godliness, I reasoned, and while I continued playing football, I was still attracted by his company, sometimes alone with him or at DVI meetings with others too.

After my assignment on Negro spirituals was assessed, our bond was closer. For the college's music lecturer was critical of it – stating that I should have written about other forms of Negro music. Ken sensed that the lecturer more than likely found the spirituality of the assignment too confronting. I agreed. We were brothers in arms against such opposition to the ways of the world.

Michael from college was of less attraction than Ken to me but I was glad for his Christian company when the freshers of the college had a week at the Mt Evelyn National Fitness Camp. Although I did not feel as bold as he about singing "Standing on the Promises of God" before the other students on the concert night. Not only feeling less bold, but thinking the song would say little to the unbelieving students. That was Michael: bold but not exactly savvy about the way to win others to the Lord. Anyhow, he taught me the bass for the song and very self-consciously I joined him on a night that was basically designed to amuse in a worldly way. Only our act was one on a serious note.

Still, I myself was of a mind to sing only something spiritual on the bus on the way back to college. A girl, who had attended Eltham High with me, begged me to sing an Elvis song into the bus driver's mike. Against her wishes I sang Pat Boone's 'Everybody's Gonna Have Religion and Glory.' It went down like a lead balloon in the hearing of all the students but I thought that in one way it would be accepted – after all, the song was on the world's hit parade. Still, it was destined to be confronting –

> 'Reading in the Bible all the things He said,
> He said He's coming back to raise the dead.
> Are you gonna be among the chosen few?
> Will you make it through?
>
> *Everybody's gonna have religion and glory……'*

Back at college, it just had to come: our first teaching round. Fortunately, at first it was only for Observation. The brash John Storey and I were paired to attend a school in Moreland. It was only the first day when, in the course of teaching his upper school class that the grade's teacher said to us, "I have to go to the office. Are you two fellows all right to look after the kids? I won't be long".

John instantly said, "We'll be all right".

He should have said, "*I will be all right,*" as he took it upon himself to suppress any noise and any 'joys' that some children may have anticipated in the absence of their routine teacher. Hoping to whoop it up in the presence of two young men who were barely and obviously seven or eight years older than them. I stood there frozen at the side of the classroom while

John, warm with ambition and enthusiasm and confidence, subjected the whole class to silence until the teacher returned. That day had me wondering if I could cope with teaching, once actual teaching in rounds became the order of the day.

As my father in the faith, 'Dad' (as I falteringly called him to his face on rare occasions) gave me a book called *In Understanding Be Men*. He was seeking to equip me with good doctrine, as well as preparing me for baptism, which I could undergo in the Anglican Church as a believing adult at the font of St John's. The Common Prayer Book called it a baptism for 'riper years,' for those 'able to answer for themselves.' Rev Moorhouse peered over his glasses on the bridge of his nose and asked me on the set Sunday morning to renounce the devil and the world and the flesh, to 'steadfastly believe' the Apostles' Creed, and to express my desire to be baptized in the faith.

Rev Moorhouse was a middle-aged man. He wore a black cassock down to his ankles, and it bore some small burnt holes from ash that had doubtlessly dropped from the cigarettes that he smoked. With drooped glasses, he used to walk around with his cassock shuffling. The moustached, rather softly spoken fellow was bent on transforming St John's into a High Anglican (Anglo-Catholic) place of worship by placing candlesticks on the altar, and getting frontals to the altar installed for the bended knees of communicants as they received not bread any longer but Catholic-like wafers during Holy Communion.

When 'Dad' persuaded me to be confirmed, to 'renew the solemn promise and vow' that I had made at my baptism, I joined a class of young people who were mostly of puberty age to ensure we could recite the Creed, the Lord's Prayer, the Ten Commandments and could answer other questions pertaining to a short catechism. I wondered about the spiritual standing of the young people who had been baptized as babies and who appeared to show no sign of spiritual life as based on the observation of the way they lived. I expressed my concern to 'Dad,' who gently but solemnly advised me not to be concerned about the other confirmees but ensure that I was in a good and pleasing standing with the Lord myself.

He said that it was not for me to judge. Previously he had admonished me one Sunday after Holy Communion, after I commented on some people taking Communion when there seemed to be clear evidence that they were not born again. 'Dad' tacitly appeared to agree that some were not regenerated but he warned me against being preoccupied with other people's spiritual standing as they knelt on the long red cushion at the altar to receive the elements, but rather to be more concerned with my own readiness to take the bread and wine at the hand of the priest.

I became confirmed in a ceremony by the laying on of hands as one 'baptized and had come to years of discretion.'

One did not have to be Confirmed to be the bellringer each Sunday morning at St John's, but 'Dad' persuaded the vestry men to select me to enter St John's adjoining church hall prior to the Morning Prayer service and there, within the bell tower, to pull hard and firmly down on the rope that caused the bell to sound out in the valley of the town as an appeal (no pun intended) to the townsfolk to come and worship. In the early days of St John's the church bell had been brought out from England and presented to a 'Charles Orme,' but it hung from a tree for fifty-years behind the church before being placed in a tower made to accommodate it in the parish hall. Once or twice I had to be checked when I swung on the bell, checked that the bell only sang and clang and rang long enough without incurring public displeasure.

Ken did not seem to be well-read in secular classics but he appeared to be discerning about the weaknesses of the logic behind Thomas Hardy. *Tess of the d'Ubervilles* had to be read for Language at college. Tess was a strong-willed young woman who was foisted on polite society that looked down on her when she became adulterous. The tragedy that overtakes her is not so much due to polite society, however, but to 'the President of the Immortals' who played sport with her. Hardy wrote novels of doomed heroines driven to tragedy by a hostile force of Fate. Tess commits adultery ironically in a paradisal garden and is betrayed so that she ends her life on an altar stone at Stonehenge. As a young Christian I was not able to handle the atheism of the book as well as I might have when called on to assess it in an essay. I cannot recall how I made an assessment of it but I found in Ken someone who was more mature spiritually and I sought his support when I wondered, out of anxiety, why we college students were being compelled to study such an atheistic, bitter, acrimonious work as *Tess of the d'Ubervilles*.

It was not long before we new students in college asked one of the lecturers in class about the way we were assessed for the sake of our career once we left college.

> "The Board of Classifiers of the Education Department will grade all of you in a list of seniority," said the lecturer.
>
> "Yes, what of our teaching training rounds? How do they relate to our college subjects?" asked one of the students.
>
> "As you know, your rounds are assessed from a grading of A down to E. The same thing happens with your college subjects. So, ten per cent of you will be allocated an A, overall twenty per cent of you B, forty C, twenty D and ten per cent E," the lecturer answered. "The college mark and teaching mark is combined". "Oh", said one fellow, "you could get a series of B for teaching rounds and end up with a college mark of A! Is that right?"

"Yes, that is correct. Then again, you could get a teaching mark of D (fair) but end up with a college mark of E, to be in the bottom ten per cent of the college overall. You can be regarded as quite fair at teaching, but weak according to your college mark."

"Oh," groaned some students.

"So, the two marks – teaching and college studies – are combined, are they? Somehow?" asked one.

"Yes, combined to give you a total mark on leaving here."

I sat there rather glum. We were all competing against one another, and we did not know how good many of us were. Success by others in teaching rounds was hard to gauge, for few spoke of how they fared. We then moved on from going out in twos for mere observation and got ready nervously for teaching rounds alone. Most students were anxious to avoid being forced to go into the country at the end of college. Prestige too was sought in gaining a permanent appointment in a city school upon achieving a high college mark. Where would I end up?

Yet we were reminded that the aim in teaching was not just to achieve personal ambition. We were reminded of what the college said – 'We, as teachers, accept a tremendous responsibility in guiding the search for knowledge which, in the future, may be used for the advantage or destruction of mankind.' In the whole of winter, weekends were spent playing football for Hurstbridge, spent in attending church at St John's morning and often in the evening, as well being at DVI meetings Saturday nights, figuring my life was well rounded apart from college life.

Come Spring, football was over, with Hurstbridge losing a final to Donnybrook. One Saturday afternoon the DVI committee was meeting at our house. Ken was one of the committee members. I happened to be down from the front door and on the lawn when the meeting ended. Ken emerged from the front door and descended the steps in a gloomy mood. Something amiss had apparently taken place in the meeting and he passed me by with eyes straight ahead, and without a word. Outside the circle of members and the committee no-one was to learn what had taken place.

The DVI – was designed, according to 'Dad' to provide fellowship throughout the Diamond Valley for evangelical believers who found that their own churches were not 'sound.' The fellowship came under some fire from a number of regional ministers who considered DVI unnecessary and an affront to their weekly ministry. 'Dad' was on the defensive about DVI, claiming that it was not in opposition or a threat to the churches of the valley – we complimented what churches already had to offer. 'Why, we only meet once a month, therefore how could we be a threat?' He maintained there was no intention of meeting any more than once a month, as well as the running of camps every Easter and Christmas at Belgrave. Yet I knew that he did not view the ministry at St John's adequate on its own, by any stretch of imagination.

Well, you may ask: Why did he attend St John's if he was dissatisfied with the ministry of Rev Geoffrey Moorhouse? He thought he could ignore the marks of High Anglicanism – such as the placing of candlesticks on the altar by Moorhouse – and even though 'Dad' believed that no matter how spiritually wanting were the sermons, there was enough spirituality in the Book of Common Prayer and the hymns to satisfy the soul. He also saw himself as one who could slowly and possibly influence the fellow-vestrymen for the good and the cause of Christ. He was seen as 'an enthusiastic and cheerful evangelist,' as well as diligently carrying out many roles – the roles of lay reader, vestryman, churchwarden and Sunday School superintendent. This, as well as being involved in the Church Missionary Society (the missionary arm of the whole of the Church of England Australia wide), and the British Bible and Medical Missionary Society, and being a committee member of DVI. Some thought he was involved in too many committees, but even if it meant at times bouncing around from being at one half a meeting one night and attending the half of another on the same evening, he thrived on boundless energy with an ever-cheerful face.

Those were the days when I loved the DVI cottage meetings that we had on Saturday nights, in various people's homes. The houses were often crowded and it served to create a spiritual intimacy among believing brothers and sisters that was missing at St John's. Even if such a church had been originally built from bricks beautifully handmade from the clay of the church grounds, as St John's was, nothing could equal the homeliness of our cottage meetings, even in any house that seemed mean in contrast to the beauty of St John's place of worship.

Our own home in Haley Street was blessed, just as many were that belonged to other DVI people. Besides our nightly family Bible readings and prayer for us, 'Dad' always had what became memorable words that I still recall, as one entertaining or being spiritually uplifting for the rest of us. Of scripture itself he was fond of quoting the promise of 'No good thing will be withheld from them that walk uprightly.' Also, that it is 'the fruit of the Spirit – not the fruits.' 'Mark the perfect man, and behold the upright, for the end of that man is peace' for its location as Scripture was memorable – it came from Psalm 37, verse 37. He could correct me without ill-feelings, such as the times when I fell into saying 'I am good' – telling me that I may be *well* when referring to physical health, but as for good, it has to do with being *morally right*. 'No one is good,' he would say – 'only God.' Often also he was fond of saying that 'Meekness is not weakness.' The book called '*In Understanding Be Men*' enlightened me much about the teaching of Scripture, and in it I was introduced to what the author

Archbishop Hammond saw as a tension between man's will and God's sovereignty. It introduced me to terms *Calvinism* and *Arminianism* – such terms that nobody at DVI, St John's or the Belgrave Convention had ever mentioned. How was I saved? Did my will determine my salvation? I heard much about the will playing its part. God's grace? I recalled how the Lord spoke to me when I was 17 and the call seemed irresistible, but Archbishop Hammond appeared to have the solution: Be an Arminian on your feet, and a Calvinist on your knees; this I set out to do.

One Sunday morning Reverend Moorhouse claimed that he had the power and authority to forgive sin. A shock ran through me to hear this claim from the upraised pulpit. After the service I could not be quick enough to express my shock to 'Dad' and, without waiting to learn from anyone else as to what to do, I made haste on the gravel drive to the rear of the church and knocked on the door of the vestry.

> "Come in," came Reverend Moorhouse's voice.
>
> "Hello," I falteringly said as I entered.
>
> "What can I do for you?" he asked, as he shed himself of the green vestment that had been around his neck.
>
> "Well", I paused, "do you believe you can forgive people's sins?"
>
> "Yes, I do", he said with confidence.
>
> "I do not believe you can – only God can forgive sin".
>
> "Well," he said, "God does forgive sin, but you must understand my position as a priest within our church."

I asked, "What do you mean?"

"I am a priest, consecrated within the Church of England in line with succession that goes back to the apostles of Christ. The apostles appointed bishops who in turn appointed bishops so that the apostolate was kept alive in what we call the episcopate succession – the succession of bishops – so that the purity of apostolic doctrine may be kept alive".

"But the apostles never claimed to forgive sins!"

"They were given the right to forgive sins".

"I don't believe it."

"Do you remember Jesus saying, 'Whose soever sins ye remit, they are remitted unto them…'?"

"I don't think that is what Jesus meant".

"What else could it mean?"

"Well…," I faltered.

"I think you'll find that is what He meant."

"Well… well…. I don't know exactly what He meant, but I am sure it cannot mean what you think it means. Only God can forgive sins."

"Recall the absolution," he insisted, "that I pronounce on you all when I turn to the people at the end of Communion. I say, 'Have mercy on you all, etc'."

"It relates to God's mercy."

"Yes, God's mercy, but as mediated through me."

I muttered that I did not agree with him, turned around, opened the large wooden door and walked out.

I discussed the dialogue with 'Dad' back home, but he was not as disconcerted as I had been. He did not agree with the vicar's claim – agreeing with me that forgiveness was God's prerogative alone – but he believed that such an unscriptural claim did not prevent us from worshipping with such a wonderful form of liturgy as found in the Book of Common Prayer. I hunted down the exact meaning of what appeared as a difficult saying from Jesus' lips, but sought to be content with the liturgy of the Book of Common Prayer that we followed Sunday by Sunday, for there was much to commend it: Holy Communion definitely stressed Christ's 'full, perfect and sufficient sacrifice.' Had I thought of leaving St John's? Much of the Prayer Book stemmed from the Bible. There were well-worded prayers that met and covered many a deep need that we the people of God had.

I felt there was a deep need of revival among believers. A book '*Lectures on Revival*' by Charles Finney attracted me at the Keswick Book Depot. I took very seriously Finney's directions that guaranteed success for revival. I longed for the extraordinary to happen in me and in other believers, and then consequently in society. Finney appeared to offer a fail-safe plan for revival : in '*Lectures on Revival*' there were twenty-two chapters on how to pray and keep praying, with excruciating self-examination to ensure that nothing whatever prevented the Holy Spirit from enduing one with power. For days on end after reading and re-reading the lectures – making certain that nothing earthly in me had been overlooked – I prayed and prayed. Nothing happened. Maybe, as Finney would say, 'God was willing, but (I) was unwilling.' Day after day passed in expectation, until I became dispirited. Had I not known enough "agony and faith?" I cannot recall how I gave up believing Finney: Perhaps I came to the conclusion that suspicion can be cast on the idea of *getting up* a revival, as gradually I was learning to despise man's efforts to bring on revival without consideration of both God's grace and timing.

When nothing extraordinary happened upon reading Finney, the ordinary and mundane things of life were being faced. Each night Peter came home from serving his apprenticeship as a carpenter, had tea, and then visited his friend Graham until he returned home late and fell into his bed alongside mine in the bungalow. We respected each other's callings, but we had little in common as far as things of the world were concerned, and certainly nothing in common in days when, despite frustration with Finney's promises, my heart was full of Christ.

Life went on in much the same way for the others in the house. Every day, Nancy, who had been a nurse at Sutherland in the time of the Smiths, left her room in the house to work in the city. Nancy was a Methodist and therefore did not worship with us at St John's. David, Peter's younger blood brother, attended school. As for 'Mum,' she stayed home throughout the week, except for attending the Ladies' Guild at St John's.

'Mum' was somewhat shy and retiring, overshadowed by 'Dad' through his strong, public personality. I found it even more difficult to address her with such a maternal name as 'Mum' when I had known her at Sutherland for some years only as 'Matron.' Yes, I rarely called her in person 'Mum.' If there had been a way to call her 'Mum' with any accompanying *sound of italics*, I would have felt more comfortable. 'Mum'? Mum? Matron? Then again, she came across to my Christian friend Michael at college as my mum, without the italics.

After college I sometimes called in at Michael's house in Heidelberg, where he would still ask me about the Haley Street family. From answers I gave, he still received the impression I had a blood father and mother and two brothers. If he probed about my 'brothers,' for me to avoid signalling that there was only twenty days difference between Peter and me, I merely told him that both 'brothers' were younger. Michael gradually probed so far, and no further, to my relief.

I certainly kept from Michael the evening when 'Dad' and I travelled to near the teachers' college and went in beyond the walls of Pentridge to see Matt Easton as called in *The Silver Poplar*. Matt was my best friend at Sutherland who left suddenly at the age of fourteen, to live with his mother in Carlton. His brothers were no help to him morally and he ended up being involved in a murder of a man at a milk bar. Matt received a ten-year sentence for the murder, though it was not known who committed the homicide among the three that raided the milk bar.

Matt had visited me after he left the Homes but I had not seen him for some time prior to the milk bar murder, and an uneasiness arose within me as I pondered seeing him in prison. I wondered what I could say to him, even though 'Dad' with his mastery of conversation always could largely 'carry the day' in any circumstances.

We approached Pentridge's high blue stone walls in 'Dad's' large black 1938 Buick, well within sight of my teachers' college.

We entered Pentridge, signed the visitors' book, then were escorted through a series of locked steel gates towards (if I recall correctly) "A" division, which was reserved for first offenders.

Suddenly Matt, accompanied by a guard, was there before us. He wore a grey lumber jacket, blue denim jeans and stood in thick leather shoes. A tin mug hung on his belt. His face had taken on gravity unknown at Sutherland, and I tried to hide my sense of alarm upon meeting him. 'Dad' opened the conversation.

"It is good to see you again, Matt," said 'Dad'

Matt slightly raised a smile, without speaking.

"You remember, Eddie, no doubt," said 'Dad'

"Yes, I do," Matt replied.

"He wanted to see you too."

"What are you doing these days? Have you left school?" asked Matt.

"Yes," I said with surprising ease, "I left only last year, the same time I left Sutherland. I am living with Mr Smith in Diamond Creek. I go to Teachers' College, which is just down the road from here."

"I would never have seen you as a teacher," he said.

"Well, that's what I hope to be."

Silence fell even on 'Dad' for a brief moment. I sought to grab at something to register my still-existing interest and concern for Matt.

"I noticed before seeing you," I said, "that there is what appears to be a school here."

He re-joined, "Yes, it's here near where I'm kept."

"Do-do you," I faltered, "attend the school?"

"Yes, I am studying for my Proficiency Certificate."

'Dad,' chimed in, "He's doing very well at it."

"That's good, Matt" I said.

"And there is the debating Matt does too," said 'Dad.'

"Debating?" I enquired.

'Dad' proceeded to tease out of him the debating that a number of Pentridge prisoners engaged in. It turned out that the debating team was considered by the outside world 'by far the best in Victoria,' and Matt was on that team! It was a surprise and it wasn't: a surprise that he could be, along with other prisoners, engaged in debating in Pentridge of all places, but no surprise to learn that he was part of their brilliant debating team. He had always been a smart person. I remembered how he would spend time skylarking at Eltham High in class and still manage to achieve reasonable scores in subjects. I envied him because while I scored better marks, I made more of an effort than he to do so.

The time came when 'Dad' and I bade Matt goodbye. Once more we passed through the locked steel gates, signed off on the visitors' book, and made our way out to the dim sight of the teachers' college in the growing darkness.

Could it have been that Matt might have ended up after Sutherland by the Pentridge walls at the teachers' college, and I after Sutherland beyond the Pentridge walls in Pentridge itself? As Ken was to say later: 'Only by the grace of God are you, Eddie, what you are.' (Yes, Ken knew of my life at Sutherland but we never talked about it, he never asked further questions, and perhaps 'Dad' had told Ken about Matt.)

Yes, the grace of God spared me of a life that could well have been ruined, brought on shame, despair and perhaps imprisonment. I shudder at what I could have been apart from the grace of God. I can say that I shudder at what I know *I would have been*. I could well have encountered danger and destruction. I speak of what will only pass between God and me. I know not exactly what the consequences of evil might have been. All I know is that I was spared before I destroyed myself. Still, some are saved when they have already destroyed themselves to some measure.

As for me, although I had not lived a life of outrageous public sin before I knew of a great lasting change, and a new life of light and joy and peace hitherto unknown until the Lord spoke to me and told me to read the Bible which I had not planned to do, it was such a new life of light and joy and peace that I wondered why I had been chosen to taste it. Therefore, I did not look down on Matt and scorn him for his downfall.

I continued to look up at the scintillating stars at night, even after moving out of Sutherland. I climbed the concrete steps in the dark from the house and walked towards our bungalow where Peter and I slept. I had become accustomed to espying Orion in the clear winter sky above me, searching too for Scorpio with its bright red star Antares, 'saw' myself sailing on what could be seen on the river of stars that ends in Achernar. Then, without first realising it, over some months I looked up a little less upon retiring for the night, for 'Dad' and 'Mum' had made the move to buy 'a television set', succumbing at last in the way that many evangelical Christians in those early days did. For some years many had resisted the purchasing of what they had conceived to be the devil's way of stealing hours from we who were supposed to 'See that (we) walk circumspectly, not as fools, but as wise, *redeeming the time, because the days are evil.*' It had been open to question if the TV programs were 'edifying' for believers. Mmm… did the edifying outweigh what was unedifying? Well, for a growing number of Christians there appeared to be enough that was edifying, and so it was reasoned that a little diversion could be harmlessly encompassed within the redemption of time.

Therefore, we joined other evangelicals in purchasing a wooden television set and, while we were attempting to not take up too much of our time viewing it, there seemed to be less time to look up at the night sky and drink in deeply the glory of God in the heavens, as tiredness from attending college also beckoned me to bed early after viewing 'the idiot box' (as it came to be called).

Yet, coming to my senses, I suddenly came one night to linger and consider more the heavens in the way I thought I should, realising the greatness of God's glory, and understanding why the Psalmist would say as he looked up at night: 'What is man that thou art mindful of him?' To gaze at the stars proved familiarity breeds amazement!

While in my latter years at Sutherland, some past inmates would pay us a visit, I felt no inclination to do the same, though I had one cause to do so after I left. To my surprise Matron Roscholler contacted me to speak to a gathering of people during Mental Health Week. After leaving Sutherland and having more to do with people of the world, particularly through teachers' college, I had acquired some confidence, though I was nervous for a particular reason about being asked to speak at Sutherland.

As previously stated, Dr Court of the Royal Children's Hospital had recently drawn public attention to childcare being more than food or clothing. He maintained childcare should embrace mental health and cover emotional disturbance, such as many a child of Sutherland had known. It was said in 1959 that a 'high retardation level at (Sutherland's) school is steadily declining.' Perhaps. Was I seen as one who, despite early suspicions about my mental stability, gave proof that a Sutherland inmate could enter high school and gain the Leaving Certificate and do as well comparatively as those outside the institution?

That was not the reason why I grew nervous about being chosen to speak at Sutherland for Mental Health Week. It was the difficulty about the subject I had to address. I was now a Christian but I did not wish to be seen as a 'Bible basher.' What would I speak on?

Through coming to know the Lord two years before, I had already known the Lord's power to grant me salvation and give peace and joy so that I had become more at ease within myself, and was growing increasingly more at ease with others. This surely had lent itself to sound mental health. Without dwelling too much on the change the Lord wrought in me, I could portray it at Sutherland in a brief way as foundational before speaking in the main about what has become known as psychosomatic illness.

I reasoned that if the audience knew anything of what was termed psychosomatic, they would know that from the way I spoke that I possessed a firsthand knowledge of God, but that they saw how trust in God helped to handle emotional stress and difficulties, and still lead to securing sound physical health. I planned to go on and refer to things such as fear and anger leading fatally to heart failure, to refer to emotional disturbances giving rise to asthma and stomach ulcers, to hypertension springing from anxiety, and so on.

After receiving a warm response from the audience in Sutherland's dining room, during supper there was a lingering look from across the room that caused an emotional disturbance of another kind. In my last few years at Sutherland a Hungarian family came to live at the institution – father, mother and two girls. The father was quite tall, strong and handsome, and became the institution's farmer. The mother was considerably shorter, pretty, and she worked in the laundry. Their two girls were also striking to look at, particularly the older one, Margaret, and it was she who looked across the room at me after I gave my address. We momentarily locked eyes more than once. She was certainly beautiful to look at that night.

With a goodbye to all and last exchange of glances between Margaret and me, I set out to walk the two miles home. I did not go home straight away but wandered around in the dark in the park at Diamond Creek – haunted by Margaret's face.

I was in turmoil. My heart longed for her but my soul, in love for the Lord, told me that it was fatal to pursue Margaret, beautiful though she was. Only recently I had heard on the record player at home a song by George Beverley Shea called simply *Because* –

> 'Because God made thee mine
> You come to me'…

I suspected Margaret was not a Christian and it was George Beverley Shea's song that I clung to tenaciously, for he was singing charmingly of finding the right woman because God has made her his. I hung on to the belief that God would one day bring a lovely girl into my life and that there would be no regrets in waiting for the one of God's choice, for the one perhaps of my wildest dreams.

I was thankful that I won out on that night in the park, though I knew that while one battle had been won over the Devil, I had not won the war.

Strengthened by resistance that night, however, I then looked for chances to be a faithful witness for Him who was blessing me so much amidst people who lifted my spirit by their own spiritual fervency.

Even teachers' college gave me believer's encouragement there in the person of our principal Miss Lowndes. In the college magazine near the beginning of the year, she included in her 'principal's welcome' a poem, written by an American, that she wanted us to peruse. It had been quoted in the previous year's graduation of 1959 exit students by the Director of the Australian Council for Educational Research. It made us ponder on the pride that we may rightfully possess in knowing we shall teach children who in adulthood would help in a distinguished way to form the fabric of our society.

The poem was read to all students, and reminded us to seek to answer the question 'Why teach?'. Among students in the classroom we could have, in years to come, 'that minister who will speak the word of God,' and one who could 'lead a stumbling soul to touch the Christ.' Quoted Miss Lowndes, "We may not see the church where any man we taught will pastor but we will be able to say proudly 'I knew him once'."

Miss Lowndes also had us singing various hymns regularly in our assemblies. Unbelieving students by far formed the majority of us, but we all joined in and sang such hymns as 'The Lord's My Shepherd,' 'God Be in My Head' and Blake's 'Jerusalem.' The song of 'God Be in My head' would ring out, commanding definite consideration –

> 'God be in my head,
> And in my understanding;
> God be in my eyes,
> And in my looking;
> God be in my mouth,
> And in my speaking;

> God be in my heart,
> And in my thinking;
> God be at mine end,
> And at my departing.'

With such Christian leadership and courage, we, who could only form a relatively small number of believers in regular Christian fellowship meetings, were emboldened to speak up for Christ. I recall in a morning break once, when a small number of students were at the foot of the steps at the northern end of the main part of the college's complex, there arose a spirited conversation about God. I felt emboldened to speak in defence of the gospel. Dissenting voices became louder and louder. More students from outside the circle congregated. The bell rang for us to attend the next lecture. Before anyone moved, I said something in brief to congregating students that I cannot remember but, as we climbed the steps to go inside, I marvelled not at what I myself said but what *the Holy Spirit* did. As I say, I cannot recall what I said but I will be bold to say: The Spirit spoke something that could not be refuted.

Bewildering though college was for me, in adapting to life after Sutherland, slowly but surely I gained confidence. The presence of Miss Lowndes as college principal, living with 'Dad' and 'Mum,' together with the brothers and sisters in Christ of DVI, the friendship of Michael at college, and Ken on weekends, all inspired me to walk carefully in the Lord.

I remained enchanted with J.B. Phillips's *Letters to the Young Churches*. Among many other passages that made God's Word appear more forceful were those found in Romans 6 and 1 Corinthians 1 –

> 'Now what is the response to be? Shall we sin to our heart's content and see how far we can exploit the grace of God?

What a ghastly thought! We, who have died to sin – how could we live in sin a moment longer?" "He has chosen things of *little strength and small repute*, yes, and even things which have no real existence to explode the pretension of things that are…"

I was of little strength and small repute but I joyed in having been saved for eternal salvation.

At college all was not exactly joy, if gauged by the editor of the students' magazine. Twice he expressed disillusionment in an editorial concerning the college. The first time found him criticizing college students for being either negative or non-committal when the public sought to know about the college's curriculum. Seeking to explain the curriculum would help the public to appreciate how it designed to 'produce receptiveness to beauty and human feelings.' As I saw it, some grappled with the study of *Tess of the d'Ubervilles*, wondering what it had to do exactly with teaching children about beauty between the ages of 6 and 12. The second blast by the editor was aimed at the marking system undergraduates for assessment, the editor offering a prize to any student who could devise a system whereby there is 'personal self-satisfaction gained' through publication of our subject marks, as well as 'having our faults pointed out to us.'

The blast at the marking system had followed a letter to the editor written by a student critical of lecturers being impressed by 'those who prettied their essays to cover up for lack of substance,' suggesting that assessments of assignments be abolished altogether.

Certainly, assessments could be at the mercy of the subjectivity of a lecturer. In my first year my essays for Language were criticized by a certain theatrical lecturer but praised by a less histrionic and more senior man in the second year. That kind of assessment left me, and no doubt others, wondering how we were faring in college.

Still, whatever we were learning, we were developing skills that could be adapted to teaching those of young minds. Lively discussion can always be ignited by teachers with 'Why?' Questioning is an art form in the classroom. Aside from being dissuaded from repeating children's answers when they were correct, we were taught never to ask a question that only required 'Yes' or 'No.' This sounds simple enough, but there are many adults of the world ignorant of the art form of questioning to engender spirited conversation that engages the interest of others. Too many in life talk about themselves, few ask questions of others.

To use George Herbert's language, we were being taught to get 'a good stock' of knowledge, and then out of college to 'draw the card' that suited best. Therefore, it is surprising the vast knowledge that one needs to possess even to teach and gain the interest of small children, surprising what one could draw on unexpectedly, or needed to draw on.

As far as my spiritual knowledge was concerned, I had my eyes opened to new things whenever I visited my sister Joyce in Brunswick. She lived over the road from a Brethren church. A true believer, she regularly went Sunday morning and night, though her foster-parents did not attend. The Brethren form of worship differed greatly from the high church sacerdotalism of St John's. There was no minister, but various men would bob up early in worship to speak when it was time to hear the preached word. Any man, who desired, also prayed. Holy Communion was called 'the breaking of bread.' Even at breaking bread there were men who felt constrained to speak a word of exhortation before we celebrated the Lord's death, unlike the chanting of the priest Moorhouse, who stood on the step above the kneeling communicants at the wooden rail, and monotoned the words to them one by one –

> 'The body of our Lord Jesus Christ, which was given for thee, preserve thy body and soul unto eternal life. Take and eat this in remembrance that Christ died for thee, and feed on him in thy heart by faith with thanksgiving'

and

> 'The blood of our Lord Jesus Christ, which was shed for thee, preserve thy body and soul unto eternal life. Drink this in remembrance that Christ's blood was shed for thee, and be thankful.'

At St John's we ate a wafer and drank from the one cup after the priest had wiped it with a cloth before another drank. The priest consumed the remains of the cup after all had participated in Communion. There was simplicity and a heart-felt earnestness among most worshippers in the Brethren church. A spontaneity rivalled the set liturgy I had known and I began to feel impromptu, informal worship may be best of all for concentration in worship.

Then, there was the time when I went with Joyce and others of the Brethren church into the city one Saturday night, when one or two of the men stood on a wooden box on a street corner and preached the gospel, while others of us handed out tracts to passers-by. Joyce told me the church often did street-preaching. Its effect was not visible but one never knew just who could be saved by such means.

As the year was drawing to a close, Joyce invited me to attend a church camp at Philip Island. I thought that for the first time, in a more informal situation, the campers may have asked how Joyce and I discovered one another. Puzzlement seemed to line the faces of not a few about Joyce and me together, so that I became somewhat self-conscious and silent among people who may have been brethren in Christ but seemed strangers in a sense. Hilarity broke some ice when, on the first morning some had overslept and they were carried out carefully, while still asleep on their stretchers, and were dropped down on the oval in sight of the rest of us, only to wake up with everybody laughing. Yet, most of all, I shall never forget the beautiful 'breaking of the bread' Sunday morning, as we all sat in a circle, with the sweetness of the silence falling on us as we broke bread and drank grape juice to celebrate the redemption Christ achieved for us. Such a solemnity, serenity and sweetness in Communion within the camp setting took me by surprise.

The year was fast coming to a close when DVI set about staging another Christmas carol outreach on Diamond Creek's football ground. A platform was erected. As managed by 'Dad,' (who worked for the SEC), electrical wires ran here and there from the speakers. When the speakers were set up, the microphone was tested. Row upon row of seats were placed before the platform. Many people were expected once evening fell and carols began.

'Dad' asked me to do a Bible reading and I became a bundle of nerves. At home I read and re-read the Bible passage to myself, hoping and praying that I would read it without a hitch. Joyce and her foster-mother Mrs Forde, who you may recall was a spiritualist, had come for the occasion – which only increased the nerves. Although uneasy, I realised to my relief on reflection, that I was to read what is the word of God, and that gave me heart to gear myself to read with authority.

The carol service was a great success number-wise, and Mrs Forde approached me afterwards and said, 'I was most surprised at the way you confidently read the Bible. I did not think you could do that!' In a way I was just as surprised. As for Mrs Forde, it may well be that she carried in her mind the difference in temperament or character between my sister and me : Joyce was vivacious, excited openly about almost anything, given to constant laughter, often thinking aloud, full of warmth when speaking to familiars or to strangers. Her disposition was so infectious that one became caught up in her mood, and always being able to bring to life even little things for conversation so that helplessly it drew one to listen to her. Everyone seemed to love her. I had a feeling that Mrs Forde thought me gloomy in disposition by comparison. Moreover, on one occasion she took offence at my opinion about her habit of reading the tea leaves in her cup after she drank her tea. I was more open about my belief in Christ than Joyce was in the presence of the Fordes, and Mrs Forde considered me over-analytical about the things of this world.

Still, Mrs Forde's reaction at the carols did much good in boosting my confidence in public speaking. I knew that if I had strong convictions – even about teaching procedure – with God being gracious, I could possibly make a fist of teaching once I left college.

However, that growing confidence was to be shaken within a few months, through a shock that was to disturb me for years.

The first year of college over, at the end of 1960, I was still unsure of where I stood in terms of academic assessment and how I fared against others after several teaching rounds. I accompanied 'Dad and Mum' to the Belgrave Heights Christian Convention a day or two after Christmas Day. It was to be my third DVI camp. Excitement mounted at the prospect of gathering with several thousand believers, anticipating eagerly the addresses of good speakers, camping with a good many Christians that I had come to know throughout the year at DVI meetings.

Ken was there – not as a camper, but on a day-to-day basis for a meeting or two. He would come down to the DVI camp on the convention's eastern side in the gully and have lunch with us in the DVI dining room.

Once, after lunch, we sat at a dining room table out of earshot of the others.

"What do you think of the convention?" he asked. He looked handsome and clean-cut as ever.

"It's been good. I thought the speaker excellent this morning."

He probed, "In what way?"

"Well," groping for an answer I said, "The way he spoke of being tired of our sin so that we then decide to give up everything for Christ in total surrender. He said that you must let go and let God."

"Well," said Ken, "that sounds fine, but I perceived that he was saying that as long as we are in Christ we will be delivered from all sin."

"Oh, I did not hear that."

"Well, it was *implied*. You make a decision, go down to the front after the message, and in full surrender you now have a victorious life."

"Oh..," I replied.

"Yes," he went on, "it is not the right approach to biblical teaching. What we call *sanctification* is an ongoing process.

It does not come through one dramatic decision to become fully surrendered to Christ. There is no end to the struggle against sin. These Keswick-type speakers – some of them – may have good things to say, but they are tied Keswick-style to having to speak on Romans 6 and 7, and Romans 12."

"Yes, I have noticed that," I said.

At this point of the conversation, I wondered why he came to the convention, unless it was the long ties to DVI, and the fellowship in lively discussion that should give rise to what he considered to be a mature understanding of what we ought to believe. I gave Ken the benefit of the doubt. Besides, he appeared to know more than I did about Christian doctrine. Also, he bore a presence that I found hard to resist, being forceful in what he believed, possibly quick-tempered if I differed too much from him.

"Yes," he went on, "Romans 6:11, for example, is a classic case of error in this Keswick approach. When it says "Likewise reckon ye also yourselves to be dead indeed unto sin…," Paul is not telling us to think ourselves dead to sin when we are not. Keswick says that, although you know you are not dead to it, become dead to it when you are commanded in a demonstration for full surrender, such as we see at the end of meetings here. The truth is: We are not being commanded to be dead to sin, for we are already dead to it, if we are saved."

"Mmm, it's a little confusing to me," I said.

Ken went back over what Romans 6:11 means, or what he took it to mean.

I made my way down to our boys' tent after lunch, rehearsing the matter: By 'reckon,' it seemed that we are to appreciate what Christ has already achieved for us so that we are dead to sin by being in union with him. In a true believer sin does not reign: because it is so, it shall not dominate our lives. Ken said (as the apostle says) that we are not under the law but under grace.

Therefore, because sin does not reign, we can be exhorted to not let it reign. It was heady stuff for a young believer. My admiration for Ken grew even more: I could see that we can easily overlook the grace and power of God in our striving with sin.

After the Convention, 'Dad' took me up country with him, although I cannot recall exactly where. It was north, and blazing hot, where we visited some of the children in remote Victoria whom he tutored by correspondence for the Postal Sunday School Movement – yet another Christian work with which he was associated. He persuaded me strongly to become a correspondence teacher as well, as we drove back home in the heat.

"I am sweating like a pig," I said.

"Only horses sweat, son", he replied. "Horses sweat, men perspire, and women glow."

"Yes, well, I'm perspiring," I laughed.

"You know," he continued, "work is one per cent inspiration, ninety-nine per cent perspiration."

I replied, "I remember you saying that in your Sutherland years."

"Well, 'Mum' and I knew a lot of hard work there."

"No doubt you did," I assured him.

"You seem to be coping well with college. You have done well. Many of the children at Sutherland were not Rhode Scholars."

I smiled, and basked in the brief, ensuing silence of several sayings 'Dad' had. He loved to describe a busy day as 'a large day;' told me again that moral strength is in terms of 'Meekness is not weakness.' He could hardly wait to get home to the dark room where he would develop photos of the people we saw up country.

The summer respite from attending college was quickly passing by, when one night after a DVI meeting, Ken invited me to spend a weekend with him and his family down at Sorrento. It was still summertime, the days had been consistently hot, and therefore I looked forward to a weekend at the beach in the company of Ken, his wife and three children, one of whom was a young teenage girl.

That same night Ken gave me a small book as a gift. It contained a long poem by Francis Thompson called *The Hound of Heaven* –

'I fled Him, down the nights and down the days;

I fled Him, down the arches of the years'…

Couched in unfamiliar language of the ninth century, I found much of it hard to fathom, but this I did discern: The poem seemed to echo what I perceived as Ken's strong belief in the sovereignty of God to save no matter what anyone as a fugitive seeks to do to escape 'the strong Feet' that follow until he is caught up by God, Who convinces the sinner-fugitive that no-one else will truly consider him worthy of love, assuring the sinner of this in such a way that he is compelled to clasp the hand of God as he arrives at knowing the truest love is only found in God, Who is the one that the fugitive has been seeking while on the run from Him. I became charmed to think that God seeks us in such a way for salvation.

Apart from occasional visits to 'Auntie Lil' in Preston and Sister Joyce in Brunswick, since leaving Sutherland I had not spent time of any length elsewhere – apart from the Belgrave Conventions. It had been a while since I had been to the seaside. I had sweet memories of times while holidaying away from Sutherland when I pestered the Willis family at Meerlieu into spending a day or two at Lakes Entrance. They would kindly give in, Mrs Willis taking the opportunity to teach me to swim, while Mr Willis stayed well clear of the beach as he had a morbid fear of sharks. Therefore, I was eager to go to Sorrento with Ken and his family, eager to see the sea and swim, allured at learning more from Ken about the sovereign ways of God to be buoyed up by fuller security. I had never heard 'Dad' or 'Mum,' or anyone at St John's, or DVI, speak of God in the way Ken did – God as King over all, unfrustrated by men's plans so that man is not able to thwart Him; in His plans hounding people as it were until He won them over. Had not I found Christ in that way when seventeen at Sutherland?

After enjoying dinner at Sorrento with Ken, his wife and children, and reading "*The Hound of Heaven*" for a time, and since it was a very hot night, Ken suggested that he and I take to a couple of stretchers and sleep outside in less stuffy air.

We fell into talking with our stretchers side by side, under a scintillating starlit sky.

As the night grew late, Ken turned off the torchlight and I lay there in momentary silence.

Suddenly he leant over and *touched me*.

What did I say by way of horror and protest, I cannot recall, but I expressed horror so that he withdrew and began to apologize. I do not recall how I responded to his plea to be forgiven. All I know is that he touched me. Stunned, and shell-shocked, I sought to go to sleep. Did he decide to go inside and leave me on my own? All I recall is that he touched me. How the night went by and became day, all is a blank, including about all of us coming together for breakfast. Yet I do recall slipping away and sitting on the sand as I overlooked the waves rolling into shore. I sat there reading my Bible – clearly I recall reading Revelation 19 – about Jesus coming again on a white horse victoriously. Still stunned, still shell-shocked I returned eventually to the holiday house.

I never told 'Dad,' or 'Mum,' or anyone at all about what happened at Sorrento, but my life would never be the same again. In hindsight I became more stressful, more withdrawn (particularly in the company of many a man), worrying myself deeply about college and the state of the church and about my future as a teacher.

More piercing at the time was the fear that I had been 'easy pickings for a bird of prey.' I had been lured and trapped by the gift of the book for my college music assignment, then by the gift of the booklet *The Hound of Heaven*, even by doctrine that seemed to have the ring of truth. The three gifts were good *but he touched me*. I had been easy prey, and I asked myself why. It seemed I was viewed as a straggler of a running herd, the young animal falling behind when the cheetah gathers lightning speed to bring down its victim. I fell, I was brought down, devoured. I was fresh out of Sutherland, sought after once by a similar predator in the past but repelled without being touched at the time. This time I was caught unawares, alarmed at the swiftness of it all amid camouflage. Fresh out of Sutherland. Weak. An innocent young man yet to come of age and learn there could be 'Christian' camouflage. For this reason I became more resolved to hide my upbringing as best I could; for it appeared to be the reason for me becoming a victim of a patient though a relentless and ruthless chase.

I think I thought Ken could be forgiven but the friendship, as it had been once, ended.

The second year of college began in seeking friendship but believing that if it were somewhat too deep it would make me wary. I sat at the back for all lectures and laughed and talked as unobtrusively as possible – still with the two girls who were the best of friends. Jill attracted me but I discovered that she already had a boyfriend. I struck up a friendship with Bob Kelsall, who happened to be a Christian, a genial fellow, well-liked by the students to the point that they happily gave him the nod for the job of editor for the college paper. His friendship was such a relief after the trauma of the month before that I hoped and prayed that he did not tire of me seeking his company as often as I did.

Bob suggested that I be Sports Editor, alongside Margaret Moon.

As the editor Bob, I am sure, was responsible for the Big Brother column, which in one issue he had a so-called male enquirer in Dorothy Dix-style seeking advice about a college girl being interested to the point of desiring to be engaged, but he feared other college girls would lose interest in him. His college work was suffering. Big Brother advised the enquirer that his college work was 'a minor matter,' and declared the girl was 'emotionally unstable and should never have entered the teaching profession.' Besides, she would understand that he could not afford to become engaged as she was a college student herself!

We students remained for our 2 years on a scholarship of a mere sixteen pounds [equivalent to $593.22 today] a fortnight, and I for one faced the struggle of being unable to afford a car at the end of the year, when it seemed I was destined to be appointed to a country school. I looked forward to a salary on exit from college as a male of 1,053 pounds but I would need a car for the country before I set out teaching. The poor girls were to exit on 717.00 pounds if under 21, and 866 pounds if over 21. The difference caused rumblings among the female students.

I especially feared being appointed to a very distant country school because I suspected my college marks, and teaching rounds' assessments, were not exactly outstanding. I was losing a degree of confidence that revealed itself in whilst desiring to play for the first football team of the college, I was too afraid to try out for it, lest I failed to qualify.

My teaching-round mark would have received a boost in spring when I spent three weeks in a staged rural school room near the college. In one particular lesson for assessment, I had armed myself with equipment that was bound to mesmerize the children – a hat with a veil, a smoker to lull bees into sleepiness, and a honeycomb frame.

How did I arrive with such equipment to 'stun' the students? Some weeks prior a vestry man at St John's – who knew that I was interested in procuring a hive of bees – told me that there was a lady at Eaglemont who was troubled by a hive of bees on a shrub in her backyard. As I had no car, I boarded the train at our local station of Diamond Creek with a cardboard box and sticky tape! At Eaglemont I found the lady's house, went into her backyard, spotted the hive of bees hanging on a branch of the shrub, held the opened cardboard box under the hive, and with a bare right hand shook the bees into the box, shut the box, sealed it and returned to catch the train nearby there at Eaglemont. By then it was peak time for workers coming home from the city. I sat in a carriage with other passengers, who were oblivious to what I had in the box, all the way back to Diamond Creek, seven stations down the line!

Mr Tonks, the teacher supervising and assessing me, could not believe his ears when he learnt of how I obtained the hive of bees, and he knew I had a captive audience for the lesson. He reported the lesson favourably.

It taught me again that when one speaks publicly, it is more successful if he or she is absorbed by the subject to be spoken on, causing one to be far less self-conscious so as not to trip, stumble, and stammer with a head spinning in fear – being successful as I had been at the DVI Christmas Carol service. This was how I fortified myself when 'Dad' obtained permission for me to preach at St John's. It was to be my first sermon ever. I kept in mind not only to centre on God's Word, but to remind myself that there were people in the congregation who needed to hear a clear word about the folly of trusting in both so-called good works and church attendance, particularly thinking of the Masons present. I built a simple sermon on one text after another, as best as I knew how. 'Dad' said that I showed some potential in preaching.

I do not recall Rev Moorhouse's preaching, but I recall his rigidity when it came to conducting the set order of service as the Book of Common Prayer outlined it. One evening I walked up the hill from home to attend Evening Prayer. I entered the foyer and then into the church itself to find that I was the only one in attendance at the set time. Rev Moorhouse stood on the top step at the front of the altar, candles ablaze. His prayer book was open, his eyes fixed beyond me. I had sat on the right side at the row behind the front pew. Not exchanging a single glance, he began the order for Evening Prayer, I still alone in the pews. I looked around – no one had entered the doors as he began to read with a loud voice a sentence of scripture.

He could have read 'Dearly beloved *brother*, the Scripture moveth us in sundry places to acknowledge and confess our manifold sins and wickedness.'… – instead of the routine 'Dearly beloved *brethren*,' as I stood alone in the church.

Then I knelt on the red cushion at my pew, as was the custom for the set 'general confession.' A quick glance and I was still alone. I read out in a flustered way the confession. I remained kneeling while Rev Moorhouse as 'priest' read the Absolution. He read from the Prayer Book about ministers seeming to have the power to grant remission of sins. My mind flashed back to the Sunday morning the year before when I challenged him about his own power to forgive. Yet did not the Absolution say that the power to forgive hung on repentance on the part of the sinner, and that God Himself grants true repentance? – yes, this is what the Absolution said.

Then Rev Moorhouse knelt. A quick glance and still no-one else had congregated yet! Rev Moorhouse and I alone recited the Lord's Prayer together.

Upon 'Amen' to the Lord's Prayer, I did not dare to turn around to see if anyone else was in the pews, instead in fear I knew that if I was still alone, Rev Moorhouse, out of his liturgical habit would sing-song the next part of the worship and he expected me to sing-song in response –

"O Lord, open thou our lips"

I in response to intone, "And our mouth shall show forth thy praise."

Moorhouse: "O God, make speed to save us."

I began to intone, "And our mouth"… and heard from behind me an accompanying voice or two respond with "And our mouth shall show forth thy praise."

'Dad' thought that we should still remain faithful to St Johns – 'Only rats desert a sinking ship.' Besides, he thought we should never go past a church that was nearest to home.

He still believed that DVI was to be regarded to our relief as a way of making up for what evangelical fellowship we lacked. As for 'Dad' he at least found further fellowship as chairman for a Christian group known as BMMF. He had strong ties also to the Anglican Church by being chairman also of the Anglican's state mission arm in the Church Missionary Society, an evangelical body.

The end of the year came and it was time for us second and third year students to graduate. Two hundred of us were to 'hit' Victoria's state schools, with approximately 120,000 children to *pass through* our hands, so long as they did not *pass out* on meeting us! Some discussion had risen over the matter of purchasing an academic gown *just to wear for one occasion*. Bob, the magazine's editor, saw humour could be drawn out of attempts to raise money for the gowns with the organisation of a soup kitchen one lunch hour. Bob wrote in the college magazine that one sole student cast suspicion on the contents of the soup for sale, sent the soup for analysis to a chemist who replied –

> "Dear Sir,
>
> We regret to inform you that your horse is suffering from tuberculosis and does not have long to live."

The graduation took place in the Coburg Town Hall early December, every graduate in a purchased gown, mainly to our cost. By now we had all received our appointments for our first school, being bonded to the Education Department for three years. I had a choice of a kind in the appointment. I was destined for the country – like it or not – and I had chosen the Bairnsdale area, and I landed with a rural school north of Bairnsdale in a timber milling place called Bulumwaal, quite close to the kind people at Bairnsdale who gave me such enchanting holidays when they lived at Meerlieu on their sheep farm when I was a boy at the Sutherland Homes.

Is That a Place?

"Is that really a place?" asked quite a few friends when they heard I had been posted to a school at a place called Bulumwaal. Dick Cranbourne on Radio 3UZ often joked about a place with such a name so that people thought it was an imaginary town – fit for a laugh. A town? – not even that as I discovered! It merely comprised two timber mills and one dairy farm. There was not even a store – instead, a fellow called Bruce ran a small van to Bairnsdale daily for the mail and for any goods that the small number of residents wanted.

Alluvial gold had attracted prospectors to the place in the 1860's, then what had been truly a town died until the 1880's, when it was revived at further discovery of gold and grew to a population of almost 1000, with five stores, three bakeries, two hotels, a post office and a school. After World War 2 timber milling became virtually the sole industry, and was so when I arrived in 1962.

The little school of number 1794 sat perched on top of a hill and out of sight of the timber mills below. Mr Riseley, who looked like a tall version of Pa Kettle, and who was the one and only farmer at Bulumwaal, drove me up to see the school in his small truck. The school appeared like half of a house, its tall roof out of proportion with its length and width. It sat on stumps and the entrance to the wooden building was past a water tank. A playground of hard yellowish gravel was on another level of ground above the school's large green door of entry.

Mr and Mrs Riseley were to have me as a boarder. Theirs was a small dairy farm and the first place one arrived at when approaching Bulumwaal downhill. They were a couple getting on in years, and had a boy who had just begun secondary school in Bairnsdale. Harry's room was opposite mine in the small wooden house. The home was quite dingy and semi dark even under the summer sun. At night several kerosene lamps were lit to provide the sole lighting.

I arrived at Bulumwaal several days before school was to commence. There were only seven children on the roll – the bare minimum for a school to exist. Only four would be in attendance until the other three returned after holidays! All seven children were of timber milling families.

My grey Morris Minor groaned to reach the top of the school hill. It only possessed eight horse power. David Graham, father of Irene who had attended college with me for two years, informed me it would prove to be a reliable car for travelling back and forth from home to Bulumwaal, and for driving from Riseleys to the school each day. I had little money and could only scrape enough for what people called 'the gutless wonder.' Irene had bought a ten horse power car of the same type and I envied the power she had in her Morris Minor. Yet 'YTO53' got me to the school despite the effort it had to make in climbing the steep gravel road to a pine tree or two for shade.

Inside the school were several wooden desks facing a rather large fireplace. My table was to the right of it. Several books or records were to be surveyed: The roll, the record book for corporal punishment, the cash book, the latest Teachers' Gazette with the syllabi for the various grades.

IS THAT A PLACE?

A rural school had to adjust to the grades each school found itself with, alongside the teaching for alternative years for some subjects. It was standard in rural schools to teach alternative years for some grade subjects. For example, grade five children in a rural school may be found following the grade six syllabus for Geography, but in grade six doing the grade five course. To some degree it eased the burden for a rural school teacher. Yet where I only had seven children, with some being the only child in a certain grade, there was as much preparation in teaching one child a subject as for teaching twenty or more in a larger school. Familiarity with the Department's syllabi made teaching easier one year after another, but as a fledging teacher it meant many hours of preparation.

Day One arrived consuming breakfast cereal topped with cream and milk, together with toast, and with a lunch prepared by Mrs Riseley, I wended my way along the road past a small public hall in my "gutless wonder" up the hill to the school.

The four children accompanied by parents arrived well on time for a close look at their new teacher. Soon the parents disappeared and the school's hand bell was rung. We all assembled around the flagpole on the decline behind the building. I looked over my pupils and recalled the advice of some of the college's male lecturers, who suggested that on the first day at school be stern and overly strict so that the children are more or less shaking in their shoes with considerable respect, and then as the days went on, let one's strictness relax so as to win their favour as well as their fear.

Could I muster up such sternness with four little children? I did my best to show that I meant to take the teaching of them seriously, but it seemed not in my nature to go in with 'guns blazing.' It seemed incongruous to be too stern with such a small number of students who did not give me the impression of desiring to try me out.

We sang *God Save our Gracious Queen* and swore the oath to serve God and country, and then walked inside through the heavy wooden door.

It was a warm day but regulations required that I wore my sports coat unless it became unbearably hot. My thin tie wound around a shirt that was a shade tight around my neck, but day one passed quickly and I was left alone to ponder over my lot. I figured that I must have done quite poorly in college assessments to have ended up in such a hole as Bulumwaal. I reflected on the three-year bond I was under to the Department. It had trained me at great expense so that I would have to repay the whole cost of training were I to resign prematurely. Still, although I had been cast into a rather strange and forbidden place, it appeared ideal in a number of ways – the quietness and easy pace of country life promised to suit me. I was my own boss (at least for one year), and I only had seven children to teach for that year of 1962.

The days went by as 'Sir' grew accustomed to sweeping the school clean, emptying the toilet can each week and burying its remains when no-one was in sight, working on the cash book for application of extra money for such aforementioned duties for the week, before returning to the dairy farm in the valley for the night. As the summer passed, the autumn came, then the nearness of winter would see the windowless house plunged into almost complete darkness in the early evening as the kerosene lamps gave so little light. Mr and Mrs Riseley were reasonably friendly but they were not the best of company, and I would spend the evenings attempting to read in the pale glow of a kerosene lamp in my own bedroom, or strain at capturing on a transistor a radio station music that would fade in and out in the remote country air.

I made up my mind to alternate between going home one weekend and staying at Bulumwaal on the other.

Of course, I returned home for Easter. It was heartening to be home, for not only was it lonely at Bulumwaal on weekends, but home also meant being with fellow-believers in Christ, particularly when the Easter Belgrave Convention lent itself to camping in the rarefied heights of the grounds in company with campers of DVI.

Such fellowship was o'so sweet as we came together to remember Christ's death for us – when we talked, sang, studied the Scriptures that touched on His great sacrifice. On Easter Saturday I took leave of the convention and travelled to Brunswick to pick up my sister in order to take her with me to see Geelong play Carlton in the VFL (Victorian Football League) for the much-heralded clash between Geelong's boom recruit in Polly Farmer and the big, bulky John Nicolls of Carlton that drew us along with many thousands to the Carlton ground.

Joyce and I stood shoulder to shoulder on the incline alongside the thousands closely gathered. Men in the main barked out loudly by way of urging on their favoured teams who ran on to the ground through large banners.

Joyce said to me in a voice not all that soft, "Which team is Geelong?"

> "The one with the blue hoops," I answered, a little embarrassed.
>
> "Then why are we hearing 'Polly,' 'Polly'!"
>
> "This is his first game for Geelong and a lot is expected of him," I laconically answered.
>
> Again embarrassed.

It was the start of any number of questions Joyce fired at me as I sought to concentrate on the flow of the game. She wanted to know why the teams could not play with a round ball, for wouldn't it bounce better? She asked the reason for four posts at either end of the ground. Perhaps the most dreaded question had to do with John Nicolls – how could he play when he seemed so fat? One expected the ire of some nearby Carlton supporters but to my relief it only raised a laugh, as by that time in the game it was plain that my sister was not actually a staunch supporter or student of the game, and not a few of the nearby male Carlton supporters were getting tipsy and somewhat oblivious to the progress of the game.

I returned to the Belgrave Convention late that evening.

After the Convention I felt inspired to set up a Sunday School for Bulumwal's children on every second weekend in the little public hall on Sunday afternoons. The parents happily agreed to the plan and I based my teaching about the things of the Lord on the wonderful books Missions Publications produced, books that captivated the children's interest so well. I eventually ran the Sunday School on Sunday mornings, once I learnt of a family called Smith that lived out at Hillside beyond Bairnsdale. Bruce and his wife were keen evangelicals, and it meant that weekends at Bulumwaal were no longer lonely times, with me spending time with Bruce's family for a large part of Sunday afternoons and at night attending their church at Lindenow. Their minister reminded me a little of Groucho Marx in looks, but he was a magnetic preacher of the Word.

I came home to attend a joint twenty first birthday with Peter mid-June. You may recall I was but twenty days older than he. On returning to Bulumwaal I told the Riseleys about my birthday celebration but never mentioned Peter. They never asked if I had family and that pleased me. Nor did I mention to Mr Riseley that I could help with milking cows if there was a dire need, for I desired to keep my past a secret. Those at Peter's and my joint celebration largely comprised DVI people, who never asked about my upbringing but I presupposed many of them knew. It seemed my company was prized most of all for my joint-life with them in Christ. Yet I would be evasive with Bruce's family at Hillside or pretend, if need be, to make out the folk at Diamond Creek were my genuine parents.

At 'home' (as I could genuinely call it) some of the weekend was spent studying books about bee life, and watching and hoping that the queen bee of the one hive would not up and leave me with a depleted colony that may not survive with few numbers.

It is said in Greek mythology that a swarm of bees landing somewhere conveyed a blessing, but people fear swarms in our time without realising that bees in such a flight are at their most passive, and some alarmed people will sadly contact the council to have them exterminated. My great hope lay in the fact that even if there were a swarm from my one hive, those that were swarming may fly to a spot close by, where I hoped to quickly capture them and have two hives, for I possessed another box to house them.

Fortune had it that just before the September holidays when I was home, about half the bees swarmed from the one box to settle awhile on a nearby branch of a gumtree on our property. I now had two hives. The ageing queen of the one box had been starved by the other bees so that upon slimming down, she was light enough to fly with about half of the hive. I returned to Bulumwaal looking forward to producing honey in the near future, as I had purchased a honey extractor, a metal cylinder that spun around at the turn of a handle and that flung out the honey from the inserted frames of the hives and left honey dripping down to a container below.

Before the holidays a family of eleven children came to Bulumwaal to live. Seven of the children became enrolled at the school, increasing our numbers by one hundred per cent! Not many years separated at least four of the very young Rickards, then there was older Billy, followed by Shirley and last of all Dorothy in increasing age. Dorothy was thirteen but in grade six – quite tall, developing into quite a mature girl physically.

At the time that the Rickards arrived in the timber milling place, I had been tutoring a 34-year-old Austrian mill hand over a period of time in evenings because he wanted to learn English. He was a sad man, depressed over being jilted back in Austria, his land of birth. I tried to witness to him about the Gospel – as best I could – but he seemed too morbid in disposition and too hampered linguistically to comprehend what I said. At each nightly session with him he was becoming gloomier and gloomier about life.

Then the shock came at school early on a Friday morning when police arrived to inform me that the Austrian had abducted Dorothy after stopping the family's car and ordering Dorothy to get out of the vehicle at gunpoint. He had fled with Dorothy into the bush.

Then on Sunday morning we received the news that two policemen tracked down the Austrian in the bush near Bulumwaal and arrested him, rescuing Dorothy in the process. All day Friday at school had been an anxious time, with the children of all but the Rickards wondering why police had come up to our school to speak to me. Something was said by me to the seven children present to have them believing that there was nothing alarming about the police presence, but for the rest of the day it was difficult to mask my fear for Dorothy.

Thankfully, the Austrian was arrested and was scheduled to appear in Bairnsdale's Court of Petty Sessions on charges of child stealing, assault with a weapon, and being armed with felonious intent. Yet, on the morning that he was eventually to appear in court, the Austrian was found dead beside a car by a pulpwood cutter. The sad man had died from firing on himself a shotgun hooked to the radio aerial of his car.

The word got around that the jilted man of Austria had wanted Dorothy to marry him. As far as it could be known, Dorothy was not sexually assaulted.

My mind is a blank when it seeks to recall the aftermath of the abduction. Such was the trauma at the time. Besides, the records would now be lost that told of the poor Rickard family staying on at Bulumwaal and the children remaining at school after their sister's nightmare. They seemed to remain stoically, for an end of the year concert had all fourteen children present.

I myself was not destined to stay on, for the appointment to Bulumwaal was only a temporary position, and I was eager to become a permanent teacher. The Teachers' Gazette was scanned and I decided to apply to be headmaster of a school called Wal Wal, north of Stawell, which guaranteed two years of settlement.

I planned to put on the farewell school concert in the public hall. The townsfolk of Bulumwaal had never known one before. There was a lady in Bulumwaal prepared to accompany the children on the piano when they sang – among other songs – Christmas carols.

The concert was warmly received, particularly the item of a shadow play that I adopted from what 'Dad' amused us with at the Sutherland Homes, when a light or two before a sheet cast shadows behind it, showing figures at an operating table opening up a patient's stomach and pulling out all kinds of ridiculous things from it. Appreciation that night was expressed for teaching the children up on the hill, and for teaching Sunday School on Sundays down there in the public hall.

With only a few weeks left for the year, one Sunday night found me travelling tired with a little too much speed down the hill near Riseleys – almost home from spending a late evening with my Christian friends, the Smiths, at Hillside. I lost control of the Morris Minor and ended up in the ditch beside the road. The car was written off, so I was bound to stay at Bulumwaal until school's final day.

On the next weekend, being car-less, I had time to help Mr Riseley bring in freshly mown hay from the paddocks. I also contacted Mr Willis, who with his family had me for holidays as a boy at the Homes. I would from time to time see Mr and Mrs Willis whenever I remained at Bulumwaal for weekends, and I thought that he could possibly help me purchase another car.

Mr Willis did find a suitable car, but it was not ready by my final day at Bulumwaal, therefore I travelled home to Diamond Creek by train from Bairnsdale. Travelling back by train from Bairnsdale I no longer felt an unsure urchin of the institution for neglected children, but as one sure that I could grow satisfied with teaching and not be troubled when thrown amongst strange people in new places, though a degree of the loneliness was anticipated at Wal Wal, as it had been at Bulumwaal.

Returning home, I camped with DVI after Christmas at the Christian convention. It was a welcomed time after the loneliness at Bulumwaal. To see Christian friends again daily in the rarefied air at Belgrave Heights and to hear inspiring speakers such as Arthur Gunn (a Presbyterian who said that if he had been ordained in the Anglican church he could have become 'Canon Gunn') found me singing longingly on the train back to Bairnsdale the day before the convention concluded, after I had the news that my new car – an FJ Holden – was ready to pick up –

> 'He leadeth me, He leadeth me;
> By His own hand He leadeth me;
> His faithful foll'wer I would be,
> For by His hand He leadeth me.'

IS THAT A PLACE?

Ken still frequented the conventions at Belgrave and would speak to me in the closeness of the DVI campers when he came up for the day. Yet the incident at Sorrento soured any fellowship we may have had. He seemed to be under the impression that I had forgiven him merely because he had asked to be forgiven on that horrid night by the seaside, but he sensed there was an uneasiness that scarcely could be reversed, as I froze still at the violation of me.

On purchasing my FJ Holden, I hardly had time to enjoy the new-found power of the 2.15 litre with its six-cylinder engine before, as a family, we set off on a Cook's tour to New South Wales in 'Dad's' large black 1938 Buick sedan. By family I meant 'Dad,' 'Mum,' David their youngest son, Nancy the boarder and me.

I believe a Cook's tour has its origins long ago in Thomas Cook, of England, who began his career as a travel agent by arranging for a special train to run between Leicester and Loughborough for a temperance meeting! Later he conducted excursions in 1855 to France for the Paris Exposition, and in the following year led a grand tour of Europe.

'Cook's tour' grew as a term to mean a rapid and extensive tour. Our tour from Diamond Creek to many parts of New South Wales was certainly such a one. Almost every morning found us laboriously pulling down our three tents and loading our belongings meticulously on the trailer and roof of the Dodge before setting off for a new campsite. 'Dad' took pride in resorting to the skill that he claimed to have acquired from his Boy Scout days (Peter, his eldest son carried a second Christian name of Baden in the admiration 'Dad' had for the founder of the Boy Scout movement). I found the constant moving on during the trip irksome, and was relieved to arrive back home after two or three-weeks' frantic journey.

Yet one sweet memory of the tour was to linger after we arrived back home – a memory of what was seemingly uneventful, but made sweet many years later by the lasting impression God's word can make. 'Dad' suggested that he and I attend a post-Katoomba Convention meeting one night when we were camping in the Blue Mountains. It was a Bible study of Colossians 3, majoring on the words –

> 'If ye then be risen with Christ, seek those
> things which are above, where Christ sitteth on
> the right hand of God. Set your affection on
> things above, and not on things on the earth.
> For ye are dead, and your life is hid with
> Christ in God.'

It may well have been lastingly linked in my memory several mornings before, because on our trip – prior to packing up to move on again for our Cook's tour – Nancy saw me reading a book that a DVI friend gave me for my twenty-first birthday – *New Heavens and a New Earth*. She thought to warn me for my good by asserting "You can be so heavenly minded that you are no earthly use." I sought to brush off her brusque remark, troubled to think that it was wrong to get caught up too much with contemplation on the Last Things. Yet on the night 'Dad' and I sat under the Convention speaker in Katoomba, I became convinced that the opposite of what Nancy asserted was perhaps true – "You can become so earthly minded that you are of no heavenly use."

Well, what lingered most of all in its sweetness that night at Katoomba was the hope of Christ appearing again because our life is hidden in Him. Surely, it was to drive me to love Christ all the more in this life, and cause me to serve Him all the better. It had been a comfort that night on the way back to our camp site to share with 'Dad' in conversation about our future and hidden life when Christ appears; to be 'heavenly minded' as we ought.

Wal Wal

....

'Mum,' David and I pulled up in a cloud of dust that drifted past my two-tone green FJ Holden as we came to a stop outside the general store-cum-post office of Wal Wal. Wal Wal was situated in the wheat-growing Wimmera district, between Stawell and Rupanyup, just north of a little town called Glenorchy. It was a stifling hot day.

Inside the general store I rang the little bell on the counter and a grey-haired man appeared before us.

"Er, hello, I'm the new teacher for the school here. Eddie – Eddie Smith is my name."

I turned around and stood slightly aside so that 'Mum' and David were visible to the store keeper.

I was at a loss as to how to introduce them, but 'Mum' spoke up by saying, "Hello, I'm Mrs Smith, and David here is the youngest of all our sons". She added a brief word or two about Peter, and then the store keeper, after welcoming us, made enquiries about my wife.

"Well, I am not married!"

"You're not?"

"No."

"How is it that you have been posted to the school. We have a school residence over the road that's for a married teacher."

"Oh!" I exclaimed. "I didn't realise this was a school for a married teacher."

"This is a bit awkward, unless you're getting married soon."

"No, I am not," I said.

"Well, would you occupy the residence?"

"Oh, well – I"…

"I mean, can you fend for yourself?"

"Uh" –

Mum came into the conversation, "Eddie has never had that experience. At home he has relied on me in particular. Even in his first year out teaching only last year he lived on a dairy farm and paid board to the dairy farmers there at Bulumwaal."

"Mmm," mused the storekeeper. "Maybe, just maybe, he'll have to live with people here. I don't know who, but we'll look into it and let ya know."

He excused himself to find the key for the school, which was situated just one hundred yards or so from the store.

After we saw the school, and I sized up, as best I could, what was to be the centre of education for twenty-one children with me as headmaster for two years, we went back to the store for further conversation, with the dilemma of where I would live for two years around Wal Wal. The matter was obviously very much on the storekeeper's mind.

Yet before 'Mum,' David and I clambered into my car, later on to return home, and before farewelling the storekeeper, he appeared keen to give his opinion about the previous teacher, Murray Dale. I knew Murray at Coburg Teacher's College, a chirpy student who was engaged, at what many thought was a young age, to a pretty female student at the college. Murray excelled in sport at college, and his fiancé was obviously the light of his life. As soon as they had finished college, they planned to get married.

What was Murray like as Wal Wal's headmaster? The storekeeper admitted Murray's wife did much without reward at the school and was loved by the children, but he thought Murray did little to advance the children's education. Instead, he extended their recesses to extraordinary lengths, which the children grew accustomed to, many of them delighting in it. Perhaps he had no fear of the District Inspector suddenly appearing on the scene and catching him out on his layback way of teaching. He appeared cunning in creating what he styled as learning through outdoor activities, but what were dubious means for students' progress in the three R's in particular. Anyhow, such was his vibrant personality that any doubting parents were won over to his unorthodox methods of learning.

A week before school was to begin in 1963, I returned to Wal Wal to prepare the year's work for all grades. A certain frustration was discovered on learning that some grades had only one or two children, which meant much preparation to teach certain subjects for just a few pupils. Such were the demands of a rural school.

The storekeeper had alerted the school council about the need for farmers to billet me over what was to be at least two years for me at Wal Wal. It was decided that I would stay one school term at a time with a number of people. The first place of lodging was to be with a fellow called Max, his wife, and his two children, who were in attendance at the school. Max was a farmhand working for a farmer who had acquired his property as a soldier settler after World War 1, when returned soldiers were given farmland that had been formed through the subdivision of large rural estates. Max was often bleary-eyed through his fondness of strong drink. He and his wife were poorly educated and they did little to expand their children's learning at home. All the same, in a stolid kind of way they welcomed me for the term, as money for board promised an increased income for the family in its struggle on the very low wage for a farmhand.

Living with some children of the school threatened to dull the effect of appearing stern, for the plan perhaps could not help but mean that one term after the other were destined to be spent with only people whose children were at the school. The ploy on my part was to play the game of aloofness in Max's house in the evenings and mornings, for does not "familiarity breed contempt?" Max and his wife asked me if I could have their children accompany me in my car each day, as they had no transport of their own.

My car was to cover considerable distance as the first term went by, for I continued the practice I had while at Bulumwaal – staying up the country one weekend and returning home the next. Therefore, there were a number of oil changes required for the FJ Holden in the course of the term, particularly when the car was burning up more oil than normal.

Max and I came to an agreement: he would change the oil in my car and I would milk the cow as he was supposed to do. Only once did the bargain fail. After he had emptied the Holden's oil sump of the filthy black oil one time, I started up the car to drive off, and the red light flashed on – Max had not put the new oil in the engine!

I grew fond of my little school of students but the weekends at Wal Wal were lonely ones. I did not have the blessing of fellowship that I had while at Bulumwaal. I attended the Stawell Presbyterian Church only to be appalled at the minister preaching in his sermon about "the spark of divinity" in every man's soul. I turned to a church of the same denomination at Rupanyup – found the worship bearable but lacking the fire of devotion that I craved. All the same, I myself had lost some of the fire I once had. Satan played games with me every now and then as time passed at Wal Wal. I would seek God's forgiveness with salty tears. He would graciously forgive, only to find me slip once more.

'Wilt thou forgive that sin, through which I run,

And do run still: though still I do deplore?'

Yes, I did not always deplore what I had even done – there lay the aggravation. What believer has not known that in a falling, fallen state?

I still attended St John's when I went home, but with reluctance. A new vicar had replaced Moorhouse but all was not well, if not worse. The new man was not Anglo-Catholic in ritual and belief, but proved ecumenic. The Mothers' Union celebrated its jubilee with the presence and blatant blessing of Roman Catholic parishioners. An inter-church Men's Group of St John's began meetings that saw Catholic priests attending.

The second term at Wal Wal found me boarding with the Milligans, a sophisticated and well-educated couple. At the time they had one child at the school and a younger son. Their knowledge of farming did not appear to be as well-rounded as others in the district, but they were doing well.

They had good taste in dress and mingled mostly with people of similar class in Horsham. Mr Milligan was a true gentleman farmer and his wife a glamorous socialite. A grown-up sister of one of the boys in the school became a kind of servant-girl to them. Not infrequently they left the girl to look after their two boys at night while they went to town. I spent the evenings completing some bible courses with the London Bible College, and also learning much from weekly magazines simply called *Knowledge* to help become a more educated teacher.

The third term saw me at another home of children at the school – three of them. Their parents were the ones Max worked for. Mr Kingston was a returned soldier as already stated, handicapped perhaps by the war and limped pronounceably. His wife had been a nurse, and was fastidious about hygiene. Their three boys were scholastically bright, particularly the youngest one – Robert. He was a prolific reader – reading the set books two grades up from his class. I took pride in little Robert being such a good reader, and giving him extra books to challenge him to be even more exceptional. As for George, he had the misfortune of being a stutterer. It seemed that both of his overbearing parents played a part in George stuttering, though it could not be proven. I would seek to put George at ease in the school in front of others, but in his attempt to avoid stuttering the muscles would tighten in his face and throat, so as to make his defect worse. Reading in unison with the other children, singing the songs of the radio magazine *Music for Schools* helped him to a degree.

I did not feel at ease living with the Kingstons and was relieved when the school year came to an end, just for that sake alone.

A book called *Holiness* by J.C. Ryle had been purchased late that year and it helped to arrest any backsliding on my part. Up to that stage I had not read any spiritual book of note, save one about Hudson Taylor, and another called *One Thousand Miles of Miracle*, both of which were not exactly gripping. I spoke to a friend of 'Dad' and 'Mum', Helen, about the book *Holiness* at the Convention. Helen was an exceptional believer, beautiful in Christlikeness, and so dear to the heart of Christ but a few years on she died in a car accident. I was convinced that like Enoch, she walked so close to God that He dearly wanted to take her for Himself – this world was not worthy of her.

"Helen, I have just read the most wonderful book."

"What is it?" she asked.

"It is called *Holiness*."

"Tell me about it," she said, prepared to listen intently, as she always did.

I told her about the chapter *A Woman to be Remembered*, concerning Lot's wife who looked back in defiance of the angel who warned her not to look back when the destruction of Sodom was impending. J.C. Ryle spoke of Lot's wife having a secret love of the world. Our body can be outside Sodom, but the heart is in Sodom. Ryle urges believers to beware of half-hearted religion. 'Some darling evil habit' that cannot be torn from the heart was not to be cherished any longer. 'Remember Lot's wife' thundered throughout the whole chapter.

Helen thought that my knowledge of theology had to be used somehow down the line but after reading *Holiness*, I felt I was only in the shallows when it came to an experiential sense of the holiness God requires of us.

In the following year at Wal Wal, I waited for that fearful day when the district inspector would knock unexpectedly on the large wooden door of the little school to enter and assess my teaching. As someone had said, the inspector would flit from one school to another "to take unsuspecting teachers in the midst of their sins and unpreparedness." One sought to teach each week as if all was normal, but the uncertainty of the inspector's appearance often held one tense in trying to keep up the drill of the students to meet the pleasure of the man who came merely for an hour or two but who held in his hand the fate of one's promotion for the following year.

"Has the inspector been to any school nearby you?" I asked the Glenorchy teacher down the line some months into the second term. He had heard that the inspector had visited Lubeck, but he added to the tension by saying there was no pattern to his movements, as if to make his visit to any school the greatest surprise and produce the greatest terror possible.

A well-acted drill was to be followed upon the inspector's visit. On the inspector being introduced the children were tutored, in response to him greeting them with "Good morning, children" by answering "Good morning, inspector," as if they were glad to see him. In a larger school, and where there was one prized sizeable class, the children could be strategically placed so that the bright ones were sitting in the front desks to field the questions the inspector asked in order to gauge the children's intelligence – rather, to gauge the teacher's ability to successfully feed them the set knowledge as required by a grade's syllabi. Yet, in a small rural school no children – be they struggling or clever academically – could escape the inspector's roving eye. The students were instructed in the inspector's presence to keep busy if they finished the set work early – for instance, to look at my increasingly large set of prized colourful *Knowledge* books that were bound together in dark red hardbound covers I had been collecting. Before the inspector finally arrived at the school, there was that fearful day at home one weekend when I had decided to begin attending the Greensborough Baptist Church.

I told 'Mum' of my decision. She was lost for words and I suspected that when 'Dad' learnt of it, he would not exactly be lost for words.

I was lying on my bed the next morning, ready to rise, when he knocked and entered.

"What's this I hear, son, about you going to Greensborough Baptist? Do you intend to go *there* from now on?"

"Yes – yes, I do," I replied nervously.

"You shouldn't desert the sinking ship, you know".

He was nervous as he stood at the end of my bed.

"It's not that," I said.

"You know, I believe one should go to a church nearest to where you live".

"Well, it's not that," I said, groping for an answer.

"Why are you leaving St John's then?"

"Oh, it's just that I am finding it hard to worship at St John's. The set service, the set prayers become too familiar, so that it is hard to worship that way without it being mechanical".

"Well, son, you must understand that the Church of England with her set order of worship, set prayers and readings in her early days arose because of the people being illiterate, and needed the spiritual guidance of learned men. Repetition meant that they could become familiar quickly with what learned men spent so much time forming into a well-ordered form of worship."

"That may have been so, but that kind of worship does not suit me."

"Well, I am disappointed to learn of your decision."

'Dad' turned around and walked out of the door of the bungalow. The ill-fitting door grinded against the floor in his attempt to close it.

While I found it difficult to prevent being mechanical in worship at St John's, there were unspoken theological reasons for leaving St John's: I had come into conviction about believer's baptism and regarded it as a surer way of having a regenerate church membership.

A certain silence passed between 'Dad,' 'Mum' and I for some weeks.

I even wondered if it would be better to live elsewhere in the forthcoming year, and yet I chose a school from the Teacher's Gazette that would mean I could still live with 'Dad' and 'Mum,' even though I would be travelling for hours each day across Melbourne. I chose Sunbury and got notice of my success not long before Mr Hird, the district inspector, came to the little school to assess me.

Little did I know at teacher's college that when, with a smile I read in one of the college's newsletters the humour of seeing "A Hird in the hand is worth two in the bush," that it would be Inspector Hird one day assessing me!

I knew nothing about Inspector Alan Hird, except that he had been a VFL footballer with Essendon, and had played in the side's 1942 flag team. He went on to become the president of Essendon.

He came knocking on the school's heavy wooden door. He was a tall, lean man, somewhat beetle-browed, with dark hair parted in the middle. He was rather grave and I quickly became nervous.

I anticipated that Hird's greeting of the children would be cheerful and that the drilled children would be cheerful in their response. His was a quiet and rather indifferent greeting, and therefore it did not turn on the charm on the students' part that I'd hoped the inspector would encounter.

He sat down in the chair at my desk. He took to viewing my work program for that week. He eyed the students and me as we continued with the work they had been doing before he arrived. An unusual quietness came over the children.

He then rose from the chair. He looked at the blackboard. Then he began to pepper my pupils with questions. When he questioned them to his satisfaction, he walked up and down between the desks scanning the children's work books in silence. Time appeared to roll slowly until midday, when it was time for the children's lunch break. They went outside in the heat of the day while he began to grill me about what I was seeking to accomplish with the children, and to cast his opinion on various aspects of my ways of teaching.

I thought he would be pleased with little Robert's remarkable ability to read beyond his grade level and how I catered for his capacity to read exceptionally well, but it seemed that our solemn and grim-faced inspector thought Robert's ability had more to do with little Robert's genes than my guidance.

We lunched together around the work table as he came to his conclusions about the way I was faring. He was not considering me for a promotable mark.

> "By the way," he said as he rose to leave, "those *Knowledge* magazines that you have in those binders and which you seem to use quite a bit with the children ... they are a waste of money".
>
> "Oh," I reacted.

"Much of the stuff is out of date. As soon as any recent things occur, they are out of date as quickly as they are published."

He stunned me with his opinion but I was not so surprised as to be lost for words; I simply thought it better not to refute him. I mean, if I used *Knowledge* to teach children the structure of the eye, was that *Knowledge* information outdated? History too is never outdated; it lives again – often unfortunately to be lived again.

I was glad to see Hird go. His parting opinion left a bitter taste in my mouth, but I continued to drive to Stawell on Friday nights to buy the latest *Knowledge* magazines, and continued to make use of them in my teaching.

Meanwhile, the history of President John Kennedy's assassination of the year before was destined to be always 'indated.' A year later, my final year at Wal Wal saw a Dallas jury finally convict the Dallas night-club owner, Jack Ruby of Lee Harvey Oswald's murder. He had shot Oswald two days after John Kennedy's assassination as Oswald was being transferred to a country jail in Dallas. It had taken 10 months of investigation after the assassination of Kennedy for a commission to conclude Oswald acted alone in sniping on the president to kill him. Theories still abounded after the commission's conclusion, and it seemed that there would be no end to any argument about the tragedy of Kennedy's assassination.

History of some kind is ever living. So was a Hird in the hand worth *two* in the bush of Wal Wal?

I made ready for "two" in the satellite city of Sunbury – that is, I first made ready for at least two years also in Sunbury, and secondly was putting rural school teaching behind me.

To the Satellite Town

After one or two mornings I learnt to shoot down the steep decline of Bulla Road at top speed so that my EK Holden could then climb from the hollow to the upward direction towards Sunbury, without being forced into the lowest of its three gears. It was a beautiful car to look at, but I felt that its body was too heavy for the engine.

At the end of the year before (1964) I bought the three-year-old Holden on hire purchase for two years at that time. Such a car when new was normally the equivalent of more than ten months of an average wage, but I needed a car as close as possible to something new to cover the considerable distance between Diamond Creek and Sunbury each day.

In the preceding year I became quite settled in the Greensborough Baptist Church under Jim Paice, and I decided to enquire about the ministry. There was no distinct call through a divine voice, but perhaps inspired by several people to believe that I had a sound knowledge of the Scriptures and a desire to see others become grounded in the word of God as well, I decided to make a secret phone call to Whitley College.

Denominational differences can cut deep. You may attend an interdenominational convention where the banner is 'All One in Christ Jesus,' but deep-seated differences must be submerged in order to be 'all one', at a convention such differences over what major issues can be. They can be divisive in a home too.

At home the one and only phone sat on a phone table in the lounge room, where conversation into the handset lent itself even to unintentional eavesdropping. To avoid ill-feeling, I made a call from a public phone box in Greensborough to Whitley College and got through to Professor Watson, who informed me that he was scheduled to preach at Rosanna on a certain Sunday evening.

I learnt that to be eligible to enter Whitley College I must gain Matriculation.

As the year progressed, I began to pay regular visits to Whittington, east of Geelong, where a family named Shorts had a dairy farm by the Barwon River. I had met them over the Christmas holidays early in the year. They had been friends of 'Dad' & 'Mum' but they had seen little of them since the family left Diamond Creek to live elsewhere quite a few years before. Dennis, the younger of the two boys, invited me down to Whittington. I took up the offer and it was the beginning of many weekends with them.

The Shorts had moved from a farm in Northern Victoria to Whittington, where they lived in a blue stone house. The lounge room window overlooked the slope of green paddocks down to the Barwon River. A small front garden faced the driveway that wound around the property's entrance to the dairy shed, east of the house. They had a fair acreage of land – sufficient for the medium-sized herd of cows to graze on, and ample enough for growing produce such as potatoes and carrots.

The family was made up of two grown sons and two grown daughters. Mr Elton Short was a quiet man, who shuffled around in overalls, ever conscientious in his management of the farm. He was a devout deacon at the Fenwick Memorial Baptist Church, which all the family attended.

His aptness to chuckle at mealtimes, when he was amused, chimed in with Dennis's similar brand of humour. He could not tolerate fools. As for Mrs Dot Short, while it was generally considered in society to be unladylike to whistle, it was easy to forgive her, as she was one of the most cheerful persons I have ever known. Whether she was cooking or helping to milk the cows, she was found whistling tunes of various hymns. She had a hearty laugh as well. Both parents were no doubt proud of Philip, their eldest son and who was reputed to be the youngest applicant the Melbourne Bible Institute had ever had, but they were not ones to boast of him. Their other son, Dennis was an apprentice electrician. As for their daughters, Lynette had entered a nursing career, while Margaret was in her final year of school.

The initial visit to Whittington took place before the new school year commenced. Once school began, a late Friday afternoon would for some weekends see me arrive at their house while Elton, Dot and Margaret were still milking. It would not be long to wait for Dennis to arrive home from work, and over dinner we would engage in lively chatter and laughter. He could tell the most amusing yarns and had some favourite sayings: darkness for him was 'like the inside of a cow;' 'You can tell a Pom but you can't tell them much.'

I shared much in common with the Shorts and that gave rise to the attraction. They were Baptists, they were evangelical Christians, the boys enjoyed football and cricket, and we shared a hankering for better days when believers had more of an influence on a society that was fast becoming very materialistic and immoral. They had no TV to steal the good times of sharing our news and the longings dear to our hearts. Meals for dinner were simple but ample, although Elton was finding it tough financially to make do, and was working part-time with International Harvester. Both he and Dot never complained about any hardships they may well have been going through. They phlegmatically pressed on, unshaken, not only because of their temperaments but because over the years they had proven the Lord to be faithful, perhaps in times even more trying than they faced at Whittington.

Travelling between home and Sunbury was going to eat into my time if I were to study as well as teach my class of 36 children. Besides, after only a few weeks, the time spent travelling across Melbourne was wearing me down. Therefore, on discovering that a fellow ex-college student of Coburg was teaching nearby Sunbury at Rockbank, and was interested in boarding nearby during the week, I tracked down a farmhouse that was available for rent and invited him to join me in the venture.

I thought that I knew little about cooking and all else that makes a place orderly enough to live in, but my friend Nigel seemed to have learnt much of how to be disorderly it seemed, as well as knowing sweet nothing about cooking. One hit song that rang out from my transistor radio at the time said it all –

> 'Accept me for what I a-a-am, (Nigel),
> Accept me for the things that *I* do-oo-oo (me)'

He left me to do almost everything so I called it quits.

Not many days later I enquired about staying at Sunbury's Railway Hotel. The tall, largish wife of the proprietor consulted her man of smaller and leaner appearance if I may live in the hotel five days a week, and one was given the impression that the burly lady was the boss in the running of the place. They had to counter "the six o'clock swill" when time came around to closing the bar each night at that time, and when some men had one or two drinks too many, it was the burly lady that would bawl out the order for the lingering few to exit with a firmness that few could resist. My rather small room was above the bar; therefore she would please me by swiftly putting an end with her loud voice to too much boisterousness and loud high-spiritness that would ascend through the floor between the bar down below and my room above before six.

Thanks to the lady, I could then nestle in the room for my studies in Matriculation English Expression and Greek History, having decided to do the required numbers of subjects for Matriculation over two years – a minimum of four had to be passed for the certificate. Adjustment to the new and unfamiliar teaching of a very large class caused me to be cautious about doing the four subjects in one year.

At first it was daunting to begin teaching at school number 1002 of Sunbury. The brick school was old but still attractive – established in 1869. I was to face a class of 36 children, after being at Wal Wal, where at the most I had 25, and that had been only for a brief time. I was to teach a composite of grades four and five pupils. I was no longer a headmaster and was subject to the principal, Mr Rush. Moreover, for the first time I was in a school with other teachers, and had to adjust to working in unison with them.

It was said that Sunbury was designed to be a satellite town of Melbourne, expecting to grow so that the school could well be bursting at the seams in the near future. It was a situation where it would seem more in place for me to come on tough and stern on the first day – to cower the 36 into submission from day one.

In the staffroom, on the day before school had begun, Mr Rush introduced himself and came across as an amicable principal. Phil, who was teaching a composite class of grades five and six – numbering 42 – lit up a cigarette as Mr Rush spelt out plans for the year. Norma, who had been an infant teacher for years at the school, lit up a cigarette too. It was not an overly large staff room and whirls of white smoke circled us all as he spoke.

To get a hold of the 36 in the composite grade also required the learning of their names. One could hardly get a hold of names by beginning to solicit answers to questions through calling out 'the boy on his own in the second last desk' or 'the girl in the white jumper, second from the front.' Learning names quickly would gain respect and knowledge of them. One trick was to use the roll, call out someone's name, quickly look up at the direction of the reaction – presuming none of them were inattentive and had failed to react. Or, you could call out a name of a child as if you knew them. It was fatal to mistake a pupil's name – particularly for boys, who at that age were often more contemptuous than girls.

On the first day I attempted to work up sternness, but it was hard to sustain. Besides, there is always at least one pupil that has the gift of perceiving such flakiness. In my case there was one girl, Polish, stubborn, and who was bent from the beginning in treating me with contempt. There were others who would at times misbehave, of course, but none had the malice of Stanislava. She would prove to be the only one that would cause me to lament that I no longer had the sole power to give her 'the strap' on occasions. Mr Rush had joined a growing number of teachers who desired the abolishment of corporate punishment. Writing lines was considered an option. Some fumbled for any alternative discipline to corporate punishment, such as reasoning with the child – a possibility, though there were always parents who, if they were brought into the issue, came to their child's defence come what may, as was the case of the Polish girl.

Still, overall, as a class we made good progress, even though my disposition and temperament restricted me considerably from being as hard as I first appeared. I loved teaching and the children enjoyed my enthusiasm for Nature Study when I came across what I regarded as an interesting approach to the subject. What happened initially when I asked them to bring snails along to school to study underlined my inability to create the kind of first impression that any envied sanguine teacher can without much effort make. My effort underlined even more the handicapped disposition of being a melancholic person.

I planned a 'hands on' Nature Study lesson about snails, desiring that the students each bring along snails in containers on a certain day. As it was, in two days when Nature Study was to be done, only one or two students had brought one or two of the creatures. I made an impassioned and agitated call on them all to make a greater effort the next day.

I retreated to the hotel that afternoon, being envious more than ever of teachers who had the charismatic ability to spur and excite students into action. I seemed doomed to be too introverted for my own good; cast down and an easy prey for disappointment. I had felt exuberant after the prospect of what was a unique 'hands on' approach to studies in nature but thought that mine was not the make-up whereby I could 'sing' my way through teaching as some others could, so that I could get my class 'singing' along with me through an infectious style. Those I envied remained unshaken by anything that looks like failure because of their belief that yesterday's failure does not mean that tomorrow they will not succeed.

Rain fell on the hotel roof that afternoon and into that night, as I wondered about my future life as a teacher.

The next morning beggared belief. Even before the electric bell rang to assemble outside the classroom, my students came dashing in excitedly with their jars and other containers enclosing dozens of snails! I had to hold back their excitement until the more basic subjects had been done that morning and before we could lay plain paper on all the desks so that they could shake out the snails and let the slimy creatures crawl across the desktops. Then while I sought to teach the excited students about the coiled shell creatures and their anatomy – how snails have a heart, a kidney, eyes, tentacles, mouth, stomach, tiny teeth, a digestive gland and intestine, etc. – there were snails that crept along with their strong muscular organ of a foot to the edges of desks and dropped onto the floor. Some even slimily crawled up the walls of the classroom, no doubt due to some mischievous hands setting them there. What with 36 pupils all having brought snails, the slimy things were all over the place – on the floor, on the door, dropping from desks, crawling on the windows!

Still, much was learnt of what was normally a common thing in nature and which was too easily passed over in life as simply a garden pest.

Rain had fallen to my fortune the day and night before, so snails were around in abundance. I found solace and hope after that. Even though I did not possess the temperament I had envied, and that I had to be quite fiery to get the students to respond, I bonded better with the students as they perceived how education can be exciting to pursue. Even Stanislava was being to some degree won over. In the matter of teaching, it was more about what was to be taught and less about me; in that my confidence still grew. Get absorbed in what to teach, so be less tempted at the fear of failure.

There was in some other ways less cause to envy other teachers. I was blessed with insights, traits and a temperament and innovation that those I envied did not necessarily possess. Snails had played their part!

Each day saw me drive back to the hotel for lunch. On opening a side door to the kitchen, the smell of beer would permeate the air to my dislike as I sat down regularly to the requested steamed fish. The lady, who as the hotel's housemaid served me at the kitchen table, once asked me if I ate fish so much because I was Roman Catholic – a strange question!

After school each day I would drive back to the hotel where I studied in my room until dinner, after which I would study more. Each Thursday I had a break from study, and in the lounge room, alone and content, watched television, particularly enjoying 'Green Acres' and Zsa Zsa Gabor – a city woman along with her husband comically attempting to be sophisticated but all at sea on a farm with her slightly more adaptable husband. The Beverley Hillbillies as a comedy was in reverse: country hicks in city life.

As the weeks progressed, the cost of my board at the hotel became less and less! There were only two of us boarding upstairs at the hotel – the other person was a man named George. On the first day I saw him I recognized him as one of two linesmen who worked for the SEC (State Electricity Commission,) and who were working on the electricity poles at the southern corner of the Sutherland Homes at the junction of the Diamond Creek and Plenty Roads when I was eleven or twelve years of age. I remembered him well because Matt Easton (as he is known in *The Silver Poplar*) and I used to beg George and his workmate for cigarettes. Matt and I went 'out of bounds' to plead for 'one, just one each.' Then we would retreat and when the opportunity arose, we crept into the upper school's cellar where we lit up and smoked what we agreed was better than lighting up strips of cane of the school's handcraft material, which often disappointed as there was no smoke to actually inhale, and the cane would burst into flames often when we inhaled the lit cane stick.

What did this memory have to do with the decrease in cost of board at the hotel? I did not acknowledge any recognition of George and he would not have remembered me thirteen years on. I did not tell the big lady of the hotel that I knew George and how I knew him years before. I rarely saw him, but would often hear him as he not infrequently stumbled up the stairs after the six o'clock closing of the hotel and staggered past my room to his own, reeking of alcohol. As it was, he did not pay heed to the lady hotelier's order to keep his room tidy. So, what did the lady do? She put his board up and brought mine down – not just once, but on two or three occasions. By the time George was to feel any pain about the increase in board, the cost of mine was quite nominal.

At home on Saturdays I still studied, and did so in the bungalow. We all regarded Sunday as a day of rest, and I did no study out of observance of the "Sabbath."

I was attending Greensborough Baptist regularly, usually for the morning and evening services, so that the pastor Jim Paice asked me if I desired to be a member of the church.

> "To become a member, Eddie," said Jim, "you must be baptized."
>
> I told him, "I have already been baptized."
>
> "Yes, yes, I understand what you mean but, when you were baptized at your Church of England, *you were sprinkled*, were you not?"
>
> "Yes, I was, but as a believer."
>
> "I have no doubt that you are a believer, but as a born-again believer you were merely sprinkled. Full immersion is the biblical way."

I bucked at the need to be fully immersed in water but in order to become a church member I submitted to undergo a series of studies as written up by Jim Paice himself, and which were endorsed by the Baptist Union for churches to use across the state.

Jim baptized me on 20 June in that year of 1965. Ironically, although I had come to believe baptism ought to be by full immersion upon profession of faith, I felt more moved when baptized by sprinkling at St John's five years before, perhaps because it followed closer in time on the heels of first knowing Christ.

On becoming a member, and encouraged by my friend Keith at the church, I began to do some preaching on Sunday evenings at the Judge Brook Village at Eltham. Keith and I were of similar age and we joined in leading the elderly in worship of God. We had fun and frustration in attempts to ensure the deafest among them could always hear what we said and when they were called on to sing. If a poor man rose to his feet to sing when Keith or I announced we were to pray – as one did – we learnt a degree of patience as is fitting for worship leaders.

On Mondays I packed up for the week and left home for the trans-Melbourne drive to Sunbury where, for the five days there, I found relief from a certain degree of uneasiness at home on account that I was no longer attending St John's, and that I had decided to go straight into Whitley College for theological training once I obtained my Matriculation. Nancy was somewhat alarmed at my ambition to go to Whitley College. Why not go to the Melbourne Bible Institute and become evangelically equipped to face what would be thrown at me by the liberal lecturers of Whitley? When I broke the news to 'Mum' and 'Dad' about going into the Baptist ministry, they gave little encouragement. Through the body, as it were, we could talk and laugh over many things, but the denominational issue proved to be a sensitive and sore point for the soul. I did not even feel like telling them about the day I was to be baptized. I did not tell them at all.

Curiously, all was well, save the issue of forsaking St John's. 'Dad' kept referring to me as his son to various people, and 'Mum' loved my company. In the two years I was at Wal Wal, when it was time each fortnight to return to the school, she would try to have me stay a little longer though I wished to return early to the country to be fresh for teaching the following morning.

Some people have said, "If you continue with satisfaction in any other occupation, don't take up the ministry." Was I satisfied with teaching? Yes, I was. Still, though there had been no clap of thunder, as it were, to convince me about the ministry, I felt driven inwardly about the matter. Some people thought that I could well serve the Lord by school teaching for life – that thought would unsettle me a little, but then I grew all the surer in my heart in navigating myself through what was any channel of uncertainty. Was not secular teaching preparing me for the greatness of spiritual teaching?

The world has always been a disquieting place, and 1965 was no exception. There was the issue of black voting rights with its riots in the U.S., the space race between the U.S. and the U.S.S.R. to see which country would have the first man walk in space, the Vietnam War with the Western fear of the southward march of Communism, and the horrific murders of seven children (the Moor Murders) by a couple that became the most hated people in Britain to close the year. To become a preacher in view of the turbulence of the world seemed to me a more paramount calling than to remain a secular teacher.

Near the year's end, I sat for my first two Matriculation exams at the Salesian College across from the state school. The college was situated on the grounds of 'Rupertswood' which was a grandiose Byzantinian style mansion that had been built for Sir William Clarke. 'Rupertswood' itself was the reception centre for the Roman Catholic College. The college at the time was a boys' school amid magnificent gardens that covered 60 acres. The beauty of the place lent serenity to an examinee like me who entered the grounds confident and eager to sit the exams for English Expression and for what had been an intriguing course in Ancient Greek History.

A few weeks before I sat the exams, we learnt that our Principal Mr Rush, to our disappointment, was retiring.

Just before school ended for the year, we teachers made our way one-week night to a restaurant at 'World's End.' We used to tease one of the infant teachers called Dawn about living at Woodend by nicknaming it

'World's End.' It seems that some thought Dawn was unwise to get herself pregnant when unmarried, and to put an end to her career before the three-year term for the bond was completed.

Apart from Dawn, the other teachers were staying on for the next year. At the restaurant Dawn was formally wished the best for the future by Mr Rush. He then formally said farewell in a short speech, obviously glad to retire from teaching. A young fellow with an acoustic guitar then sought to entertain us by singing *The Hucklebuck*, a song that called for just a few chords and just a few words –

> 'Here's a dance you should know
> When the lights are down low.
> Grab your baby,
> Let's go.
>
> *Do the hucklebuck, do the hucklebuck,*
> *If you know not how to do it,*
> *Then boy you're out of luck!*
> *Wriggle like a snake, waddle like a duck –*
> *That's the way you do the hucklebuck.'*

After singing the same words several times over, he invited us to get up and dance, as he sang the same words several times once again. The song blended or 'blanded' in with the standard of the meal at 'World's End.'

I said farewell to the hoteliers at the Railway Hotel but indicated that I would like to stay there in the following year.

I attended my seventh Belgrave Christian Convention. The conventions in those years were still attracting the calibre of some fine Presbyterian ministers, such as Arthur Gunn and Graeme Miller. The fellowship of the DVI campers was once more a joy, though it was disturbing to see two young fellows who were not believers being badgered by too many spirited campers seeking to witness to them. The two openly championed Bob Dylan, whose views were unsettling to a good number of young Christians of the camp. They branded Dylan rather leftist, inciting revolt among the young against their seniors. Dylan was anti-war, so he was fostering a protest against the Vietnam War that was supposedly being fought to stop atheistic communism in its tracks. The boys, in answer to what was said against Dylan, claimed the influential folksinger was only posing questions, with 'Blowin' in the Wind' serving as an example of mere questioning.

I felt sorry for the two boys. I knew little about Bob Dylan, and thought obscurantism on the part of some did not help the two young fellows in desiring to know Christ, who actually is the only One Who in contrast to Dylan could effect a change in this ever-troubled world of ours, as to bring in universal righteousness and peace.

After the convention Philip and Dennis Short and I made a trip to New South Wales. We went in Philip's 'guards van' (Vanguard). The ute would break down, stubbornly refusing to move into second gear. Philip had to get out and manually tamper with the engine to 'click it into second gear' so that we could move on from first to third gear without a hitch. How we got to the Sydney Cricket Ground in one day to watch England play Australia is a wonder. Peter Philpot was playing for Australia, one spectator under the weather kept yelling out for 'Pheter Pilplot' to bowl.

Upon returning to Sunbury in 1966 it was not long before I got the news that a lady across the road west from the school wished to have a boarder. Even if it meant higher cost in board, I was keen to be closer to the school and not have to contend with the noise of the drinking bar of the Railway Hotel rising through the floorboards to my room. Better and quieter hours for studying after school and before were promising.

Mr and Mrs Collier were Roman Catholics, and both worked at the Salesian College across the road. They had a daughter of around 20 years of age who was living at home. I cannot recall what the daughter did, except she was no longer at school.

Mrs Collier gave me a worn copy of *Pride and Prejudice*, which her son had studied at the college but who had since left home. For English Literature I also had to possess copies of *King Lear* and *Great Expectations*.

I felt immediately at home with the Colliers. Mrs Collier kindly suggested that I may even like to have a cooked light lunch during the week, being prepared to come home from her work to do so. As the weeks went by it became evident that she loved to make large lots of wine trifle for dinner, and for lunch I sometimes had the leftovers of the sherry saturated dessert.

I had scruples about wine, holding alongside Christians of the day that we should not consume strong drink. Certainly, we of DVI held to that, but I firmed up to convince myself that I was not drinking wine directly – besides I enjoyed its taste in the trifle!

We teachers at the Sunbury school did not feel at home, with our new principal, Mr Bruce Spratling. He had ideas to shake up the school with the latest theories and practices that were in circulation among some places of primary education. His manner was rather brusque, and he was bullish by nature. This was in contrast to Mr Rush, who perhaps did not assert himself enough with authority, and who stayed staid and satisfied with all the old ways of learning.

It was not long before the majority of the staff began talking of applying for another school at the end of the year. I shared their feelings about the disquiet Spratling was causing, and rested content to know that at the end of the year I could apply for another school upon completing a compulsory two years at Sunbury. Betty Ham, one of the infant teachers and who claimed to be a Christian, called our new principal a 'sod' because, while it may mean an unpleasant person, it is an abbreviation for 'sodomite', a person engaging in sodomy.

I got along well with Betty, who was always very jovial. She was fond of quoting Paul the apostle's words to Titus 'To the pure all things are pure' to justify any double entendres she uttered. I would return to her on such occasions when opportunity provided it, by quoting Paul's words that followed on from 'To the pure…' I would quote Paul seemingly in jest, the kind of jest that appealed to my jovial friend, but praying it would be viewed as a true word spoken.

It was put forward by a journalist at the time that, in view of prescription for public examinations, such as Matriculation, young minds were being unfavourably safeguarded from what was allegedly 'defiled.' He bucked against things that were too easily deemed in the eyes of the education authorities as 'impure' – things that deal for instance with 'sexual experience and imagery.' A book called *Six Voices* was prescribed in my English course. Among the Australian poets under consideration was A.D. Hope. My eyes lit upon another newspaper article one day by the same journalist in mind that seized my interest, for it was one about the poetry of A.D. Hope. It was written with annoyance about what he saw as the puritanical selection of Hope's poems for *Six Voices*, because it only had 'an eye to prescription for public examinations,' but it was claimed by the journalist that many of Hope's best poetry dealt with 'sexual experience and imagery.' Indeed, the literary critic claimed that many of the selections for *Six Voices* could be criticized for avoiding superior works that made use of good 'esoteric, recondite' adjectives.

In the year before this, I had studied Chaucer with selected works of his that omitted *The Miller's Tale*, a tale that Chaucer warned any would-be readers to pass over if they considered themselves too refined to read it –

'So if this tale had better not be heard,
Just turn the page and choose another sought...'

Of course, Chaucer put forward what he regarded as good reasons for including the story in *The Canterbury Tales*. Yes, our literary critic had proof for believing that, in the minds of the prescribers for public exams, Matriculation students were being needlessly protected from what they, the authorities saw as an obscene, bawdy tale of Chaucer's miller.

The three set books of English Literature in 1966 consequently were free of anything deemed suggestive, sexually explicit or blasphemous – *Great Expectations, Pride and Prejudice* and *King Lear*.

My landlady Mrs Collier was a devout Catholic. She had a framed medieval picture of the Virgin Mary where we dined. A suggestive or vulgar word did not drop from her lips. She was concerned that her daughter might be loose and indiscreet, chiding her loudly one morning when she was walking past my closed door from the shower with only a towel draped over her body. A devout Catholic in all things? One day a lady visitor was sitting with Mrs Collier and me at the dining table when the phone rang. The caller on the other end of the phone wanted to know if the lady visitor sitting with us was 'at home.' Mrs Collier told her that the lady sitting by us was 'home' – creating the false impression that the lady was in her own house. The caller hung up her phone. Mrs Collier chuckled as she came to sit down. 'Well, you are 'at home' with me!' she said to our lady visitor, and added that she had mentally qualified the whole truth under her breath while speaking to the caller – 'My friend is 'at home', 'my home.'

I heard that not a few Catholics' such as Mrs Collier, still practised then what historically was called 'lie of necessity,' which had been banned by Pope Innocent XI as far back as 1679.

So life was quite full and eventful in my second year at Sunbury – in living with the Colliers, studying wonderful books for Literature, juggling one's philosophy of teaching with what Spratling sought to innovate, going out occasionally with my fellow-teachers for ten pin bowling at Essendon and such like, then driving home Friday nights with my little leather-cased transistor radio sitting on the dashboard, sounding out the new songs of the Beatles and Rolling Stones.

It was a relief that Mrs Collier never asked me about my parentage.

Also, it seemed I was in love. The pastor's eldest daughter took a liking to me. She invited me for a Friday evening spent with the family to watch a regular series for them – *The Untouchables*. It centred around a federal agent who learnt the hard way to deal with both underworld crime and police corruption in Prohibition Chicago. As machine guns rat-a-tat-tated with gangsters mowing down one another, I would picture Pastor Jim in the pulpit on Sunday, and was not sure if he could use anything from *The Untouchables* for illustrations for the sake of the gospel. Then again, watching Eliot Ness in the name of justice seemed harmless enough.

My friend Keith at the church was right. He had warned me about the pastor's daughter being flirtatious, that all too soon she would ditch me. Keith pointed out to me the young fellow attending the church that she had recently ditched. He was from the U.S. Not that it is relevant to the pastor's daughter dropping him but it was interesting, all the same, that a rumour was going around that the young fellow, along with his friend, had fled the States to dodge the draft for the Vietnam War.

It was tempting to ask the young Americans about the reason for being in Australia, to probe and discover if the rumour had any semblance to truth. No-one knew much about the young fellows and that made their movements in Australia a mystery. They did not remain long at our church.

There could have been any number of reasons for dodging the draft in the U.S. in the 1960s. Some challenged the morality of the draft, in addition to the morality of being in Vietnam. Some believed the draft was a restriction of individual liberties. Conscientious objectors also held that the rules to determine objections were too narrow. There were those who railed against the Selective System because there was allegedly too high a number of poor men being drafted. Some burnt their draft cards in open protest, but many draft resisters were imprisoned.

When the young men moved on from joining us at our church, and it appeared that they would be seen no more, it seemed to clear the way for me to return the interest that the pastor's daughter had for me, without taking Keith's warning too seriously. Yet, he was right: after only a little more than six weeks, the pastor himself rang me up one Saturday morning and informed me that his daughter wanted to concentrate more on her studies for her final year for school. It dented my pride more than anything else, as I had had no deep attraction for the man's daughter, so I was not 'cut' for too long.

Even if I had wanted to continue viewing *The Untouchables* on Friday nights, it would have been out of the question, as 'Dad' and 'Mum' were not the kind to watch violence as they defined it. 'Mum' and I had something better to view on Friday evenings: Two or three football shows consisting of so-called experts predicting the outcomes of the VFL matches for the next day. One jingle lingered –

> "Kevin Dennis, Kevin Dennis,
> How we love your football show!
> Kevin Dennis, Kevin Dennis,
> Tell us how our teams will go."

As 1966 began to close, most of the teachers had not changed their minds about leaving Sunbury on account of Spratling, and made applications for other schools.

I managed to secure a position at Watsonia for the new year.

I went to the Salesian College to sit for the final Matriculation exams of the two remaining subjects. I went full of confidence and eagerness to display my knowledge of the three books I had studied for English Literature.

We teachers celebrated the end of the year by going one evening to a Japanese restaurant in Victoria Street in the city. After the many farewells at school and leaving the Collier's house with good memories, was I then bound to return home with years of teaching over, though expected at Watsonia for 1967? I mulled over resigning and seeking entry to Whitley College for the Baptist ministry.

Watsonia

Over the holiday break my friend Dennis and I took a trip to Adelaide, at the time when Matriculation results were to appear in a Melbourne newspaper. Could I be assured of getting the paper in Adelaide, and if so, would my exam number appear for both subjects so that I matriculated and could apply for entry into Whitley College?

We had a great time together camping, and it was even more delightful when I discovered that I gained my Matriculation.

My pastor of 1966, Jim Paice, anticipated that I would gain my Matriculation and he advised me to enter Whitley College the following year of 1967, that is, to apply even before I had gained the qualification.

"Why not apply this year (1966) for Whitley?" he asked.

I replied, "I think I will wait another year."

"Why?"

"Because I need to save for another twelve months to cover my needs while a student at Whitley for the three years."

"Just trust in the Lord, my friend," the little chirpy man said, "for He will provide for your needs."

I refused his advice, but it left me with a sense of uncertainty: Was I showing a lack of faith in the Lord? Recently I had bought a book about Hudson Taylor, the famed missionary in China. His home base of the Chinese Evangelization Society could not support him. He was only 22 years of age – younger than me even – but he lent on God through faith and prayer, resulting miraculously in support until he returned to England invalided. Yet despite setbacks there, he returned to China, when his work was so effective that many missions were to follow his example and become faith-missions.

Apart from Bishop Ryle's *Holiness*, the only other Christian book outside the Bible that I had read again was the one about the life of Hudson Taylor, and it had a profound effect on me. Still, I became convinced that not all believers are called to 'live on faith.' Paul tells us that some in the church are given the gift of faith. While there have been those who view the so-called living on faith as a superior trust in God, I slowly but surely became convinced it was wise for me to save enough in twelve months to meet all my needs of three years at college. Theological students were blessed in not having to pay board, or to pay for meals, and received free lectures and tuition within Whitley as well as at Queen's College. However, there were personal expenses naturally enough.

Before he left the pastorate of Greensborough – once I learnt that I qualified academically for Whitley – Pastor Paice still considered that it may not be too late to seek out the possibility of going before the candidates' board before the academic year that began in March of 1967.

I remained resolute about teaching one more year, and therefore I began work at Watsonia – school number 4838 (the number given to the school when it was built.) Do recall that Sunbury was number 1002, and then appreciate that the Sunbury school was old but possessed character – built, you may remember in 1863 – and set solid in brick, having light pouring in to each classroom through what were something like French windows, a platform that stretched out in each room across the whole width so that the teacher's table and the wide backboard was elevated in front of the desks, and there stood large wooden doors for entry. Watsonia by contrast was composed of two long grey-painted buildings, each being parted in the two blocks of buildings by corridors that ran right down the entire middle of classrooms on both sides. Watsonia in contrast to Sunbury was treeless too.

One similarity shared by the two schools was that each of the two blocks of buildings divided the infant grades (grades prep to two) from the more senior ones (grades three to six).

To my surprise I discovered that one of the infant teachers at Watsonia was Miss Luxford, who had taught me in grade two at the Sutherland Homes! I could not mistake her face. We were glad to see one another. Our reunion made the move to Watsonia less unsettling – not only because I had known her as a child but that she was a fervent Christian. (She goes under the name of Miss Buxon in *The Silver Poplar*.) Besides Miss Luxford, I knew no other teacher, though a certain fellow of an upper grade was the husband of a female teacher who came in my second year to Sunbury. His wife was an avowed kleptomaniac. I recalled that several of us at Sunbury were gathered one time together in my classroom after our students had gone home, and in casual conversation she unashamedly admitted that she was given to stealing clothes from stores. We were flabbergasted at her confession.

Mr Hicks, the head teacher of Watsonia, proved to be not all that amenable but he took an interest in me because he had been head teacher at the Plenty school, a mile or so from the Homes, and I told him of the sporting connections we had with the Plenty school when I was in grade six. It was not like me to admit that I had been raised at Sutherland but I felt he had some empathy for the kind of start that I had had in life. Since he responded in the way he did, I became a most dedicated teacher to his satisfaction. He ran a good ship in a school that was quite large in numbers.

There was a kind of temptation to continue teaching beyond that year at Watsonia, but the urge to go to Whitley proved stronger as the months went by, particularly as I began to seriously study theology of a kind that lit a brighter fire than previously. Nancy still regretted that I was not attending Melbourne Bible Institute before Whitley, but her regret fuelled my desire to equip myself well evangelically before Whitley all the same, and in my anxiety to be well equipped, I purchased John Calvin's *Institutes*.

For those who are unfamiliar in our day with the *Institutes*, John Calvin wrote the work in the 16th century with a dedication to the King of France, Francis 1. Calvin hoped that such a work would convince the King that persecuting those who had adopted the Reformed faith was wrong, even though the faith had shaken the foundations of Roman Catholicism. As a work in its final edition, it comprised four books and a total of seventy-nine chapters.

One scholar maintains that apart from the Bible itself, the *Institutes* form 'the most important book ever printed on the subject of Christian faith.' Yet I do not ever recall the *Institutes* being mentioned by any Christian people I knew, and I certainly had never heard of anyone (with the exception of Ken) who believed in the doctrine of God's sovereignty in salvation; the doctrine often would be quickly dismissed in conversation if the subject ever was raised. Still, the subject of election, as Calvin raised it, opened my eyes in wonder at why I had not seen it before in the Scriptures. I embraced it and my heart was overwhelmed by the security found in such a salvation.

It amazed me that despite there having been a Reformation once 'affecting nearly every European' and '(forcing) almost everyone to make a choice between the old and the new' – 'changing the course of Western civilization' – I had not learnt or heard of what had given birth to such an astounding movement. It is true that Ken – who still kept his distance from me after he had scarred my life – had talked to me about the doctrine of election, and also that 'Mum' had gifted me a book called *The English Reformation* two or three years before, but it was only upon reading the *Institutes* that my eyes were opened to understand and believe in election with a joy previously unknown.

Such a new-found belief gave me confidence in mastering whatever was theological, for quite suddenly there was a master key that opened many doors. The doctrine of God's sovereignty in salvation helped plumb the depths of 'the deep things of God.' A number of earnest Christians wondered about my decision to go to a 'liberal' Whitley.

Reactions varied. 'Dad' and 'Mum' had learnt at last to accept that I had become a Baptist, and for them it seemed a natural thing to go to a Baptist theological college if one wished to be a Baptist minister. My sister felt the same way. I never learnt if Mr and Mrs Short thought that I should have detoured by going the way of MBI in order to reach Whitley, but they had a high regard for MBI, since Philip their son was studying there; they were sceptical of Whitley but said nothing about my aim to attend it. Yet, there were some from DVI, who like Nancy, wondered if, as a hunted bird in flight, I may be winged by the shots of liberalism – being shot at over the three years at Whitley – so that it caused me to fall from full flight evangelically.

Finally, it was time to meet up with the dignitaries of the candidates' board. I took the day off school and travelled to Albert Street, East Melbourne, to the headquarters of the Baptist Union.

We all sat around a large round table, and after brief introductions to each member of the board's gentlemen, the conversation passed on from questions of my years of teaching to that of my church life.

> "How long have you been at the Greensborough Baptist Church?" someone asked.
>
> "For three years," I replied.
>
> "Where were you before then?"
>
> I replied, "I used to be in the Church of England – St John's of Diamond Creek."
>
> "How is it that you became a Baptist? We presumed that you have been baptized by immersion, otherwise you wouldn't want to be entering this ministry."
>
> "That's right," I answered, "I was baptized by immersion. I desired to be a Baptist as I was convinced that only believers should be baptized."

There was further questioning and probing about my understanding of Baptist belief, but then it dawned on me that nothing had been asked about me becoming a Christian, therefore I seized the moment to draw attention to how I came to trust in Christ without going into what could have been a complication. I did not mention being raised in an institution for neglected children – for I was self-conscious about such a matter and felt that it could prejudice the case for applying to be a ministerial candidate by it suggesting that I may not be a well-rounded person.

"Actually," I said, "I was baptized as a believer at the age of eighteen at the font of St John's, Diamond Creek. I was given an unwanted Bible when I was seventeen. The Lord told me to read it when I was on the point of burning it in my anger. I began to read John's Gospel. I believed in Jesus for salvation and crossed over from death to life."

"Interesting," said one or two men laconically.

"Have you been happy teaching?" asked Professor Watson.

"Yes, I have been, but I believe I can do more for the salvation of people by becoming a pastor. I think the Lord led me into secular teaching to prepare me for a spiritual work."

"Now," said one of the other men as he leant back in his chair as if to make a casual remark, but straightened up to ask me, "We believe you have been associated with a group of people who go under the name of the 'Diamond Valley Interdenominational Fellowship.'

"Haw, that's a mouthful," interjected another fellow.

"We want to know what the organization is all about," continued the fellow who was interrupted, "and how involved you were in it."

There followed a spirited discussion when I explained the purpose of DVI. Why was there a need for such a group? They wondered why I needed to be part of it when I joined Greensborough Baptist. The question cast a doubt about devotion to Baptist work, but I had learnt to fellowship with

Christians that differed with me over certain doctrines, and said it was to my favour that I could tolerate differences without compromising my own beliefs.

I departed from Albert Street a little uneasy about how some of the direction the interview took. On reflection it appeared that it was not only my link with DVI that created some uncertainty about Baptist loyalty, but because DVI was linked to the Belgrave Heights conventions, some men hinting at a conservatism that did not meet much approval of a number of those of the board, if one could judge by some rather snide remarks. On reflection, I thought that it would have been better not to have merely said that I tolerated differences between Christians, but that I should have emphasised how I knew sweet fellowship with many believers of other denominations. Yet, would that have suggested also that I was not sufficiently Baptist to be a candidate for the denomination?

When there is a degree of uncertainty, it makes the thing that one waits for seem longer to eventuate, yet with relief eventually I received a letter that stated I had been accepted as a theological student for 1968. In tendering my resignation from the Education Department, I sought permission to remain with the Department until March 2 of the following year, and was allowed to remain at Watsonia until then.

Near the end of 1967 I was due to be assessed by the District Inspector. The assessment had been arranged months in advance as part of a general assessment of the school, as well as that of individual teachers. I had heard of Christians who, before entering what is falsely called 'full-time service,' received alluring promotion in their secular work, it being a possible form of temptation to forgo entering 'full-time service.' The method of assessment of teachers had now changed: The district inspector no longer alone assessed a teacher, for the headmaster (where applicable) could recommend a teacher on observation of him or her for the whole year, and not just on one day (or, even less than half a day) as the past appraisal had it, when all power once lay with the lone inspector. As it was, I received a promotable mark. Was I tempted to turn my back on the ministry? By no means!

Although on paper the time to be spent at Watsonia in the new year appeared short, in reality it ticked by slowly. I had no grade to teach. I spent much time cutting up paper for teachers, sorting books in the library, and running off work sheets for teachers on the spirit duplicator that reeked of methylated spirits. There was much time doing such mundane things with another teacher called Anne, who was in excess at the school, and who would ask me, "How can you give up teaching? Didn't you find teaching to be a secure job?"

Still, while time ticked by slowly until I finished teaching, I often had pleasant thoughts about my future as the month before school closed in the previous year, I received a small parcel in the mail at home. I opened it and lo and behold! there was a little book called *New Testament Greek*, one of a number in those days of *Teach Yourself Books*. Also, there was a note from Professor Brown of Whitley College, which explained that learning New Testament Greek was demanding and that it was necessary to become acquainted with the rudiments of it before one entered Whitley, and before one began facing the task of translating the Gospel of Mark right from the start of the academic year.

The introduction to the book stated that "If Greek was good enough for Jesus and His disciples, it is good enough for us to take the trouble to learn it." As I glanced at the book, I noticed that there was a certain familiarity about it: the alphabet possessed letters similar to those in English; and many words in its vocabulary were known too. Respecting vocabulary, the author of the book included a list of fifty words that had crept into our language, almost unchanged.

I could hardly contain myself at the thought of learning the language of Jesus, and hardly needed any further spur from the professor to begin the book.

It spurred me with confidence to master the New Testament Greek. As previously stated, that to do a language when I began high school had been called into question when I discovered that out of the three groups at Eltham High of First Formers (Year 7 in those days) two groups were to learn French and the other was to do Art and Craft. It was easy to see that the brighter students were learning French. Do recall that my group consisted of those who were less bright overall. Why had I not been placed in any of the other groups? I had become dux of Sutherland Homes School, scoring higher marks than my friend Stewart, who did not live in the Homes and who was going to the prestigious Scotch College after Grade six. I took it to mean that I had only been seen as dux of the Homes' school, a school viewed as one only for institutionalized children. The passing over of me for studying French also led me, even beyond into living outside the Homes, into concealing as far as possible the fact of a boyhood spent in the institution.

I was to learn that Professor Brown had headed up the preparation of counsellors for the Billy Graham evangelical crusade in Victoria in 1959. If I could judge Whitley College by the presence of an evangelical in Professor Brown, I took some heart to know that all was not as grim as a number of fellow-Christians had painted: Some, as you know, had been alarmist and warned me against entering Whitley altogether. Some were wary and warned me to be careful of facing and falling for the Higher Criticism of the Scriptures (said to be alive in Whitley), commending me to the Lord's care with trepidation.

Nevertheless, I was thankful for the concern that not a few had for me, as it was good to be cautioned, and heartening to know many were praying that I would 'stand firm for the faith that was once delivered to the saints.' 'Was Whitley not in the shape of a colosseum?' it was wryly asked. Mmm….

Meeting the Queen

With all my belongings packed, I said 'Goodbye' to 'Dad' and 'Mum,' with the feeling that Whitley College was to be my home for the next three years; though it seemed to them, as well as me that I would never return to live with them again. They wished me well. Even though I had become a Baptist, they were proud to think I had chosen to enter the most rewarding vocation of a Christian ministry.

I headed for Whitley College in 1968 in Parkville, still possessing my EK Holden.

Whitley College was quite new. Previous to 1965 theological students trained at a property in Errol Street, North Melbourne, before the college moved to the colosseum-like, new building at Parkville, where it became affiliated with the University of Melbourne. It was named Whitley College in honour of its first principal. As a college it was only in its fourth year at Parkville, when I arrived and called on the office to the left in the entrance. Then I was directed to the Common Room where, eleven of us new resident theological students, met and were greeted by the principal and some of the theological faculty before the opportunity arose to become familiar with the other 'theologues' already studying there.

It was an all-male college, comprising by far in number Melbourne University students pursuing secular degrees, though a small lot were combining theological studies alongside their secular ones. We new eleven theological students in the main had theology as our sole pursuit.

It was hoped that we 'theologues' would have a Christian influence on the secular students and therefore we were sprinkled around the college in rooms not too close to each other. I was allotted a room on the inside of the college's round walls – being on the first level overlooking the circular expanse of lawn that was somewhat akin to an English village green.

The rooms for all students were either on the inside wall or the outside wall on two levels above the height of the entrance, which entrance on ground level may lead one round in clockwise direction from the office to the Common Room, on to the dining room, then to a small lecture room, followed by the college dean's living quarters, then the library that took one further on to another lecture room, and concluding the circuit with a chapel.

I had barely settled in on that first day when there was a knock on the door. I answered the knock by opening the door to three seasoned theological students, who briskly walked in and welcomed me to the college. Once a few pleasantries were expressed, I was subject to a fusillade of questions in order to size up my stance on the Bible. They grew agitated to learn that I was evangelical, and sought to plant doubt on the veracity of the Scriptures, seeking to belittle me for what they saw as ignorance of the latest scholarship.

They left as briskly as they came. I guess that I was anticipating only an enemy in 'battledress' at Whitley in the form of a liberal lecturer or two in an academic gown – and did not think the enemy could come in student dress from among those who were studying theology part-time, one of whom was contemplating a future ministry full-time. That first-day visit by the three liberal students came with such shock tactics that they left me reeling, because I had never had to confront such an interrogation of that kind before; I had only been accustomed for the most part to the warm climate among evangelicals. Interchange of theological views at teachers' college had been mild by comparison with those of Whitley. The episode with Rev Moorhouse had been one where I was on the offence. When it was a matter of being completely on the defence, it compelled me to become even more grounded in 'the faith once delivered to the saints.'

I had been stung suddenly by the students' attack, a little similar to the day some years before when I was keeping bees at home. The lid to one of the hives was taken off in my keenness to gather honey. A heavy frame of honey was lifted out of the hive. The bees became a little agitated. Then, when the frame of honey broke and fell on to the hive, the bees became more than a little agitated, suddenly shooting up in increasing anger and attacking my bare head. I had not bothered to inspect the hive with the net on my face, nor had the smoker first been used to put the bees at ease. I ran. I raced for the bungalow to escape them but they chased me, ever stinging as I darted into the bungalow and slammed the door shut. That Sunday my face had become too swollen for me to drive up country to my school at Wal Wal for the next day.

I had been stung by the student's attack, but not so much that I could not recover. I only missed one or two days of school from the bees, and their attack did not deter me from returning to the hive; the prospect of gathering honey from it drew me on. Those three students caused me only to study God's word all the more – yes, to see it even clearer as honey for the soul.

> 'The fear of the Lord is pure,
>   enduring forever.
> The ordinances of the Lord are sure
>   And altogether righteous.

> They are more precious than gold,
>> than much pure gold
>> they are sweeter than honey,
>> than honey from the comb (Psalm 19:9-10).'

It was discovered that the three liberal students had also gone around to the other new 'theologues' to interrogate them. Among we eleven new ones were two who became certain friends when it was learnt that we had passed through the same ordeal. We quickly learnt of each other's love for evangelical truth.

I became acquainted with another 'theologue' in Murray, who was also doing an Arts degree. He had already spent a year in the college. He, most of all, helped assure me of the whole truth of God's word for he held to the sovereignty of God in our salvation too. He introduced me to Jonathan Edwards, who was described by the historian Perry Miller as 'The greatest philosopher-theologian yet to grace the American scene,' even though Perry Miller said of Edwards that "Because of his faith Edwards wrought incalculable harm." I do not ever recall having heard of Jonathan Edwards before entering Whitley.

Gradually I was to learn that the theology I knew through St John's, DVI and Belgrave Convention was somewhat backwater theology. I had been an evangelical believer for almost ten years but had never heard of the likes of the towering philosopher-theologian in Edwards. I had been surrounded by those who held to 'the simple gospel' with all its shortcomings. Calvin's *Institutes* had certainly opened my eyes. So now there was to be a great spurt in my knowledge of truth, and not merely through becoming acquainted with the profundity of Edwards, but through those of kindred minds to Edwards. While there were not a few who feared I took a bad turn when headed for Whitley, there was Murray – and to a lesser extent, newcomers to Whitley in Alan and Geoff – that caused good growth even if the soil seemed infertile at the college on first sight.

Alan and Geoff professed to be evangelical and they, along with Murray, were drawn together with me after the bruising we received from the three liberal students on our first day. We shored each other up with the consolation that the Scriptures possessed a veracity that proved them to be reliable for accuracy in not only the matter of salvation, but in science and history.

Among the books we had to purchase for our courses of study was *The Introduction to the New Testament* by a scholar called Kummel. I thought it promised to be an actual introduction, thereby enlightening us about essential truths of the New Testament, so that we may be fired up for our future Baptist ministry in the churches, but it was clouded with shady terms and names of various scholars hitherto unknown. Such a book served as an introduction forced on us by other works that were predominantly written by those of strange European names – Bultmann, Barth, Kung, Dibetius, Bornkamm, Gunther, Conzelmann, Kierkegaard… We could have had authors of Bornkamm and the like that of 'Bunkum', and it would have seemed apt at the time! Many of those scholars lost us in wrestling with processes belonging to names such as Source Criticism, Form Criticism, Redaction Criticism.

I for one was bewildered by such an approach to study for the ministry, and sought to balance my reading with what I considered edifying for my spiritual good against what seemed dubious but deemed essential for credentials for the ministry as governed by the exams set by the Melbourne College of Divinity. My brief course in rapid reading in the city promised to help me out with all the reading coming up on the horizon.

In just a few weeks at Whitley, I made my way to the city and sat for two or three sessions with others who also desired 'to read as quickly as possible' and still possess an understanding of what we read. We each sat before a machine that had a bar set to lower itself down on the page we were reading – set according to the required speed we desired. Back at college Murray thought the idea ridiculous, but the advice we were given seemed to have merit when reading a technical book –

    A. Read the technical book three times

    B. On the first reading, race through the book to get the gist of it

    C. On the second reading, read even more slowly, make some notes as desired

    D. On the third reading, read even more slowly, make more elaborate notes, summarize what is read.

The fear of rapid reading often lies in the dread of missing out on essential knowledge, but what may be unclear at some early point through a first reading often can 'come together' down the line.

I do not think it is demeaning to state that Alan and Geoff found the maze of liberalism even more confusing than Murray and me. They did not consider themselves academics. Alan's entry into Whitley came with the anticipation of him gaining his Matriculation but he was admitted, all the same, though he had to complete Matriculation by re-sitting the French exam while doing Theology, which included a new language of New Testament Greek. He was to take it in his stride with infectious humour. As for Geoff, his was a farming background but who tilled the soil of the liberalism he encountered as best he could and pronounced it infertile – he had seen too many people whose lives were far better by being changed by 'the true truth' (as Schaeffer called it) so not to doubt the power of the gospel.

I quickly became attracted to Alan in particular. Apart from our shared faith, we had much in common when it came to everyday things and sources of amusement. Yet, it did surprise me that he was pro-Labour in politics. How could that be? Every keen Christian I had known voted Liberal. He came from Altona, from a working class family. Geoff was for the Country Party, naturally enough. Murray was definitely Liberal. Some lively discussions arose as a result when Alan was around. After a time I began to see Alan's point of view to some extent: that campaigning for the rights of the poor and the oppressed could be seen as a Christian thing to do. Any difference in opinion did not cool our friendship. In fact, I admired Alan for what he stood for, and our friendship became firm.

Now, Alan, Geoff and I were 'freshers' and we were to undergo initiation at Whitley, along with all the 'freshers' amongst the secular students. One night found us all pressured by the seasoned students in taking off our day clothes straight after dinner and putting on our pyjamas. Then, with the paper bin from our rooms and a wooden stick of some sort, we were made to walk down busy Royal Parade for about 900 metres and past Princes Park in the growing dark to Cemetery Road West, until we arrived at Queen's College, where we were told at last to take to our paper bins with the wooden implements and begin banging the bins on the way back to Whitley, walking past St Hilda's College, a residential college for women university students. The banging was meant to be maintained all the way back up Royal Parade to Whitley, but there was no objection to it dying away once we had created the loudest possible racket at St Hilda's. It certainly achieved the object of embarrassing us, but who among us could not wait until next year when we initiated those destined to be 'freshers' then at Whitley?

Queen's College was where we 'theologues' would regularly attend lectures in Early Church History. Students from other colleges were present as well to hear a balding professor mumble his way through his notes that centred on the history of the post-apostolic era through to that of the fourth century. It was the only subject for lectures outside of our own college.

Inside the college among the lecturers were: Professor Brown, who took us for Greek and New Testament Exegesis; Professor Watson for Systematic Theology; Ron Ham for New Testament studies; and Alex Kenworthy for Pastoral Care. The principal did not give us lectures at all. Our lecturers were an interesting lot of men. Concerning two of them, Murray was fond of saying, "One is an evangelical trying to be a liberal, the other is liberal trying to be an evangelical."

Professor Brown loomed large in our lives. He was relatively short in stature, but he seemed to assign us too much work outside his lectures. He appeared to be oblivious to the work required for our other subjects. He would enter the lecture room praying as he entered. Then he would ask us for the 'homework' he had given us in the lecture before. After that, sitting in a semicircular arrangement, we were expected to translate a verse each in our own words from the New Testament book of Mark under study. "My, that's an incredibly good King James' translation," he would occasionally say, and equally with cynicism "And you have really missed the bus." He would give a chuckle and demand we translate accurately and in our own fresh way. He could easily discern if we knew the Greek, of course. However, Alan and I, pressed for time in the week, put it over Professor Brown with our 'homework'– Alan and I did the 'homework' together, he contributing to the deciphering of any grammar, I to the vocabulary. Others were pulled up for cheating, but he never suspected us, as we mixed up a few errors to make the 'homework' different from one another's. Professor came across as rather acerbic in manner to existing 'theologues', but it was said that he proved affable to them once they were exit students.

I will always remember Professor Brown saying that the only students who would go on to use their knowledge of New Testament Greek in their ministry, would be those who struggled with the subject in college! There was probably some truth in that.

Professor Watson took us for a good part of the week, for Systematic Theology. He was an affable fellow, but getting on in years and growing forgetful, sad to say. His lectures were rather dry, though to us they were given sparkle when students "took him up the garden path" and snared him into reminiscing about his experiences in the U.S.A. For one thing, he amazed us by telling of the exorbitant fees preachers could get for one sermon as an itinerant there. Some of our Australian ministers were going to the U.S. for pulpit exchange in a few months' time and we wondered at the monetary surprise they may get just for a twenty minute sermon.

Despite being a dry lecturer, Professor Watson was clearly a man of prayer, and he would always get one of the students to close in prayer at the end of a lecture.

Dryness of a lecture could cause sleepiness and that in turn could cause a risible unreadiness for prayer. At the end of one lecture, Professor Watson, without being all that conscious of us listening to him at the best of times, called on a certain student to pray without looking up at we students. For a laugh a student poked a sleeping fellow next to him in the ribs, and said to him, "The professor wants you to pray." The fellow woke up slowly, drowsily but mumbled audibly enough something incoherent in what remotely resembled a prayer to much laughter while the Professor was speaking.

Although the principal, Mervyn Himbury, did not loom large in our lives, in that he gave no lectures, he often took chapel in the mornings. He loved to preach after the style he used to captivate quite a few churches whenever the opportunity came his way. He was humorous, demonstrative with his hands and stentorian in voice. Once in chapel he began with an intriguing story – as he was apt to do – about a man who fell in love with a woman, and married her. However, she became a prostitute. She cashed in her husband's possessions to pay those who made love to her – unusual in that she paid men to have sex with her. We college students were entranced with the story right to the end, until our principal revealed that it came from Ezekiel 16. In modern dress it had been disguised, and together with the theatrics of our principal helped to hide from us what was probably an unknown or unfamiliar parable of an unfamiliar book of the Bible to most of us students.

Much of my experience at Whitley was becoming 'grist to the mill.' In more ways than one I had met 'the Queen' – in the days when science was used as a broader term than it is now. Someone once said that theology is the queen of all sciences. In the Middle Ages the Schoolmen, who were teachers of philosophy and theology, regarded arithmetic, music, geometry and astronomy as the fourfold way to knowledge, and to a lesser extent held that grammar, rhetoric and logic were the actual keys to knowledge. While I could hold that the above liberal arts may be essential in varying degrees, theology was the Queen of Knowledge. I do not know who made that claim, but I believe it is true.

From early on at Whitley I was sure that there was so much more to learn than what could be gained from the Melbourne Bible Institute. Early Church History introduced me to Eusebius 'the Father of Church History', and I branched out into learning of our Baptist history through a book called *The Anabaptist Story*. I became acquainted with the Puritans through my friend Murray – by reading what were known as Puritan Paperbacks, many that opened a vast treasure of some of the most spiritual works one could ever encounter. There was *The Rare Jewel of Christian Contentment, The Great Ejection, The Lifting Up of the Downcast, Heaven on Earth…* One of them was titled *The Plague of Plagues*, telling of sin being such a plague and an affront to God that for several days after reading the book I did not want to live for fear of sinning. Still, that could be the problem with some of the Puritans: too much of an accent on the disease and not enough on the remedy.

The Puritan Thomas Watson had me so enthralled with his insights that I decided to copy him by making up a sermon with fifteen points as he had done. I preached the message at Bacchus Marsh Baptist, no doubt leaving them bewildered, even if out of grace nothing was said after the service. At least no-one could say that my sermon was pointless! It was a far cry from the sound advice we students were to receive a little later in Sermon Class: If you cannot express in one sentence what you intend to preach on, what you wish to say is not worth preaching.

Another intriguing theological student was Keith. He was not a residential one, as he was married and serving as a student pastor at North Carlton. Tall in statue, very handsome with a slick of black hair frequently falling down over his forehead. He possessed a somewhat rasping voice, yet it carried an exacting confidence and knowledge that the rest of us envied. He was a first class scholar, but showed traces of a mind that was probably too liberal for the Eltham Christian Fellowship, with which he had been associated. He was to say "There is no black magic in the Bible."

"There is no black magic in the Bible." One day as we walked back to Whitley after attending an Early Church History lecture at Queen's College, the conversation turned to the subject of reading the Bible. Keith said that we should not fall for the superstition of believing it to be most spiritual to first read the Bible upon rising from bed every day. Since Keith had come from the same kind of evangelical setting as me, I knew what he was getting at. He wanted to kick against the traces of what was an evangelical proverb: "No Bible, no breakfast." No guilt ought to be felt if we did not follow that rule. It also related to the practice of setting a time limit of at least fifteen minutes in "quiet time."

Keith's thoughts freed me up and was to give rise to what became a favourite sermon of mine in those early days when I stumbled on an arresting expression used by the Puritan Thomas Brooks: "They were to lick the glass and not the honey." Brooks was referring to barren practice born out of ritualism (superstition) when maybe one seems to be in touch with God. My sermon was based on Israel taking the Ark into battle against the Philistines. Israel thought the presence of the Ark ensured victory – they were only licking the glass. The presence of God is honey, and they were not tasting that, consequently the Philistines defeated them. It was my way of attacking the ritualism and superstition Baptist people, of the congregations I preached to, could easily fall for. Brooks in his *Heaven on Earth* had captivated me with his sense of the presence of God.

My time to preach a sermon in Sermon Class was coming up and I vowed that my sermon 'Licking the Glass' was to be protected from the criticism expected in that class. I learnt that some of the other 'theologues' were intending to preserve their best sermon from what could provoke a barrage of fault-finding and nit-picking. Stewart, who was a devotee of Roy Orbison and who cannily enough resembled 'The Big O' with his rather thick-rimmed glasses and dark hair, wanted to make a protected species of his sermon 'A Bag With Holes' that was inspired by a text found in Haggai.

Still, Sermon Class could have its use. With criticism coming from the principal and from even your own fellow-students, one could learn with profit of his faults. Apart from being advised to follow the dictum that "unless you can put down in one sentence what your sermon is about, it is not worth preaching," we learnt that our mannerisms could be distracting to our listeners. Our voices also may not have been projected sufficiently. Were we exegeting the text correctly? Was our application of the text convincing? Were we building up our voices in volume too early, so that our final words lost their effect and formed an anti-climax?

Around the time I was scheduled to preach at Sermon Class, the principal thought it profitable for us to have a radio announcer come along and run several classes in order to teach us about speaking with controlled breathing, pausing, etc. Alan and I attended all classes bar one – we decided to skip a session as we thought that the number of lectures set aside for the radio announcer were too many. The business of correct reading as understood by a secular fellow was over-rated and too theatrical, we pompously concluded.

A semester had arrived before I was set to preach at Sermon Class. All the residential theological students had to vacate the college during the semester. Where was I to go? I had misgivings about asking 'Dad' and 'Mum' about staying with them, for I felt there was still some tension about me belonging to the Baptist denomination. They may well have received me but I remained apprehensive. I was even apprehensive about asking the Shorts, whom I still visited on some weekends, but there was no-one else to turn to with confidence. No-one at Whitley knew of my dilemma. Neither Alan, Geoff nor Murray knew of it, for they had no notion about my upbringing. Could I seek permission to have my room in the semester, plead special circumstances? No, I had no confidence to ask, as the directive to move out temporarily seemed fixed.

Out of desperation I contacted Mrs Short and she assured me that I could stay with them.

I took with me a book called "*The Source*" which Keith had recommended. Besides filling my days at Geelong with helping milk the cows, enjoying dinner at the end of each day when Dennis came home from work and when we exchanged stories and shared in evangelical fellowship, during the day I would sit in my car in the sun, out of Geelong's biting wind, and read "*The Source.*" It was an intriguing story to do with archaeological digs in the Middle East, interwoven with portraits of lives of the archaeologists.

Then it was back to college, too soon it seemed.

We residential theological students discovered that we were being compelled to move rooms further away in some cases because it was thought that we ought to mingle more with the other fellows residing in the college – many of them being non-Christians. We "theologues" were seen as being too cliquey. Did we not know that once in the ministry our mission was to evangelize outsiders and 'bring them into the church?'

The 'segregation' did work to some degree but we evangelicals still gravitated to one another when we could and to our satisfaction. We hoped that the 'segregation' would not blunt our evangelical fervour that sprang from seeing each other as often as we could. It did not appear to.

My own evangelical fervour threatened to be dampened by the Puritan influence when my sermon for Sermon Class was eventually delivered to the critical audience of the principal and the students in the chapel, to such an extent that some became suspicious and quizzed me after I delivered it – "Was that sermon your own, or did you borrow it from somewhere?" I chose for my text Psalm 8:4… "what is man that you are mindful of him, and the son of man that you care for him?"

Most of the criticism of the sermon was levelled at the subject matter, for some thought that the view of man that I projected was somewhat demeaning. The view was one shared by a number of Puritans and was considered more than Scripture warranted, so that indirectly the Puritan view of man was scorned to my fear.

"I say, Eddie, was that your own sermon?" asked Derek, one of the three liberals who interrogated some of us on our first day at Whitley.

"I'll leave you to work it out," I replied.

"Go on, tell us."

"No, I'll keep you guessing."

I left the chapel somewhat ashamed. While I took pride in causing most to wonder and to be uncertain if I had perhaps plagiarized, I felt sheepish because it looked like I was mocking the concept of Sermon Class, as well as making it appear that I was more intent on escaping the fear of personal criticism. Well, was it tantamount to mocking the principle behind the class? Was I telegraphing that the whole thing was of no benefit?

On one hand the critics of the trial sermons could give healthy advice, but the more liberal students could cloak what antagonism they had towards the evangelical students without their criticism appearing overtly unhealthy. Yet, secretly I knew all was "grist to the mill" and I had actually learnt much from Sermon Class, so that when I came to do my first morning devotion in the chapel before all the students, I was in possession of better preaching ability than I ever had before. Dr Noel Voce, principal of the Western Australian College, was present that morning and he made a favourable comment or two about my devotion on a testing passage from 2 Kings 7, where it says that Elijah told the Syrian captain that he would see God doing the impossible but would not literally eat of what seemed improbable to come to the famished city.

As a circular college, Whitley had its peculiarities. If one had a lecture in a certain room, particularly if your room was an outside one, you would have to think twice about which was the nearest way in your hurry for some lectures – to the right or to the left in the passage way?

If you had an inside room – as I did when I first entered Whitley – and some student turned up his music to full volume, the music would circulate and reverberate right around the inner part of the whole college. An architectural student was known to turn up his music in his own inside room and go see a friend several rooms around from his and listen to it there! A popular instrumental piece of pop music at the time was *Love is Blue*.

Another student from an inside room played it over and over for many weeks – some of us could have wailed in unison against the version that had the words 'Blue, blue, my world is blue,' for the endless sounding out of it was making our own world blue.

A little later in the first year a social was arranged at Whitley. Murray, Alan, Geoff and I anticipated more than the usual reverberating noise around the college that particular night, for the university students were allowed (?) to bring alcohol onto the college grounds. We felt sure that many Baptist churches would have been horrified to learn that alcohol was to be on the Baptist College premises, therefore two of us thought ourselves justified in hurriedly grabbing bottles of beer from the fridge and tipping their contents down the plug hole of the bath when no-one was in sight. In the evening we went into the city to see the controversial film *In Cold Blood*, and afterweards Murray planned for us to stay at his parents' house in Altona for the night.

The evangelical bond between we four saw us light-heartedly make our way down to Swanston Street, then to the Capitol Theatre to see the adaption of Truman Capote's book to the film about the story of two young killers who had slaughtered an innocent Kansas farm family in cold blood. It was a black and white semi-documentary that followed the murder case from the moment the crime was reported until the execution of the two killers. When we walked out into the street's bright lights more than two hours later, we were confused: Had Capote too much sympathy for the killers, or did he simply display an even-handedness about the controversial issue of capital punishment?

The issue generated a lively discussion between us – Murray, Geoff and I believing execution is a fitting crime for murder, while Alan did not appear convinced that we were right and thought Capote's portrayal of the murder case lent a sound argument against capital punishment.

It was not the only time that Alan and I ventured to the city. We were avid fans of Glen Campbell, the American country vocalist. Once we could not wait to buy his latest album at a record store closer to Whitley, but found out that Allen's music store in Bourke Street in the city had it on sale. I drove my EK Holden to Allen's and waited outside while Alan dashed in to buy it.

Alan's parents, as well as Murray's, lived in Altona and I went with Alan to Altona once more, when he had to call in at home. By the time I had joined him to travel to his parents' place, I had grown so fond of our friendship that I felt a strong urge to tell him of my upbringing even before Alan stepped out of the car. The urge to tell him of the neglect suffered in my childhood in an institution was strong, but to work myself up to telling him deserted me. While I waited for Alan to emerge from his house, I attempted to console myself with the thought that there may be another time to tell him, and yet it seemed that golden opportunity to do so was there at Altona. There was no-one else at college with whom I had such a longing to speak of the past.

There was more of an affinity with Murray in a deep and shared belief in the sovereignty of God in salvation, but at the time no affinity with him in respect to music. Alan and I conceived some mischief, deciding to take out a tape of some classical music of Beethoven in Murray's player when he was absent from his room and put in a tape of the craziest rock music possible. We would have loved to have seen the shock on Murray's face when he played the supplanted tape, but he guessed who the culprits were. He recovered soon enough.

Soon after, all of us – yes, the 'theologues' and the secular students – were caught up in a common protest against the quality of the meals served to us by a company called Nationwide Catering.

I think Nationwide had been catering at Whitley since the inception of the college, but perhaps it was the mischief of one of the former residential 'theologues' named John Hicks that caused discontent to grow beyond his time, whereby the decision was made to boycott dinner one evening.

John had been a prankster. Few students had cars when John was a college resident in a year or so prior to my time there. John had a car. You may recall that the college circled around an expanse of lawn. He decided one day to point his car in the direction of the stone steps that formed the entrance to the college from the street's footpath. From the road the car shot forward, climbed the steps with some shaking and he sent it speeding around the round lawn with John happy at the helm. One would think that he was admonished for his devilry. I guess he was. His devilry became etched in the college folklore. He particularly became known for what was called The Hicks Test.

What was the Hicks' Test? It mainly had to do with the dessert that Nationwide supplied for dinner. To earn a little money, dressed in a white shirt and a black bowtie, I was one of student waiters who took turns to serve everyone present for dinner, except for the dignitaries who ate at High Table with Principal Himbury. The object of the Hicks Test was to pass the dessert upside down from one student to another and discover if the dessert would not flop out of the plate under the test before all of the ninety students had passed it on inverted. I recall that as a waiter one night I triumphantly carried out a dessert that passed the test to the kitchen but as soon as I said "Look! It's passed the Hicks' Test!" it dropped and splattered on the bench in front of the Nationwide staff.

I had some misgivings about joining in the mass boycott. Overwhelmed by the thinking of the majority, I joined with the whole student body and chanted a protest as the college dignitaries entered the dining room. Along with everyone else, we sat down on the grass in the courtyard facing the dining room and ate bought fish and chips.

I regretted protesting, for after all, we residential 'theologues' did not have to pay any fees for the theological courses we were doing. All that we ever paid for were the necessary books for our courses at the beginning of the year – we did not pay for room occupation, for lectures, for use of the library, for electricity, and certainly not for our meals. The secular students alone paid fees, considerable fees.

One tutor said once as he passed me by on the steps leading up to the second floor of the college, "Hello, here is a man of God!" There were times when we 'theologues' were not men of God, on occasions when we thought we were.

The end of the academic year drew to a close, with exams being sat at another college down the road. They were set by the Melbourne College of Divinity. On the very day when the Melbourne Cup was being run mid-afternoon while a certain exam was being done, the supervisor provided us 'relief' by writing on the board behind him the name of the horse that had won the Cup! Then, there was Alan, who was completing his Matriculation by sitting for a French exam that year, who became confused between the study of French and New Testament Greek and either wrote down French answers in Greek, or the other way around in one of his two exams.

Once more the residential 'theologues' were required to vacate Whitley during the semester – only, it was a long one from mid-November to the beginning of March. Where could I stay for that length of time? If I did not stay with some kind friends, I would be pressed to pay board at some unfamiliar place somewhere. And while we paid nothing for college accommodation, the money that I had saved the year before I entered Whitley – was dwindling at a considerable rate.

Where could I stay? My mind was set on Whittington and Diamond Creek as options. I took a chance on asking the Shorts for permission to stay with them during the coming summer month. Whittington had more pulling power because the Short boys had become fast friends of mine, and the open air on the Shorts' farm with the nearby picturesque Barwon River promised a good break from the sometimes-claustrophobic city life in a circular college with the ninety students.

My life as a boy in an institute for neglected children was spent on forty acres and included helping with the daily dairy milking of cows to supply milk for sixty or more children. While for most of my time strict boundaries within the forty acres were imposed on us, preventing us from straying into most of the property, it was always a blessing just to see a large green paddock or trees beyond the set boundaries, and the beautiful blue hills in the distance. Thus, the Shorts' invitation to live with them for the summer on their dairy farm was eagerly anticipated.

Between helping milk the cows twice a day, Philip, Dennis and I often played cricket up against the house wall. Once or twice the ball was hit into the windows of the shed where the milk was stored for the pick-up by the milk tanker, smashing and splintering the glass. Elton accepted it calmly to my surprise. He and Dot complimented each other well: Elton being phlegmatic and easy going; Dot sanguine, either laughing or whistling cheerily some hymn. Elton was trying to make ends meet by both dairy farming and working for International Harvester. When we all sat around the table, much conversation was often spiced by the Shorts' recollections of where they lived before Whittington, Dennis being as usual a lively raconteur, while I joined in with telling of the light side of college life, which virtually was all I knew since entering Whitley.

One day during that summer break Elton said to me, "We are collecting bales of hay from a paddock we have down Wilson's Road."

I replied, "I can help you."

He said, "The bales are heavy, in case you don't know."

"Well," I answered, "I helped to bring in hay for the dairy farmer where I boarded at my first school."

"It's up to you," he said, "but you don't have to help."

"I'd like to," I said.

In hindsight it is of particular interest that hay-carting at Bulumwaal only came to mind, not the number of times I had helped to hay-cart at the institution. Thoughts of Sutherland, the institution had flown from my mind. While living with 'Dad' and 'Mum' my mind was ever conscious of having been an inmate of the institution with 'Mum' as the Matron. It was not her fault that I thought that way, for the association was inevitable. Whenever I stayed with the Shorts, they never asked me about my upbringing; they must have known something of it since they had known 'Dad' and 'Mum' for some years before I met the Shorts, but my upbringing did not seem to interest them. They lived for the present and, God be praised, for our future at Christ's return, a subject that Elton loved to talk and read about.

Elton and Dot were not the kind to greet you with "Good to see you!" or "How have you been?" upon visiting them for the first time even after months of not seeing them. For an instant it would disappoint you to not be greeted in such a way, but conversation quickly began to roll and one knew they were happy to see you again.

The college got in touch with me that summer for an opportunity to preach at Wangaratta. The church there kindly put me up at a motel in the town overnight, and in the morning I preached from Ruth on the text "And she *happened* to come to the part of the field belonging to Boaz." Back at college I had become entranced with a Puritan paperback *The Mystery of Providence*, written by John Flavel.

Flavel had been a powerful preacher in his time. An example of it lies in the story of a farmer in New England of America, who had reached a hundred years of age. One day, as he sat in a field reflecting on his long life, he recalled a sermon he had heard in England as a boy before he sailed to America. As he meditated on what he heard so many years before, the horror of dying without having made peace with God struck him. With that dreadful realization dawning on him he placed his faith in Christ – eighty-five years after hearing John Flavel preach!

Now, can you not wonder at Flavel's "*The Mystery of Providence*" being so rich to a young man ready to embark on the ministry?

An opportunity also arose to preach at the Shorts' church – Fenwick Memorial at East Geelong. It was a different matter from proclaiming the Gospel and preaching to many who were receptive at a church such as Fenwick, than to strain to sell encyclopaedias. For I had sought short-term work in Geelong but, with nothing promising, I drove up to Melbourne one day to attend a seminar conducted by Collier Encyclopaedias, to join young hopefuls who desired to perhaps become salespersons. An aggressive American headed the seminar. He wore a large ring on a finger with the initials 'SS.' He spoke more about the methods one ought to adopt to sell the encyclopaedias than the value of the books. He was quick to wax lyrically not about the books so much as the big money we could all make. Objections flew at him about the tactics he suggested, and then the conversation curiously turned on the philosophical side of life.

One young fellow piped up, "So what! You burn yourself out making big money, but where does it get you?"

Boomed 'SS,' "Just think of the house you could buy, or a luxurious car, or maybe a yacht."

"Well, is it worth it?" persisted the young fellow.

"Of course, that's what life is all about!" said 'SS.'

As he groped to enlarge on his answer, several were at once shouting out about their views on life's purpose.

However, 'SS' still held most of us in his hand. After all, we hopefuls were there because we needed good money without having to make too much of an effort to earn it.

I set out for the city from Geelong a few days later, armed with a sample of a Collier's volume and an eye-catching brochure. Night was falling when in a certain suburb I hoped that people were home from work. At one door a man appeared. I did not put forward my foot quickly in the doorway to prevent it from being shut as 'SS' suggested, believing I would create an impression of awkwardness if I were to do what was unnatural for me.

"Yes?" he said.

He ushered me inside to my surprise, where I came out with my spiel, and further to my surprise he seemed most interested in purchasing a set of the books. Yet his wife appeared in the lounge and when she learnt of what I hoped to sell so easily, she put a wet blanket on any prospect I had, then left the room having settled the matter – the husband and I stood there alone. Yet, as I turned to leave, he began to be philosophical in a similar way to that of the young hopefuls at the seminar, only he spoke of the vanity of acquiring much of the knowledge such books as Collier's possessed. I sensed a yearning in his soul, so much that I wanted to tell him about the eternal truth in Jesus, but my mission that night was to move on straightaway and to go house to house in the hope of landing a sale, was it not?

Solomon speaks of 'Making many books there is no end, and much study wearies the body.' He goes on to say 'Fear God and keep His commandments, for this is the whole duty of man.'

I had no success whatsoever at being a salesman. I possessed a temperament unsuitable for an occupation that calls largely on lively chat laced with open charm. Still, I stored up in my memory the seminar with 'SS,' and in a few months down the track I would include within a new sermon my experience of 'SS' on what was to be the second most momentous day of my whole life.

I returned to Whitley College in 1969 for my second year. It seemed that life as a theological student would be similar to the year before, apart from doing some demanding translation work with Professor Brown in Greek, and several other new subjects such as Pastoralia. I expected more preaching in various Baptist churches throughout the year, as did the other 'theologues,' but little did I know what lay ahead by way of a great surprise given by God.

When one is doing the will of God, you can never predict what is in store for you, when perhaps for years you have met with disappointment. David tells us in one of his psalms that 'my life is consumed by anguish and my years by groaning,' but says in the same song –

'How great is your goodness,
Which you have *stored up* for those who fear you'…

Even before the academic year had begun, I was invited to preach at Wandin North, east of Melbourne and up country. It was on March 2 that I set out to preach at the 9.30am service. I had the sermon that was influenced in part by the experience of the seminar for selling Collier's encyclopaedias and about 'SS' being challenged over his materialistic outlook on life. The written sermon also had the resounding words 'the siren sounds but we sleep on.'

Upon entering the pulpit of the little wooden church, I cast my eye on the small gathering of people, when all a sudden I became transfixed by a beautiful young lady in the back row, looking intently at me. She was with two other young ladies but her eyes and mine were interlocked so much that as the service began, I found it difficult to concentrate on introducing the first hymn. The most testing time was when I launched into my sermon. I had hoped and prayed back at college that the Spirit of God would give me a telling word for the people of the congregation of the danger in being caught up with materialism, but to be inspired to serve God wholeheartedly.

On coming out in my new sermon for the first time with the words "the siren sounds but we sleep on," what should happen but the siren of Wandin North's fire station sounded! It seemed providential that the siren should sound, for the congregation paid even more attention to the preached word.

Was it providential that I met up with the beautiful young lady with the blonde hair? We exchanged more than a momentary glance when all the people filed out at the end of the service and shook hands – ours was a long glance at each other. We seemed to be tumbling into love even though it had been only an hour that we saw one another for the first time.

It was with an anxious heart that I parted from her, as she mingled with the others of the little wooden church, while I headed for Millgrove to preach there also.

After preaching at Millgrove, I slowly drove through the main street of Wandin North hoping to catch a glimpse of the young lady. She was not to be seen but such was the longing to meet her again that back at college, I wrote a letter in the hope of passing it on to any student who would be preaching at Wandin North in the future. For it was at the time when the three churches of Wandin North, Millgrove and Lilydale were being served by us 'theologues' as that circuit of three churches was without a pastor. I wrote the letter, but could not bring myself to give it to any student who was preaching at Wandin North. I became impatient: Would I get another chance to preach there again?

Murray returned from preaching in that circuit in mid-April and said that whoever was to preach next time was only to preach at Millgrove and Wandin North. The college asked me to preach at both places, based on Murray's information.

Firstly, I travelled to Wandin North, but was dismayed that the young lady was not present! Would I ever see her again? I set off sadly for Millgrove. On arriving there, I entered its small wooden church and began enquiring about the service arrangements at the front porch when I discovered that a Mr Harry Blake was scheduled to preach. There at the front of the church, and without observing the congregation, Harry and I entered into discussion as to how the confusion about preaching there had arisen. It turned out that Murray had got it wrong: *I was not to preach at Millgrove, only at Wandin North*. Harry was gracious enough to offer me the preaching, but I thought it was fairer to allow him to do it.

Therefore, I sat down at the back of the church, when suddenly I caught sight of the young lady, who had turned around at the front seat. Her eyes lit up at seeing me there, and I did handsprings in my heart.

After the service, and after the awkwardness of seeking her attention when she stood in the midst of other people, I learnt of her name and where she lived.

At her home up the Mount Donna Buang road and down a narrow lane, Kerryn and I sat and talked, after meeting her mother and her three siblings.

My heart was full on returning to Whitley. Surely, life was never to be the same.

I was in my second year at the college and, although it had been known for four years or so that I had an ambition to be a pastor, the one and only opportunity I had to preach at my home church at Greensborough came merely a month or more after I had met Kerryn. Despite it taking a long time coming, I did preach, by using my favourite sermon that was built around the words of "licking the glass and not the honey." It was well received. It was on that day that I travelled down to 'Mill Valley Ranch' at Tynong North, where Kerryn's church's young people were attending a weekend camp.

When the camp finished, I took Kerryn home to Warburton. As I travelled, the same desire, that I had felt the year before, when taking Alan to Altona, came to the surface, except that with Kerryn I felt more comfortable expressing it. I told her on her curiosity about my past that I was an orphan, had lived in an institution for neglected children between the ages of six and eighteen, that I knew nothing about my parents and I had no way of finding out. My sister Joyce was discovered when I was 15. We had a great aunt in Canada who tracked us both down, but claimed that she knew nothing more than that our mother was 'VERY YOUNG' (capitalized by great aunt in a letter) when she married our father whom our great aunt thought had died – "He was old, you see." My sister had our paternal grandfather's death certificate but she said that is all the knowledge she possessed.

After many years it was a relief to talk openly about my upbringing – not just about the scanty facts I knew of my very early life before entering Sutherland, but of my feelings about the frustration of knowing so little about the past. It was a great relief because I found someone that I fell head over heels in love with, and who had sympathy for what I had faced in life. I sensed no shame or embarrassment in telling her. What was revealed made no difference to her – she loved me and I drove back to Whitley with a heart over-flowing with happiness.

It was a corny song Doris Day had sung some years before, I suppose, but it captures somehow what one can feel when at last you find someone you will love till the end of time –

> 'Everybody loves a lover,
> I'm a lover,
> Everybody loves me,
> Anyhow, that's how I feel,
> Wow, I feel!'

Even though what I told Kerryn had not freed me so that it inspired me to reveal about my upbringing to anyone at Whitley, I still 'stood tall' among the students at Whitley – all the students. As well as being in love with certainty, there was a feeling of self-worth unknown before.

Confidence filled my days, with a mixture of ever-occurring thoughts of Kerryn in the middle of lectures to do with New Testament Greek, Church History, Pastoralia, and Old Testament Exegesis. Principal Himbury contended that since we 'theologues' were Baptist, we should become acquainted with Baptist history. Was he not the author of *British Baptists* –

A Short History? He arranged to have the first lecture in one of the lecture rooms in our own college, only to tell us in the one and only lecture that he had too many pressing commitments to further lecture, and jokingly concluded that Baptist history was too short to warrant extended learning by us!

Professor Brown continued to walk through the door of the lecture room praying as he went, and then would have us opening our Greek New Testaments for translation. As we sat in the usual semicircle around him – doing a verse each – whenever we bungled, he would still allow his right hand to go hopping away customary from his shoulder as he said somewhat grimly, "You have really missed the bus, Mr ……." Or, "That's a very good rendition of the King James, Mr……" One student, who was not 'a Rhodes Scholar' (as 'Dad' would say of anyone lacking in intellect) had bungled excessively once with translation that Professor grew annoyed as the student pretended to look at his Greek New Testament on the desk while actually looking down anxiously at a Pocket New Testament in English under the desk. The student blurted out in exasperation, "Professor, the only Greek I know is the fellow who owns the fish and chips shop down the street!"

As the weeks went by, my fellow 'theologues' suspected that I had a girlfriend, for regularly on Friday afternoons I set off for Warburton and would not arrive back until Sunday evening. Also, at times during the week the one and only phone of the college for all students would ring for me and someone would yell out, "Eddie Smith! Phone!" Their voice would echo around the courtyard. Then, when I or anyone reached the phone at the bottom of the college stairs, you had to look up while answering it because often some student would tip a bucket of water over you from above. Yet, the risk was worth taking when I suspected that my phone calls were likely coming from Kerryn. It was not that the Baptist college was one for sprinkling but immersion by drenching!

As for students' meals in our second year, they had improved. Some desserts passed the Hick's Test. All the same, after dinner on some nights Alan and I would head for Lygon Street in Carlton where we would order a pizza, watch the pizza base spin in the air at the hand of a skilled Italian, and see the chef deftly decorate the base with toppings. We then left the shop to eat our purchase in my car outside while it was piping hot.

On July 16 of that year Murray rented a TV to watch the momentous landing on the moon. Kerryn was there with me in Murray's room. His room, of course, was only fitted out for one student, but quite a number of students had packed into his tiny space on Murray's invitation. The landing on the moon by the U.S. astronauts, Armstrong, Aldrin and Collins was said to fulfil a dream that had existed for centuries but, while Armstrong was seen as making a 'giant leap for mankind' on the Moon's Sea of Tranquillity, it was a nightmare in various places around the world at the time. The Vietnam War was taking a horrendous toll on lives – 1200 soldiers being killed on average per month – with the West fiercely divided between Hawks and Doves over the conflict. The U.S. was still reeling over the assassination of Robert Kennedy. Students all over the world were rioting in great numbers for any number of causes. In West-Africa a civil war left millions dying of hunger. The Sexual Revolution of the early Sixties was still evolving, with the stage production of *Hair* causing consternation among Christians everywhere. The fulfilment of the dream on the Sea of Tranquillity had been eclipsed by the nightmares on our planet Earth.

The only other TV seen at Whitley was that set up in our common room, where students would gather in the evenings to watch *The Avengers* and *The Frost Report*. *The Avengers* was a clever British series – a form of escapism built around a male secret agent who, with a beautiful woman equal to the occasion, tackled quirky crimes and dastardly evildoers. As for David Frost, he was adored by many a student because he was a skilled satirist. He was a master at interviewing well-known figures with the technique – someone said – of "caress, caress, nod, smile, kidney punch, smile, smile." His wife was once asked if Frost was religious: "Most certainly, he thinks he is God."

By mingling with 'the secular students' in watching *The Avengers* and *The Frost Report,* there was a way of breaking down any barrier that could exist between the 'theologues' and the others in the college, though we were eyed with disdain and suspicion by most of them. Besides, our study life and lectures were within the confines of the college alone – so many saw us as not having the status of attending Melbourne University for learning. Still, we regarded theology as Queen of the Sciences, with Jesus being truly the Way to God, the Truth and the Life.

After the second year exams of 1969, as usual we 'theologues' had to vacate the college until the beginning of our academic year in early March. Once again, I had to find a place to live during the summer semester. I toyed with seeking accommodation with 'Dad' and 'Mum' at Diamond Creek but I learnt that they had become carers for some children in Box Hill, and that people unknown to me now lived on their property. Still, I sought accommodation there because a summer job was available for me at Eltham – under Alistair Knox, who was a renowned mudbrick architect. The unknown couple, at what once had been home to me, grudgingly allowed me to live with them but only wanted me there for a short time. As it was, it became a shorter time than expected because my back gave way to considerable pain after a mere few days of wheeling barrow loads of mudbricks for Knox, who gladly got rid of me, though Pharaoh in Egypt might have forced me to press on alongside the Israelites.

What was I to do? Where was I to go until March? I longed to be near Kerryn, and her mother kindly took me in at their tiny ten square house while I recuperated from my ailing back.

Fortunately, a leader at Kerryn's church at Millgrove landed me work with the Forestry Commission, and I got accommodation at Adanac Lodge in Yarra Junction. The Forestry Commission was out to kill creatures known as phasmatids, since they were destroying the forest around Powelltown. A deadly spray was used, and there had to be no wind when "the agricultural aviator" (not to be called "the crop duster," thank you) flew over the trees and spewed the spray out on the gum trees below. It meant rising early each morning in the hope of spraying. I joined others holding up markers on the ground so that the aviator knew where to sweep in with the spray. We had masks on for safety purposes.

That job dried up and then I worked for a few weeks at a timber mill at Powelltown. I had never been so bored in my life, and it was a relief to sit in my car at lunch break and get my mind active again through reading.

Kerryn and I saw one another whenever we could, with Kerryn at times calling at Adanac Lodge. Once she came dressed up to go out with me one evening while I was having dinner. I shall never forget the young English fellow, who was also at the Lodge and who said to me when he saw Kerryn: "She's smashing!"

In the new year of 1970 Kerryn and I became engaged, and in early August I penned a letter to the principal to seek permission to be married early in the following year on February 27. I anticipated gaining my Diploma of Theology at the end of the year so that I could possibly get a ministry in a church somewhere for 1971. I also wrote that I was seeking permission to live in a college flat should an opportunity not arise to gain a pastorate. Whatever he circumstances of 1971, I was to serve out a probationary year before I was available for ordination in 1972.

Meanwhile, I served for a few months as an assistant to the pastor of the Korumburra-Wonthaggi circuit. Kerryn and I would travel down each

Sunday for me to tandem preach with the pastor Brian McKelvie, both of us alternating week by week to preach at one of the two churches.

One Sunday, Kerryn and I were heading for Wonthaggi, where the church had a stubborn lady organist. Brian (the pastor) warned me that at times she would begin playing the organ to accompany the singing of the congregation, only to break off and exclaim, "We don't know that hymn!" Before the sermon I announced the hymn to be sung. She played the introduction. The people rose to sing. We all began singing to the organ. Suddenly the lady stopped. Silence. Then she called out to me, "We don't know that hymn!" The congregation looked up at the pulpit. "Oh, well," I called out, "I am sure we can sing it without the organ!" I began singing and the congregation began the first verse again in unison with me. With only a line or two sung, the organ's notes resounded and continued until the end of the sacred song! Now, that was another story to tell and amuse my friends down at Geelong!

Before 1970 came to a close, I received the news that Kerryn and I were able to get married on the desired date and that I was to become the student pastor of West Coburg Baptist church after our honeymoon.

Until we became married, I managed to get work at the Seventh Day Adventist Sanitarium in Warburton. At first I worked with a small team on 'the Hydro,' up in the mountains and revelling in the open air, where we were to ensure that the channel running down to the breakfast cereal-making factory was clear of rubble. I happily engaged in witnessing about the Lord to the team, particularly to a young Samoan man. The SDA boss of the factory got wind of my witnessing to the SDA Samoan, and I was pulled out of working on 'the Hydro' and put in the factory for humdrum work in the stuffy warm to hot air but was permeated by the inviting scent of toasted weet-bix.

MEETING THE QUEEN

I worked at the Sanitarium up to the day before Kerryn and I wedded. On our actual wedding day I had cause to go down to the milk-bar in the town to buy milk. The milk-bar owner said, "It's going to be warm. What do you hope to do today?" I hesitated and then said, "Mmm… I think I'll get married!" He chuckled when I told him that I was getting married.

After a three week honeymoon, we moved into the West Coburg Baptist Manse on busy Bell Street. After living in the quiet of Warburton all her life, it was a little unsettling for Kerryn to live on Bell Street. Not only was the traffic dense day and night, but there was a bus stop outside our weatherboard house, with only a small expanse of lawn separating the bus stop from our bedroom window, so it left us open to the noise of the screeching buses and the continuous roar of other vehicles.

During our time at the West Coburg church we had little to live on, and we acquired essential things only after exercising patience and enough money to purchase them. We borrowed a double bed from Kerryn's mother until we could afford our own. After a month from moving in, we purchased a second-hand refrigerator and a reconditioned washing machine. We had no lounge room furniture until our second year in the manse, when we bought a used lounge suite through 'Trading Post.'

Still, people were kind to us. We were given a belated wedding present of a top class dining room suite to replace a kitchen table we had borrowed from Warburton. A couple from the church had lent us kitchen chairs – and gave us a spare Astor TV set to use. A lady of the church made white terylene curtains for the house, and someone mysteriously slipped under the front door twenty dollars (the equivalent of one hundred and twenty odd dollars today.)

It was necessary for Kerryn to find work. One day after visiting Victorian Football League house near Melbourne Cricket Ground in the hope of a successful interview, the phone rang as soon as we entered the front door of the manse on our return from Jolimont. The timing was perfect – or, God's timing was – for Windsor Smith, the shoe company where Kerryn had a job interview a few days prior, offered her a job as their receptionist.

In those days, I appreciated the advice of Keith the fellow collegian at Whitley that there is no black magic in the Bible. However, I found that life by rule is not to be scorned. We must not become superstitious or guilty in insisting on having a time of devotion in Bible study and prayer first thing in the morning, while the balancing of attendance at Whitley in my probationary year with that of serving the church, and of spending time with my cherished wife.

It is common to scorn life by rule, but we expect rule and accuracy in many things of life. George Herbert, the great English poet says this –

> 'Slight those who say amidst their sickly healths,
> Thou liv'st by rule. What doth not so, but man?
> Houses are built by rule, and common-wealths.
> Entice the trusty sunne, if that you can,
> From his Ecliptick line: becken the skie.
> Who lives by rule then, keeps good companie.'

It was in my early days at West Coburg that I had lived by Sabbath rule. I bought myself a book written by Paul Jewett called *'The Lord's Day.'* It claimed to be *'a theological guide to the Christian Day of Worship.'* I was curious about how we believers should conduct ourselves on a Sunday. My suspicion had been aroused by some things that were prohibited even from when I was a boy at the institution. Was it right not even to clean shoes on 'the Sabbath' (Saturday)? I was no longer watching Saturday football on TV only, for the VFL (Victorian Football League) had introduced Sunday football. Was it wrong to watch football on the Sabbath? Remember that the same dear folk who were my godly guardians in the institution were the people I knew and lived with after I left it, therefore it seemed that the only right things to do on a Sunday were to either visit relatives of 'Mum' or sit on the front porch while overlooking the town of Diamond Creek and reading things spiritual. In fact, after becoming a believer at aged 17, it appeared that it was quite right and proper to 'observe the Sabbath.' As youngsters in unbelief and under 'Dad' and 'Mum' in Sutherland, how bitter and angry we would be because we were not allowed to kick a football on Sundays! And was it not beneficial for people's bodies not to work on Sunday, or to open up shops?

At that time, I read into '*The Lord's Day*' more than the author intended, but there was a setting loose for freedom of a Sabbatarianism that proved more of a burden than realised over the years. On a distinct day I sighed – sighed with relief at the lifting of the burden of legalism.

Of course, as a pastor I did not desire that church people waive attendance at West Coburg, and spend Sundays in a worldly sense elsewhere, for I held to the conviction that in the present world Sunday was the most convenient day for we believers to gather together for the essential fellowship we needed for the study of God's Word –

> 'Let us not give up meeting together…but
> let us encourage one another – and all the
> more as you see the Day approaching' (Heb 10:25)

As I thought on my days at the institution under religious legalism, and while we were newly married with the memories of our three-week honeymoon still fresh in my mind, I reflected on a strange thing that occurred on our honeymoon which caused me to look back at institution days even more.

Naturally enough, Kerryn had bought for herself new clothes for our honeymoon. Yet, when she put on one of her new dresses for a certain occasion, I became alarmed and asked her if it were possible to change into a familiar dress she had worn before our wedding. Naturally enough, she wanted to sport the new dress and calmly said so. Yet I then begged her to change. She wanted to know why I insisted. What answer could I give her? There was none but I pleaded with her, and she graciously gave into my wish.

It surprised me as much as it surprised Kerryn to think I longed so strongly for what was familiar. I suspect that it was related somehow to my early life in the Sutherland institution. I did not tell her that there may have been a possible link, because at the time I myself was confused and a little ashamed of my request of her. Of course, it is common for many of us to love the familiar, to love memories to do with long associations with people and places we have known, but I had been alarmed and fearful until I saw something familiar. As for memories, I longed to consider something troubling that lay deep down in the past at that time. I had to go on to consider with Alan Bennet, an English actor, who once said –

'Memories are not shackles, Franklin, they are garlands.'

I shall always have good memories of Alan, Geoff and Murray at Whitley. Even though I was now married and not living at Whitley any longer, I still saw Alan and Geoff for the few lectures I was required to attend. As for Murray, he had left Whitley to attend the Geelong Reformed Presbyterian College, because he had become a dubious believer in paedo-baptism. Before leaving Whitley, he was honest enough to admit to someone that he could not counter what I told him in defence of believer's baptism. Still, while he had been a student at Whitley, I had prized him for the support given in defence of truth related to God's sovereignty. He also showed confidence in me by arranging for me to speak once at the Evangelical Union for students at Melbourne University.

When you are raw in the ministry, it is a blessing to get all manner of support. I dearly prized the calls that Rev Bob Pocklington paid on me – an experienced evangelical who was a good listener and proffered sound advice.

'All manner of support'? While at Whitley we had not learnt how to conduct church business meetings. One would have thought that in Pastoralia that we should have been taught such a thing. (Strangely, the thing that remained most memorable about Pastoralia lectures was the ringing laughter of Rev Alex Kenworthy when he talked of old men trying to control their bladders while they sang in church "Wide, wide is the ocean"…!)

The news of the first church business meeting, which I as pastor was to preside, was sprung upon me. I panicked. In haste I bought a small and hopefully simple book on the matter. I did not even know what a 'quorum' was, much less about my presiding role, nor the role of a secretary. Then, to read of 'motions' – seconding them, changing a motion, amending a motion, 'tabling a motion,' 'disposing a motion.' Well, the meeting did not end up as one of such motion as *commotion*, as those present were well aware – and I mean *well* aware – that I was new to the game.

Indeed, I learnt how church meetings can be a thing that need to be endured graciously. They have ramblers. There are those who fail to keep to the point; those who have had an assigned task and after a year or two regret the appointment and wish someone else could take over the assigned duty; those church members more occupied with things such as paint rather than pastoral matters, and so on.

Only after the first church meeting, and discussing the matter with the likes of Alan and Geoff, did I learn that many pastors dreaded church meetings. Still, they were seen as essential and, as one became more adroit at presiding over them, much could be achieved for the progress of the members' spirituality and evangelization of the community around us.

My progress in preaching, teaching and pastoral care was readily observable to myself, as it well could be since I was in my early days of ministry. As for preaching at that time of life, texts were pulled out from the Scriptures here and there, though they were often from Hosea, Mark and John in the early days when I had to prepare two new sermons for each Sunday. Teaching midweek in people's homes saw me lean on books in Scripture already explored at Whitley, such as the book of Amos. With respect to pastoral care, I set out to regularly visit those attending church in afternoons and evenings, setting aside the morning hours for sermon preparation.

They were good years in the Baptist Union of churches. While there was disquieting news, such as the possibility of a certain female being ordained for the ministry, and the scoffing of not a few about those men who out of concern for revival in Baptist churches formed the Baptist Revival Fellowship, and as well the lifelong tenure of Whitley's principal, one felt part of a large family of countless believers of many churches. The paper *The Baptist Witness* did much to create the family feeling. It is disturbing to be a pastor made lonely by an isolated church, and I was sure that country pastors and their people sensed they were 'family' on getting the monthly Baptist Witness.

Yet harmony had to be worked out in the local church. My predecessor had grown-up children who magnetized many young people to the youth group, but the youth group was purely social, with many of the young people not attending church and not showing any interest in spiritual things. I sensed this when one night I gave a devotion to the youth at an outside activity. Slowly I drew together a group of young people whose parents were of the church, and I began evening Bible studies for them. Eventually several of them were baptized to the joy of their parents.

Towards the end of 1971 Kerryn and I decided to go down to the Brighton beach. It was not an overly hot day and we sat on the sand for a few hours after swimming. Well, that night our bodies were burning red and stinging us with pain and stiffness that no number of remedies could counter. We were in so much agony that we could not walk, and all evening we were forced to crawl about on our knees in the manse!

I had to ring Bill, the church secretary, to tell him of our dilemma and that I was unable to preach in the morning. Bill told me that the principal of Whitley had decided with little notice to come and hear me preach! He had never heard me preach at all.

Before the college year closed one of the 'theologues' thought he was giving me good advice because it was hardly likely that Kerryn and I would stay at West Coburg, since I was but a mere student pastor there.

"Say, Eddie, I hear you are going up to the Convention."

"That's right," I replied. "What is on your mind?"

"When you're up at Belgrave, make sure you are seen by as many Baptist people as possible, particularly deacons."

It was in days when gaining a church as an evangelical was not exactly hopeful, but in my heart I despised the student's advice. It seemed an unsanctified way to secure a ministry somewhere.

The object for attending the Convention was to hear sound teaching, and yet some of the teaching left a lot to be desired. We met Murray at a meeting and he was bemused by one of the speakers appealing to the audience to surrender to Christ with the words: "You have got to be willing to be made willing." Murray chuckled: "Yes, you have to be willing to be made willing to be willing to be willing…"

In a house at Selby, where the owners kindly allowed us to stay while the convention was on, there took place in my heart one of the greatest moments of my spiritual life. I had come across the writings of Francis Schaeffer. If ever I had confidence to witness for Christ before that time, I had far more after reading Schaeffer's *The God Who is There* and *He is There and He is not Silent*. He showed how one can broach the subject of God in everyday conversation. He had his finger on the pulse as to what was happening in the world of philosophy, music, art and films. I was falling over myself in eagerness to get back to West Coburg in order to implement what I had read.

The beauty of Schaeffer's approach to 'true truth' was also his belief that the evangelical church should live out the truth herself. It is so easy to blame unbelievers for the evils of society without looking at ourselves. Did not Jesus say: "By this shall all men know that you are my disciples if you have love one for another?"

Still, the fellowship with many fellow-believers well compensated for whatever lacked in some of the things to do with the Convention. To see the friends of DVI once more was a prized occasion. 'Dad' and 'Mum' were not present at the DVI camp, as they were still living at Box Hill and were busy foster parents to underprivileged children. (I had not seen them for some time but Kerryn and I had paid them a visit once or twice at Box Hill, since our marriage.) Ken was no longer on the DVI scene; therefore I was more at ease at Belgrave.

It was only a little under two months after the Convention that Kerryn and I celebrated our first wedding anniversary. In order to spread the joy of how Kerryn and I providentially met each other, I took what I regarded, as a good parallel to our experience, the passage of Genesis 24, when I preached the day after our anniversary. The passage tells of Abraham's servant being sent to what formerly was Abraham's country in order to obtain a wife for his son Isaac. The Lord led the servant to a woman who proved to be a wonderful choice for Isaac.

Bill Hornby, the church secretary, took me aside after the service.

> "It was a good sermon, Eddie, but you should keep in mind the likes of Miss.... And how she would feel about what you said of marriage.
>
> "Yes, I guess you are right," I said.
>
> "Marriage is not for everyone," Bill said, "and she should not feel inferior about being single. At her age it is highly unlikely that she will ever marry."

Bill's counsel was taken on board. It taught me when preaching to consider every situation or circumstance people of a congregation may find themselves in. I sought to carry out such good advice for the rest of my days.

Bill called a spade a spade but he was a good man. He was small in stature, had a wife noticeably taller than him. He possessed a rather nervous disposition and a raspy voice. Yet he was solid in his devotion to the church. Quite earnest, but whenever he chuckled, Bill showed a sense of humour that reflected his considerable intelligence.

It was 1972 and months were drawing nearer to the end of the year when I was to be ordained for the ministry in the Collins Street Baptist Church in Melbourne.

As a student pastor, time at West Coburg soon had to come to an end. This became clear when the Baptist Union asked me to consider a pastorate in northern Victoria. Would I be willing to go there?

I had decided to get a Bachelor of Divinity with the London University – just by finding out by mail the syllabi for the many subjects one had to do in Australia to get the degree, and sit for both the preliminary exams and, if successful, proceed with the final ones at Melbourne University. It would mean hard work, even for the preliminary exams. For instance, Greek Grammar would require mastering the irregular verbs of New Testament Greek. The final exams would see me sitting through ones that lasted for two weeks. There was no second chance: every exam had to be passed on one attempt to gain the degree. Two men of the college had been successful, but they warned me of the hard study required. Now, would I be willing to go up country for a pastorate? If I agreed to do so, would it make study and research for the degree more difficult to gain?

The temptation was to turn my back on a possible move to the country, wait for an offer of a church closer to the city so that study and time-efficiency for research in access to library books was a better alternative.

I turned down the offer of the move to the country but not without great anxiety. Would the Baptist Union think I was too hard to please? Had I ruined my chances of getting another church at all? Was I even in the will of God by not moving up country? Was my reluctance to place an albatross around the neck of the congregation at West Coburg, who no doubt would desire a more experienced pastor? The Union had been good in enabling us as a temporary measure to fill the pastorate made vacant by an experienced man – close to the college for my final year at Whitley. Turning down the offer made by the Union so quickly caused me to feel uneasy.

Nearing my ordination, I still felt uneasy about my image in the Union's eyes, and wondered if I would ever become a settled pastor somewhere.

My ordination was held on October 3. Four of us were ordained for the occasion: Kevin Forbes, Joe Sherriff, Barry Wollmer and me. Barry had finally won through for ordination – he had been wrongly tutored for one year because his Baptist College lecturer was not acquainted with the year's syllabus for the subject studied. It was jokingly said that after three or four attempts to pass Early Church History Barry was fit to be a professor of the subject!

A good number of Baptist dignitaries lent solemnity to the occasion: Professor Brown, Principal Himbury, the General Superintendent Manley, Reverends Farmilo and Hinton, Dr Ithel Jones and the guest preacher Dr Noel Vose.

Among the verbal responses we four ordinands had to make, one arose from Paul's statement to do with every Scripture being 'inspired,' we responded by vowing to 'diligently study and practise God's holy word' so that by example and preaching we promised to be a worthy witness.

At college there had always been heated discussion about Scripture and its inspiration. One lecturer argued that we cannot claim every word in the Bible is inspired by God because Job's three friends said things God did not approve of, suggesting the door was open to question divine inspiration! It was claimed by the same lecturer that some parts of Scripture could not possibly be sound because Scripture erred in its doctrine of cosmology, contradicting the findings of modern science. It was claimed by others too that the Bible is not a book about science, nor is it a history book.

(Only God knows how many Baptist ordinands all those years ago believed what they vowed, as it was not only lecturers but also students who became ordinands and who were followers of what is known as Higher Criticism.)

Anyhow, there were still a considerable number of Baptist churches that were evangelical and held a high view of Scripture in 1972. Despite concerns over liberalism, I could still feel proud to be a Baptist.

It surprised me to learn of the pride some had in me at the time of my ordination. It deeply touched me to receive a letter from St John's of

Diamond Creek; to receive congratulations from the vestry of the church, even though I ceased to be Anglican eight years before; and to learn from the letter that "Mr Cyril Smith remembers you with great joy and pride, as do several of other members." Two telegrams were received also from the Sutherland Homes, and another from Alex, the dear brother and secretary of my home church at Greensborough. The telegram from the Homes and the letter that included the thoughts of 'Dad' were certainly heartening. 'Dad' was to be seen as having a Catholic heart in the true sense of the word. As for the telegram from Sutherland, it was clear that there were those who were proud of what I had climbed up to, despite being raised in the institution.

Fanning into Flame God's Gift

The President of the Baptist Union at the ordination had exhorted we four ordinands with the words of Paul:

> "Now I remind you to stir into flame the gift of God which is within you through the laying on of hands."

Reverends Farmilo and Hinton then laid hands on the four of us.

Symbolically the gift of God had been bestowed on us. I felt I was gifted, otherwise why was I considered fit to be ordained? And yet, strange are the turnings on the road when God leads us, though the turnings had been made stranger and more difficult to navigate through rejecting the offer of a full-time pastorate.

As it was, with nothing coming my way in terms of full-time ministry, I had to accept East Malvern's offer of part-time work, beginning in May of 1973. However the income from such a ministry had to be supplemented by other employment, therefore I fell back to teaching when I found out that I could get full-time work with the Education Department.

The Baptist Union did the best they could by obtaining a ministry for me at East Malvern, and West Coburg was kind enough in allowing us to stay on there until May. We were thrilled that Kerryn had become pregnant before the ordination and our first baby was due in February.

Belinda Rachel was born in February. We were showered with gifts, particularly from the West Coburg parishioners. What a blessing to be parents of our dear baby girl.

Nothing had been gained from turning down the offer of the full-time country pastorate in more ways than one. Time-wise, things were worse: I had to wrestle with full-time teaching at a very distant school at Frankston, run a part-time ministry mid-week and on Sundays at East Malvern, sit up at night doing research and study for the London degree, and also adjust to a new life at home, now that there were three of us to love and support.

If the service history records of the Education Department are correct, I was only at the Ballam Park school of Frankston for 13 days, before I was moved a little closer to Chandler Primary School, serving as what was described as an 'Outside Assistant.' My service history record of the Education Department is riddled with error. Perhaps those days were all a maze to the Department as well as to me. The time of one teaching post remains correct: the move close to home to teach at the Alamein school, where there were only 10 teachers, together with the principal.

The service history was all mixed up – recording that also I went to Alamein and then had a length of time at Greythorn in Balwyn. In fact, I was only at Greythorn for 2 days, before I determinedly made my way to the city to the head office of the Department to meet the Director of Education.

> "Yes," he said as I sat before him at his desk, "what can I do for you?"

"Well," I answered, "I have been appointed to teach at Greythorn in Balwyn but it is hard work travelling all the way each day from East Malvern."

"Well?" he uttered.

"It is taking one and a half hours at least to get to Greythorn."

"You can't be too choosy, you know. You're lucky to have a job."

"I know. I realise that."

"I could send you to Mildura! Did you know that?"

"Yes, sir," I answered as I dreaded being sent to the northern extremity of the state.

"Well?" he professed.

"I guess I am in your hands."

"All right, all right. We'll see, I suppose, as to what we can do."

I got the posting to Alamein, where I remained until early in 1975.

We were delighted to welcome Janine Maree to our family. She was born 19 months after her big sister's birth.

By the time I taught on my last day at Alamein we had received the good news that I had secured a full-time ministry in Ulverstone, Tasmania. Belinda's second birthday was the day we flew to Tasmania, with Janine only 5 months old.

We flew out from Melbourne in a Fokker Friendship, though our Labrador 'Monty' had to fly out on another plane bound for Launceston, where I had to drive to the airport to pick her up a few days after we had arrived.

We reached the humble weatherboard manse of 13 Hope Street, Ulverstone, early in the afternoon, but the place was not ready for us to move into until the darkness of 7.30pm, as people of the church were still preparing the house for us until then. All the same, they seemed excited about meeting us.

In 1975 Ulverstone was a town of about 7000 population. It is situated on the north-west coast of the Apple Island, the eastern part of the town separated on the western side by the Leven River. If I remember correctly, the town was bedevilled everywhere by 20 railway crossings! The Baptist church possessed an outstanding spot at the top of the main street, where at the centre of three converging roads stood a three-legged zenotaph-cum-clock tower. To call the zenotaph 'three-legged' and to imply it appeared a little odd in its structure says something of its asymmetrical shape, depending on the angle you viewed it. Anyhow, it was an outstanding feature and did much to draw attention to the centrality of the Baptist church in the town.

The church was a beautiful red brick building – at one end with its rectangular shape of a tower seeking to dwarf the zenotaph at the middle of the roundabout for the three streets at hand. Almost the whole of the church's front wall was lined with French style windows through which the sun shone softly when, in the first few weeks of my ministry, I had cause to prepare my first sermon in the church's porch by the windows.

In the course of the early days in Ulverstone, the deacon we got to know quite well was Eric Smith. He was a deacon and secretary of the church, and proved keen to give an insight into the kind of church to which I would minister. Retired, he had been a dairy farmer on a fertile property of flat land east of the town. The property became subdivided, leaving Eric a wealthy man who had a house built on top of a hill west of the town, with a beautiful, wide outlook of the ocean. He had similar beliefs to ours concerning God's sovereign mercy, and told me that it was a grievous issue in Tasmania's churches in the Fifties, with churches all over the state still recovering from the bruising that took place in those years ago. He and his wife Ruth were childless, and they loved our two little girls. In our pastorate at Ulverstone, they proved kind and only too glad to mind them from time to time.

Eric had a lovely nature. He was quietly spoken and calm in temperament. He carried a grin that attracted you into wanting to converse with him. He was a good reader of the nature of his fellow-deacons, saying nothing in malice but what was instructive and worth treasuring up in handling prickly situations that seemed bound to arise.

Eric loved the sea and fishing. He owned a sea launch that could be called on for sea coast operations and rescues. We were not long in our new state when Eric invited Kerryn and me, and one or two other deacons, to go out fishing. It was April, the sky overcast, the sea a little choppy for the three and a half hours spent in the water, but Kerryn and I had some success – I caught a flathead of moderate size, and Kerryn caught a four-foot Barracouta!

Eric told us that later in the year he would be going south in his boat, down to the Tasman Sea, where he aimed to catch a kind of tuna known as 'Chicken of the Sea.' Such a fish would live up to its name – if one followed Eric's advice and wrapped the tuna around with slices of bacon and put it in the oven. On one's plate you could not tell its taste from chicken.

We told Eric that Kerryn and I had been dairy farmers, like himself.

> "I didn't know that!" he exclaimed.
> "Oh, yes, we were on a farm down near Geelong," I said.
> "Really?" he said, "You're joking."
> "Oh yes, we milked about twenty cows."

Eric joked so much himself that he thought we were trying to out-joke him.

> He laughed, "What sort of cows did you milk?"
> "Oh, some Friesians, but mostly Guernseys."
> "Go on!" he laughed.
> "Really!" I laconically replied.

Then it looked as though Eric had had enough of what he thought was a joke, and merely smiled.

> "Well," I said, "Kerryn and I looked after our friends' dairy farm for a week – not all that long after we married. I had learnt to milk early in life so I understood about cows when I was young. Our friends therefore had confidence that we could manage their farm while they had a badly needed holiday. Just for a week…"

> Eric laughed. "Guernseys are good cows," he said.

He told us that it was Guernseys that he had specialised in on his farm, and proceeded to tell us that in every two years he took an overseas trip to the Guernsey Island in the English Channel to find out the latest in research about dairying, where sleek Guernseys at their best graze on an island of only 62 square kilometres.

As we encountered our first winter in Tasmania, we soon learnt that it was deceiving to think Ulverstone had more hours of sunshine than Melbourne. Yes, there were more hours of it, but it was made weaker by the very bitter cold winds that blew over the state. Moreover, more rainfall fell in Tasmania than we ever knew on "the mainland" (as the Taswegians called the rest of Australia). Kerryn was to write to her mother that it rained for 80 percent of the time in that first winter.

Still, we grew so busy with church work and other interests to think overly much about the cold climate.

As time went by Kerryn and I were caught up with innumerable things, so that she recorded that at one time, quite early in our ministry, there were nine nights in a row when either one of us were out for the evening. Related to the church there were two sermons to prepare for each week; ladies' meetings; Young Marrieds' evenings; the midweek prayer meeting at which we could expect 25 people at times; the teaching of Religious Instruction at three schools; the beginning of a program called 'Search' in early June when ministers of the town put on a Christian feature once a week for the local high school assembly; Homemakers' meetings for womenfolk; the conducting of services at the 'Eliza Purdon' nursing home; all this, as well as pastoral visits to people's homes.

Our two little girls were not to be neglected, and I ensured that I spent some time in the middle of each day with them.

Kerryn grew interested in the Nursing Mothers' Association, through her experience she contributed much to the welfare and concern of young mothers. This she did, while taking up women's basketball in the town. Yes, this she did, while becoming involved also in the Kindergarten at Turner's Beach, when Belinda was of suitable age.

I began to play squash in the evenings until I found that I would become so 'worked up' after such strenuous activity I could not get to sleep until the early hours of the morning.

As you would expect, family members and friends made use of us residing in Tasmania. Kerryn's mother, her sister Sheryl, my sister Joyce, Kerryn's brothers Irwin & Graeme, and David my foster brother was among the family that stayed for a week or so with us, and also made use of the occasion to visit many of the beautiful towns and the country side of the Apple Isle.

We took full advantage of residing in Ulverstone and visited "The Nut" at Stanley, the Devil's Gate, the big blanket of tulips when in bloom at Table Cape, and the delightful little town of Penguin, where a wide array of pretty flowers sprang up in the spring along either side of the railway line in the direction of Ulverstone.

Besides keeping in touch with "the mainland" via our visitors, we sought to do so by the normal means of the newspaper and television. "The Age" newspaper cost 25 cents on Saturdays and that was seen as expensive! There were two TV stations only – Channel 9 and 3, with 9 being a mixture of Melbourne's 7, 9 and 0. TV programs were a few years behind Melbourne's as well.

Yet nothing took the place of the desire to be in closer touch with relatives and friends in Victoria. Belgrave's Christian Convention was also sorely missed. There was a hankering to return to our native state. It was hoped that a few years in Ulverstone may well prove to be a stepping stone back to Victoria and a church there.

We sought to remain positive, however, and make a fist of ministry at Ulverstone. In addition to my own preaching and teaching, I sought to capture the congregation's interest in the things of God by having a guest speaker one Sunday morning each month. Yet I soon realized that there was a spiritual apathy among many that proved to be a cause of concern to one lady, who was most fervent in prayer at midweek meetings, as she exhorted and reproved us with the use of a favourite expression: 'spiritual paupers.'

Mrs Bingley claimed that we should not be content with what we know of God in our midst thus far – that God desires us to make access through prayer to greater riches that there are in Christ. She stood out as someone who shared my ambition to 'Never be lacking in zeal, but to possess spiritual fervor.' (Rms 12:11). Why not get her voted on to the diaconate?

At the time of contemplating the possibility of Mrs Bingley becoming a deacon, I came under the influence of the teaching of John Murray, a Scottish theologian who taught at Princeton Seminary in U.S.A. In his work *Government in the Church of Christ*, he caused me to see that 'in the institution of the New Testament those exercising the ruling function of the church of God are (either) elders (or) bishops.' We did not have elders at Ulverstone. The all-men body ruling the church were known as deacons. They could have been elders in function perhaps, but they were appointed not so much for spiritual oversight as for administrative oversight and therefore in actuality were deacons. At times the men may have raised spiritual issues when they met, only they were mostly occupied with the church's finances and the upkeep of the building.

I contemplated teaching the people about the dual offices of elders and deacons, as I saw it in the New Testament. The teaching had to be done with gradual inculcation. This was contemplated when Baptist churches on "the mainland" also did not have the dual offices in operation.

To the praise of the Ulverstonians they greeted "the ancient innovation" (if you understand what I mean).

Still, to vote in suitable people for eldership looked like a difficult task. Just a few men met the qualifications required for spiritual oversight, therefore, in order to have a body of sufficient numbers I planted (?) in the minds of some members the suggestion of voting in, for one, Mrs Bingley for eldership. She was voted in.

Later, I was to regret the fervent lady becoming an elder, only because I came under the conviction that no female should share in such a spiritual oversight of a church. To the end of our time at Ulverstone I let things be so that the lady remained an elder. People may respect a pastor but they, as well as the pastor, are to be more acquainted with the word of God themselves so that people and pastor all do things in accord and in concord with the Scriptures – that became my conviction, particularly with regard to the proper roles of men and women in the Church.

Around mid-year I attended a 'School of Theology.' I was privileged to speak, and had chosen the subject of Job. It proved to be well-received by all the pastors bar one – he became critical of the fact that I did not refer to Christ, stating that I saw in creation that which may solve the problem of suffering, as he said that Christ alone solves the problem of suffering. The other pastors took the fellow to task, since they could see that God at the end of Job's trial appeals to creation and still leaves Job humble and at peace with the ways of God. I was not denying that the hope in Christ aids us in our suffering. Still, I travelled home from Launceston thankful for the dissenting pastor and his concern for the glory of belief in Christ, which can be woven into the book of Job.

I sought to extend a Christian influence on the Northwest coast community by offering to write for the newspaper *The Advocate* a Christmas message. I titled the article '*Taking the Reins off Santa*' but it was changed to '*Kids Need Santa Clause!*' All the same, the body of the article carried the message I wanted published, so that people were to read that Santa Claus was not 'a fourth member of the Trinity.'

The pastors' retreat at Sister's Creek, along the Northwest coast west of Ulverstone, was a momentous occasion.

It was midwinter of 1976 and we Baptist pastors of Tasmania were privileged to have Dr Noel Vose, the President of the Baptist Union of Australia as our guest speaker at the two-day event. I had met Dr Vose once as a student at Whitley College. He was destined to become the President of the Baptist World Assembly in 1980. He was a learned man, evangelical and warm hearted.

He began our opening session, after having briefly met us all individually, by saying to us –

> "I have learnt that there is someone here who is having difficulty in walking with God. He is struggling with the ministry. He is having a measure of success but in his heart, there is a tendency towards bitterness. He is frightened that his secret thoughts might burst forth and that the people of his congregation might find out what he is really like. He has a tendency to be jealous of certain fellow-ministers and has a difficulty in curbing his jealousy – afraid it could eat him up…"

Noel went on for a little longer with the man's description. I sat there most uneasy. Back in Victoria at Whitley College, he had heard me give a morning devotion in the chapel and he had spoken to me after the devotion with curiosity and searching eyes. His eyes still seem to be searching me there at our retreat at Sister's Creek. How did he arrive at such an accurate description of me? I quickly fell into despair.

Then, Noel paused. He swept his eyes around us all and quietly said, "The man I have been talking about is ….behind the table." Relief ran through my soul.

That was Noel: Beautifully honest, humble, revealing to us the raw truth that we all have struggles, sins that are not foreign to anyone, irrespective of our status in the ministry.

Then on the heels of our retreat I received a note in the post from Noel, a note that was to become the greatest encouragement I would ever receive with respect to ministry.

Noel wrote –

> "I was particularly glad that we had the opportunity to talk together during the School of Theology. It does seem to me that God has given you a significant pastoral teaching ministry, but this is perhaps one of the most difficult roles within the church, as so often it lacks the glamour of missionary or evangelistic service.
>
> Teaching is a slow business, and even within the rarefied atmosphere of the tertiary institutions, it can be very disappointing. More than most others in the work, the teacher must be prepared to plant the tree and believe that others will enjoy the shade long after he has gone. May it be so for the people of Ulverstone.
>
> God bless you in your work, and as the little Welsh woman at Yagoona used to say to me when I was a student: 'Keep the corners up!'"

What a diagnosis! What a prescription lay in that letter! I could not help but cry upon reading it, could not help but feel relieved. Yes, I also needed to 'keep the corners up' – well, I had reason to heed his words, even with its mild reproof found in the letter from the great man.

Until I had received Noel's letter, I could not understand why other pastors enjoyed more 'success' than me, why others saw people coming to faith in Christ in a way that I did not.

Congregations often see glamour in those who are evangelistic, as well as in missionaries. Baptist congregations were prone to put teachers, who were not evangelistic so much, at risk because, as congregations they had power to not only vote 'in' but 'out' any pastor who did not appear to 'succeed.' Tenure for a Baptist pastor was not as secure as in some other denominations.

Yet I was Baptist by conviction, and Noel gave me another timely word: He had said on the last day at the conference in private that while I was a teacher and not an evangelist, I should view myself as a general practitioner ('GP'), though specializing in the gift God gave me. This brought joy to my ears: Yes, there for me was 'one of the most difficult roles in the church' but it is 'a significant pastoral ministry,' even as 'GP.'

With that in mind, later in that year of 1976 I drove down to Launceston one evening with one of our close friends of the church, John Plumpton, to hear Ron Baker, who had been an alcoholic before he was wonderfully saved under Billy Graham in 1959 in Sydney.

While I had striven to be a 'GP' and do my utmost to be an evangelist as well as a pastoral teacher, I saw in Ron Baker, the opportunity for the church-goers of Ulverstone to come under a specialized evangelistic ministry, just when we had quite a number of young people in the church who had not become true believers in Christ. I invited Ron to come to Ulverstone.

Billy Graham had appealed to Ron in the vast meetings in 1959 because Billy said that no matter what mess your life is in, by being spiritually reborn you can have life anew. Ron had not only been an alcoholic, but a drug addict and an occultist. Then in 1961 he became challenged at a 'This is the Answer' meeting about serving others. He conceded that he had been practically uneducated but spent two years 'catching up,' followed by two years in Bible college, then two years at the Baptist college in NSW before he became ordained for ministry in 1970.

Much preparation had been made for Ron's crusade in Ulverstone. The itinerary included: Sunday services in our church, a NW Coast Ministers' get-together, coffee mornings around the town in people's houses, home evening groups, attendance at a Rotoract dinner, speaking at an interchurch drop-in centre, a youth tea followed by a youth rally one night, a men's breakfast, a ladies' afternoon, a family night at the high school and an interview on the 'Talk Back' program on radio 7AD-BU!

The coming crusade received good publicity in *The Advocate*, the NW coast paper.

What was Ron's approach? There was a tincture of his uneducated past, but it helped to win many people over as he would colloquially speak of his former days so that the common man could not help but see that Christ had wonderfully saved him from a wretched life. He did labour too much perhaps about his past, but he left the door open with a sufficient chink so that Christ was never entirely eclipsed by overly drawing attention to what *he* had achieved if anything. He majored on the ill-effects of sin, the abuse of the body and the dryness of the soul without the Lord.

I was a little nervous when Ron would draw on something akin to the theory of the Primeval Scream. He claimed that people may well be troubled by trauma experienced by their earliest of days, so that soon after birth they suffered from that which was in the subconscious and what cannot be fathomed. All the same, Ron claimed that no one ought to see himself or herself as hopelessly entangled by such a matter, and always offering hope through faith in Christ. Perhaps it could be said that Ron was touching on the universal effects of original sin, without ever mentioning Adam and the Fall.

Both Kerryn and I were exhausted after the crusade. I had been out every night for two weeks with Ron. Kerryn had been busy with many people calling at the manse, as well as answering countless phone calls.

The success of the crusade lay in 12 young people committing themselves to Christ for the first time in our church, and saw several others re-dedicating their lives to Him.

Ron dined often with us and one thing that was particularly destined to have a lasting effect on us were his words of "You must read people upside down." Never, or very rarely, accept what people say or do: they often mean or do the opposite. It is easy to be taken for a ride by what some say or do: the opposite is even frequently true of ourselves.

In the wake of our friend's departure, I decided to run a follow-up weekly class for the young people who were professed believers so that they might be baptized, but an uneasiness ran through me when two of the church leaders, who were fathers of some of the young people attending, had decided to sit in on the classes. Did they not trust me to teach their young correct doctrine? Did they think I may come on too heavy so that their children may be pressured into baptism against their will? Was it not better, I thought, if the two leaders stayed home and allowed their young freedom to talk about problems they may well have in being a Christian, struggles they even could encounter at home?

I sensed doom.

We took a break soon after the baptism classes and holidayed down at Hobart for a week. While on the holiday, a secret meeting of the church leaders was held, and Eric broke the news upon our return to Ulverstone. Certain elders and deacons wanted us to resign. There was no official letter to that effect, but a certain coldness and tension could be felt by Kerryn and me whenever we were present at the church. The two leaders who sat in on the baptismal classes for their children appeared to meet us with an indifference. They sought hard to mask their coldness towards us, watching with stolidness for any hint of us buckling under the strain of us having learnt, no doubt, that they were the ones who particularly longed to see the end of us at Ulverstone – so it seemed.

I had always been wary of one of the two men, as according to Eric he had been involved in a fist fight with one of the pastors before my time. Eric was never a gossiper but simply someone, who out of good intent had put me on the alert about this and that person in the church when I first arrived at Ulverstone – for the sake of my ministry. He was an honorary deacon who remained with a high regard for me to the end.

It was a bitter time in more ways than one. Our young church friends, the Heads, had to fly over to the Royal Melbourne Hospital with their second son in a mere two days after Jo had given birth to him. Stephen and Jo learnt that he had only two chambers to the heart, therefore the surgeons could not operate. On the day when Stephen and Jo were to go over to Melbourne, Kerryn and Jo cried together but their faith was such that Stephen and Jo in tears said: "We are not asking why, but just for the strength to help us through this time of trouble." I had no doubt that Stephen was not part of the leadership desiring me to resign.

There was never an official request for me to resign. It appears that the leadership was divided over the matter.

Still, it seemed best to resign.

An elderly couple, the Ryalls, had recently retired to Ulverstone from Melbourne. Mr Ryall was a seasoned believer.

When I told Mr Ryall of my intention, he said, "We are finding your ministry refreshing, and we would hate to see you leave."

I replied, "I find it suffocating here in the church."

"Look," he said, "there are more in the congregation with you than against you."

"That may be," I continued, "but I think certain people are set on bringing me down somehow."

"I think you should ride this problem out, difficult though it may be. You must remember that Ron Baker's crusade was a great success. It can happen that one can have a downer after such a success. Just think about Elijah."

"I guess that is possible," I said. "I don't know... I don't know..."

He advised, "Don't rush into resignation. Think it over."

I went away and thought about Elijah challenging the prophets of Baal on Mount Carmel and winning over the people to his side and that of God's. Then he fled like a frightened rabbit when he heard Jezebel was out to kill him immediately after the victory on Mount Carmel. Elijah became most depressed, running off to Mount Sinai, believing that he was the only one on God's side.

Elijah even wanted his life taken from him. I had not thought about such an extremity, but I was shell-shocked about men as leaders in the church hungering for my resignation. It more than likely seemed that the discontent would spread like a loathsome disease, maybe slowly but surely.

The writer of Hebrews issued a warning that seemed apt – "See to it.. that no "root of bitterness springs up and causes trouble, and by it many become defiled." The root of bitterness in the congregation seemed too deep to remove. Many appeared bound to become defiled in a short time.

Kerryn and I agreed to tender my resignation. "Some of the people here are being as sweet as pie since Eddie announced his resignation," wrote Kerryn to her mother.

I put out feelers, even before my resignation, to see if there was a pastoral vacancy in Victoria – anywhere in Victoria this time. Nothing proved prospective all that soon. We blindly put our faith in God's hands, while we planned to return to Victoria, no matter what may happen.

At such a time our little girls were a light in our life. With them we went swimming one day in late November when the water was… (you guessed it) icy cold, yet the girls loved running about in the waves, Janine getting a mouthful of salty water and exclaiming, "Oh yuck! I don't like that pepper water!" We had a wonderful candlelight dinner with Stephen and Jo one night, with a lady from across our street happy to baby sit our girls. We sought to comfort Stephen and Jo as best we could in concern for their little boy, who seemed better some days. Back home Belinda, our eldest girl, claimed that she could draw better than 'Mummy!'

I went to Melbourne to have an interview for industrial chaplaincy but thought it was not suitable, nor did I desire it all that much. I reflected on my ministry of three years at Ulverstone and concluded that by having Ron Baker conducting an evangelistic crusade, the thing might have recoiled on me. Was not Ron an evangelist? What success had he! What could be seen for my ministry at Ulverstone? Without Ron Baker, how many souls were saved in my three years at the church? I sought comfort in the letter Dr Vose had sent me the year before, but the comfort was a trifle cold, for there was talk of luring Ron back for a longer term of ministry once I had resigned.

An offer came to do an interim ministry in one of Launceston's churches. It was in the new year of 1978 at the Baptist World Convention in Launceston with the Canadian Dr Roy Bell as world president, that I caught up with Trevor Farmilo, who was the President of the Baptist Union of Victoria at the time. He was confident that I would find an opening of ministry for us 'very soon.' With that I turned my back on remaining in Tasmania.

Many attended the evening at the church to say farewell and wished us all the best. It was hard to part from a good number who had become close friends, including some from outside the church. Our next door neighbour, dear old Bill, who was always giving us fresh home-grown vegetables and who, even long after we left Ulverstone, could still be 'heard' saying with our little girls in mind: "You can't beat the kiddies."

Kerryn and our girls returned to Victoria by plane, while I made my way by car to the Tasmanian ferry at Devonport. Soon the rich chocolate soil of farms hugging the coast and the rolling sea of Bass Strait were seen no more.

The Broken Spirit, a Mending Heart

Kerryn's mother – whom I had gradually come to call 'Mum' – had moved from Warburton to Coburg. Moving to Warburton for Kerryn and me meant that the clock had been turned back. For Kerryn it was going back to the town where she was born and lived in her early days, back to the tiny ten square house perched on the slope of the road that led the way to Mount Donna Buang. For me it was going back to the days of being a theological student when I first came to know Kerryn, and when I landed a summer job or two in order to complete college, when I dreamed of securing a church to serve the Lord as its pastor.

Despite what Trevor Farmilo of the Union had said, nothing was in the offering for ministry throughout Victoria.

My spirit was broken. We had left Ulverstone in harrowing circumstances and, as months went by, nothing seemed forthcoming. I found some work at the Seventh Day Adventist Sanitarium as a gardener. Then I applied for emergency teaching which, while it promised to make us financially more stable, broke my spirit even more, as it turned the clock further back still. I had thought that teaching had groomed me for preaching. Were my years at Whitley wasted? I fell into deep despair. Kerryn did her best to keep me from being overcome by our circumstances, but Satan seemed to be finding the upper hand.

Yet, at my lowest God sent an 'angel.' It came about as the result of what the Baptist Union called 'Witness Weekend.' Some congregations of large city churches planned to spend a weekend with people of small country ones. Some from Blackburn Baptist came to Millgrove Baptist. I think my sad, long face, which could hardly be hidden 'attracted' Evelyn from Blackburn on the Saturday evening. In perceiving that I was passing through the Valley of Humiliation, Evelyn spoke on the side to me without rebuke – about God allowing all that had happened in Ulverstone for our good, and the present emptiness and sorrow, to create in us a greater dependence on Him. Yes, and before great things come our way, He 'walks you through the wilderness.' The following day soon passed and Evelyn was gone, perhaps like an angel never to be seen and heard of again.

I took some heart from Evelyn's counsel, but even greater heart, when only a few days later she sent a book after she had been 'praying hard.' She was rather afraid that I 'would not be able to accept the concepts' of the book *Bringing Heaven into Hell*, and yet believed it was the right book for me. She was even more convinced about sending it because it was the last copy of the book in the shop she visited.

It turned out that I had some of Merlin Carothers' books at home but I had not read them. Evelyn was amazed that I had not read them, but she believed that God's timing was perfect – wooing me when I was 'open and desperate.'

What Merlin Carothers was saying in *Bringing Heaven Into Hell* seemed outrageous. Evelyn was particularly taken by the chapter "Am I really glad?" and hoped it would inspire us as it had done her. In essence Carothers was claiming that we should praise God sincerely even for all the bad things that happen. Could I praise God for the way I suffered at the hands of some at Ulverstone, thus perhaps jeopardizing my chance of ministry in Victoria? Could I praise God for the underhandedness of the two Ulverstone elders? Could I praise Him for being compelled to return to teaching, to the uncertainty of regular work as an emergency teacher? Could we thank Him for being in financial straits? Thank Him for having no pastorate?

In "Am I really glad?" Carothers says –

> "Is there anyone you would rather be or anything you would rather do than be who you are and do what you do right now? Can you think of any change you would like to see in your circumstances?
>
> *If the answer is yes, you haven't learnt to be really glad yet (italics mine)."*

Was this not hitting me below the belt? Was I wrong in desiring to get another church and turn back from teaching?

> "Are you glad you have the problem? When you're glad, you are not complaining. When you're glad, it means you are sure you are a child of God. You are sure of His love for you and that He is working everything in your life together for your good in a perfect plan."

Evelyn believed God gave her "a glimpse of His wonderful plans for you." Yet, could I tough it out in Warburton without growing downcast of what may not turn out as 'better things?' Carothers talked of better things, did he not? No, I thought that I would tough it out and not be glad about our present circumstances – no, I could not be glad.

For days I struggled with the belief that I should be genuinely glad for the lot that had become ours, until it was not merely Carothers gradually winning me over with what some thought was a 'cuckoo' notion, but the Scripture itself. Paul the apostle said that he took *pleasure in pain* (2 Cor 12:10), and did I not preach once in a Launceston church on Paul's words in 1 Thessalonians – "Be joyful always; pray continually; *give thanks in all circumstances, for this is God's will for you in Christ Jesus?*"

Ah, what a cruel blow to think that one could preach on something without knowing it firsthand!

Then another blow that felled me to the canvas to the count of ten was that I professed to believe in the sovereignty of God in salvation – that God has chosen me to believe in Christ and nothing can thwart His purpose!

I rose from the canvas battered and bruised but all the better for it. I learnt not only to praise God for good things, not even just for any trauma in the hope of it leading to what is good, but for the bad things in themselves. I recall being at a strange school, feeling strange about being a mere emergency teacher, yet full of joy about our humble, seemingly degrading lot.

Kerryn was pregnant when our 'angel' appeared again to briefly see us. When she returned home, she wrote a letter and said she loved to envisage our new baby as heralding 'the springtime.' Were good things to come so soon?

Stephen James was born on Melbourne Cup Day, in November 1978, at 3.35pm. The doctor said that "we had backed a winner." Stephen brought much joy to the family, but was he a sign of other good things to come? It appeared so.

About halfway through the following year, we received the news that the chance of securing a pastorate with the Swan Hill church was promising.

Before Stephen's first birthday we moved far north to serve the circuit of churches in Swan Hill, Nyah West and Lake Charm. Swan Hill itself did not have its own building but met in the Young Farmers' Hall. Nyah West had its own church. Lake Charm did too, but its continuance was to be questioned, as a very small numbers attended, and its people were seen as possibly attending Swan Hill to bolster the fellowship there each Sunday. I looked forward to getting back into full-time ministry once again.

Sad to say, the beginning at Swan Hill was not promising, as within a few weeks we went from pillar to post for accommodation. It turned out (unknown to us initially) that the tenants living in the manse refused to move out, and a court case was pending for the end of the month that we had moved to the 'Sun Centre.' The church deacons rented a flat for us upon arrival. We were tightly packed with our three young children and our possessions for just five nights because the flat had been pre-booked for the following weekend. In haste we were shown a house on a farm, 20 minutes drive from Swan Hill, with no phone. Instead, we stayed for a tense two nights with the church treasurer. Where to next? To a caravan on the site of the church secretary's house, where we were accommodated for one night! The next day we moved – on Stephen's first birthday – because it was discovered that the Church of England manse was available until January 26. Some furniture was left in storage, so that we could avoid unpacking as much as possible. The minister who vacated the untidy manse was a bachelor, so Kerryn became very busy – with our young family to care for and making the house as liveable as possible. Large boxes of possessions were stacked up one above the other in the lounge.

It was among the boxes one evening that I moved around alone while I sang ever so longingly Keith Green's heart-searching song –

> "My eyes are dry, my faith is old,
> My heart is hard, my prayers are cold,
> But You know how I ought to be–
> Alive to You, and dead to me."

I craved to be sold out to Jesus and the work ahead. My spirit had been broken at Warburton. Would my heart be entirely mended in Swan Hill?

The court case concerning the manse was in the church's favour, and finally sometime in mid-January we were able to settle down in the church's brick house.

Yet, there was also a move to have the congregation of Swan Hill settle down in some place other than the Young Farmers' Hall for Sunday worship. This was led by the opinion of a self-styled prophetess in the circuit of churches. There is hardly a church that does not have such a prophetess – one who is eager to tell people how "the Lord has led me to tell you…"

The person concerned claimed that the Lord spoke to her from reading that little known book of Haggai. Through Haggai the Lord tells the people of Israel, who have returned from exile, that they are not prospering materially because they have not given priority to building God's house for worship of Him. It was reasoned that as the Swan Hill congregation we were not prospering spiritually and seeing our numbers grow because we were not open to getting out of the Young Farmers' Hall and seeking to find a more fitting 'house' for worship of the Lord.

Rightly or wrongly, I interpreted the tone behind the 'prophecy' to mean also that there was already dissatisfaction with my ministry. Was my temperament causing me to be unduly suspicious?

Back at Warburton, during the interval of ministry between Ulverstone and Swan Hill, I had come to believe that there are four basic temperaments that form the types of people we encounter. No less than a distinguished Norwegian professor, Dr Hallesby believed this to be true, while rightly discarding the ancient belief that the four basic temperaments can be attributed to four different bodily fluids. I saw myself in his delineation of the melancholic temperament the one that matched mine, with its strengths and weaknesses. This temperament is prone to give way to self-centredness, over-sensitivity, an uncompromising spirit, pessimism, passivity, and often proves to be impractical and irresolute. While the melancholic has pleasing strengths, his weaknesses can make it difficult in the ministry: his reserved nature, his passivity, his dreaming big and being easily disappointed may well mean he lacks resolution and can be impractical.

In short, he is not the type that a congregation is immediately attracted to. Very few melancholics have been pastors, certainly so in the modern era that calls for those who are infectiously happy, optimistic, capable of gaining the interest of others in an instant, or built of a strong will power to energise others into carrying out enterprises before they are aware of it themselves as it were.

And when I reflected on Dr Vose's diagnosis of my kind of ministry in church life, and then combining it with what may well lie true of the kind of nature I have. I wondered how I could cope. The prophetess desired an evangelist, it seemed.

It was not long before she made it plain that my ministry was more suited for a theological college as a lecturer. I took offence at this, even though there were many – particularly at Nyah West – who warmed to my teaching.

It was not as though I did not try to be a "GP" and evangelize. Other than ministry within the churches of the circuit, moves were made to extend the influence of the circuit of churches in the secular community. I landed an opportunity to write a regular column in the regional newspaper, calling the column "Path-finder – the letter "t" being in the shape of a cross. The column was an attempt to connect with Everyman, perhaps a little moralistic but thought-provoking in the hope of the paper's readers seeking the truth as it is in Jesus. Then there were relationships forming with others in the community.

The owner of the record shop in Swan Hill and I were becoming good friends, as were those of a strange Apostolic church.

As a family we had cause in mid-April to head south to the house in Warburton, which we had bought with the consent of Kerryn's siblings from 'Mum.' We had to check on a number of matters, as we had tenants occupying the place. It was a short stay before we made the six hour trip back to Swan Hill.

It was only a month later, after just seven months at Swan Hill, that a meeting was convened in the presence of the church deacons and the general superintendent of the Baptist Union that they called on me to resign. Was it a repetition of Ulverstone? – a secret meeting having been held by the deacons while we were away in Warburton? Yet more shattering was the fact that the decision to have me resign seemed to be based on a loose foundation.

Our eyes at home were filled with tears for several days – not with the sort of tears little Janine had "shed" when we had left Warburton only seven months before and she made sobbing noises, together with a licking of a finger and putting the "moisture on her eyes." No, these were tears that flowed whilst the stomach felt sickened at such treachery. I suspected that our self-styled prophetess had undone us. In a short while, we had made good friends, but it only needs one bitter root to grow up to cause trouble and defile many, yes, just as the writer of Hebrews tells us.

We packed with tears. We left in tears.

We moved in May 1980, to Rowville's vacant manse, kindly arranged by the general superintendent. We had bought Kerryn's mother's house at Warburton and, on moving up to Swan Hill, had put in tenants. (Actually, we were still in the process of paying off the house at the large interest rate of 16%, a common interest rate for housing loans in those days.)

Both my sister and my friend Alan from Whitley days had sent letters of considerable comfort, before we left Swan Hill. Alan expressing disgust at the injustice done to me, and Joyce saying that she was "deeply shocked."

Yet Joyce believed that God had a purpose in what had happened – that "the terrible trial" would produce a stronger character in me.

As I pondered on whether or not I would end up having a stronger character – doubting that I would ever get the chance to pastor a church again – my mind flashed back to Evelyn's appearance at Millgrove, when I grew to be glad in our trials at the time – thanking God, really glad for our circumstances.

We were now saddened and shattered to move down south, near the city of Melbourne to the Rowville manse. Were we grieving the Holy Spirit by being sad? I began to question Merlin Garothers *Bringing Heaven Into Hell*. Is there actually no place for sadness? Were we unthankful in God's eyes? Was there any man of God who had not been sad and had not been chastised for it?

Take note of Nehemiah.

He appears before the Persian King, sad in the King's presence when he had not been sad before. The King looks at him and says, "why does your face look so sad when you are not ill? This can be nothing but sadness of heart." Nehemiah replies that his face should look sad when the city of Jerusalem lies in ruins.

James teaches us the following –

"If anyone of you is in trouble? He should pray.

Is anyone happy? Let him sing songs of praise."

'Trouble' may be a tame word for what James signifies – for he is speaking of 'being vexed… and dejected? We may be dejected but, so long as we can work our way out of it by prayer, we can end happy or 'in good spirits'. In good spirits' we can then sing. If I read Carothers correctly, he seems to leave no room for sadness; his approach could lead to a lack of empathy for anyone who is dejected. Sadness is understandable when one is shell-shocked as we were. We were not ready to sing as we ought.

While the congregation of the Rowville church welcomed us, it became hard to work out how we were to make ends meet. No permanent positions in the Education Department were available, perhaps for a few years. It forced me to think of emergency teaching once more, and with all its uncertainties of irregular work. Although the coming winter looked like providing something more regular, there was the gloomy thought of no work at all during school holidays. We were expected to pay rent for occupation of the manse.

For more than two years at Rowville we lived in a certain state of anxiety – paying rent for the manse, as well as paying off the house in Warburton with its high interest of 16%.

It was at this time, when I was often at home for want of a call for emergency work that something moved me to reflect on my past at the Sutherland Home and created the urge to write about it. I felt coy about using the names of some people who were still living – and for most others, I decided to change their names as well. I wrote more than 500 pages to make it acceptable for the secular world, to the point where there was scarcely a hint about becoming a Christian at 17 while I was still at Sutherland. The manuscript was successfully submitted to a secular publishing company, but the company folded almost immediately after my submission. After one failure upon another to gain interest from other secular publishers, I made three major moves in a bid to get the manuscript accepted.

These included: (1) to abbreviate the manuscript for modern readership, (2) to rightly make the story of my conversion to Christ explicit, (3) to enlist the interest of a Christian publisher in the work. I pressed on because Kerryn believed I had a story worth telling. Yet *The Silver Poplar* was to take some years before it was re-worked to my satisfaction and ready for publication.

When it is said that an urge was created to write of my early life, it is more to the point to say that the crisis of Swan Hill accelerated a deep desire to heal my mind of a number of things that in the past bred anguish and unhappiness. Many of the disturbing things were mostly unconscious. In writing of unhappiness, I was giving vent to frustration and led the way to feeling some relief in writing, even though the unhappiness refused entirely to go away.

I sought to balance matters to do with my boyhood, because *The Silver Poplar* possessed the right to have the inclusion of happy times. Happiness of a sort comes naturally to children, even in adverse circumstances. Therefore, it was also pleasurable to write up my memoirs, particularly about the wonderful day at 17 when I was 'found after being lost', after being blind and then I could at last see – Amazing Grace!

Towards the end of 1982, with warmer weather coming on before school finished, there was less emergency teaching available. The long Christmas school holidays meant no money could be earnt, and we wondered how we could pay the required rent for the Rowville manse. Yet God is faithful, and one day an envelope was pushed under our front door. On it was written –

> "James 1:17
> Please do not tell anyone based on Mathew 6:1 and 2 Corinthians 9:11-13".

Inside the envelope was $500, almost enough money to pay the rent into the new year!

We do not know who gave us so much money so that it did not disturb us if we, the receivers, were given "hush money" by someone unknown. We simply appreciated the fact that some dear brother did not want us, or anybody else to know, of his 'act of righteousness'.

In early 1983 God proved His faithfulness yet again by giving me a promise in prayer and fulfilling it so wonderfully. It was related to Ash Wednesday, February 16, rated as "one of Australia's most well-known bushfire events." By 'event' I am sure that the journalist who made up the phrase, did not mean to convey the idea the fires on that day were mere 'events' and thus 'entertainment'. They were deadly serious.

In the year before, Victoria had suffered one of its worst droughts on record. In late November temperatures soared with 85 bushfires recorded across the state. It was claimed that with temperatures remaining high throughout December and January, 119 fires had been deliberately lit. With the state being a tinderbox, fire authorities became even more edgy as we came into February when 98 fires on February 9 were whipped up by winds of 110 kmh in southern and eastern Victoria. Winds drove a great cloud of dust 150 km wide from the loose soil of thousands of tonnes from ravaged farms to the north, sweeping down over Melbourne. Then a second dark dust storm changed with smoke that swept over the city on the day that was known coincidentally as Ash Wednesday of the Christian calendar – traditionally the first day of Lent and, according to Roman Catholic practice, the day when the foreheads of worshippers are marked with ashes that have been *blessed*. Ironically, the Lenten ashes are applied with the words –

"Remember, man, that thou art dust and to dust thou shalt return."

Except that the ashes of so many fires in our state were seen not as a blessing but as a curse.

Besides the untold destruction of houses, farms, and forest, 14 firefighters and 47 other people lost their lives. In terms of lives lost, the fires spent their greatest fury and fate at the Belgrave Heights and Upper Beaconsfield area.

Warburton's township was threatened, particularly in the early evening when the scorching day-long northerly gave way to westerly winds, changing the relatively long neighbouring fire to an even broader front in its menacing move towards the east of the town. This meant that fire threatened to come up over Mount Little Joe from west of the town and clean up the town in one foul swoop. Houses around the town fell victim to the fury with 57 buildings destroyed. Yet the town itself to the east of the mountain was inexplicably untouched.

We feared the loss of our house in Warburton on that day of fury but, once information flowed through about the aftermath of the fires, to our relief we discovered our house and others around it were untouched.

Kerryn and I began thinking about selling our house in what could always be a fire-prone zone because of surrounding forest. It was a wild notion, as who would contemplate buying a house that could be open to the threat of another bushfire, particularly when much of Victoria had been ravaged by that recent conflagration, described as the state's deadliest to date. Clearly, there was no hope of becoming the pastor of the Rowville church – a mere seven months of a pastorate at Swan Hill was not the best CV one could have. It seemed we would be compelled to move back to our house at Warburton, against our wishes. Another minister for Rowville was being entertained, though calling a desirable pastor can take considerable time to achieve. We would still have to quickly vacate the manse sooner than expected when the church succeeded in obtaining a pastor.

I went to prayer one day concerning the house. We felt we had put the house, surrounded by bush, on the market, hoping against hope. As I communed with the Lord, He spoke to me and assured me that we would sell it, without my eyes lighting on any Scripture about it.

People will ask concerning such instances in what way one knows that the Lord is speaking to you. What sort of voice do you hear? It is difficult to describe what takes place in such an experience; all I can say is that the Lord brings about a strong conviction concerning the matter.

I have never been given to hearing voices, allowing my imagination to run riot. Like most people I am cautious. Yet there have been rare occasions when the Lord has spoken to me in the way that He did with respect to the house – when for instance, at age 17 He spoke and lay upon my heart the urge to read the despised Bible to my salvation, and at Whitley where He gave me peace about my deep love for Kerryn when I had certain reservations to do with our relationship.

Were we surprised after only a few weeks of having the house on the market to have the phone ring and the real estate agent telling us that the house was sold! On going to Warburton to finalize matters, the real estate agent gave me a look and said –

"Gee, you were lucky!"

I smiled and inwardly gave thanks to our faithful Father.

The rest of 1983 was spent with me still trying to support the family through sporadic emergency teaching, and with both Kerryn and I seeking to make ends easier to meet by selling World Book Encyclopaedia, until late that year. In early 1984 Kerryn found work with a small company called Weightcare in Keysborough. She was one of four who included a dietitian, who assessed customers of the weight loss needed, put them on a diet programme, and counselled them to encourage them in their efforts.

However, the job with Weightcare was short-lived, as in May the company closed its doors.

As time went by there were people who wondered why I could not obtain a pastorate despite my efforts since 1981 to do so. It became even more obvious that Rowville Baptist were looking in another direction for a pastor, even though the leaders appreciated what ministry I had in the church. I preached occasionally. I produced an integrated series of studies called "*The Unclosed Door*" that went for a month – studies for children and adults, for church and homes, which caught the attention of the Baptist Union Christian Education Department. There was also a night series done in the manse on The Four Temperaments that generated much interest. Still, there seemed little hope of being a Union pastor anywhere again. It was particularly those of other denominations that wondered why my prospects had come to not so much as a standstill but to a dead end.

We had increasing appreciation for 'Dad' and 'Mum' Smith – who I called 'Cyril' and 'Beryl' when speaking about them to others – for their constant love for our family. They were puzzled by the uncertainty that could arise within Baptist ministry, as tenure for ministry was more certain in the likes of Anglican and Presbyterian ministry. In fact, while we were living in Warburton, before the disastrous move to Swan Hill, a Presbyterian elder did his best to persuade me into becoming a Presbyterian minister. It had been a tempting proposition.

In mid 1984 Kerryn had already found another job with Veith Transport. It was owned by a Mr Eugene Lincoln Napoleon Veith! His business had been Melbourne's biggest parcel-delivery company and Kerryn worked there in Accounts Receivable.

Mr Veith was a most unique Christian man. His object in life had been to set up a business called Mission Enterprises Limited, challenging rich businessmen to help provide relief for the hungry and homeless children the world over. Apart from his Christian convictions, he may have inherited a trait for generosity from his father, who, during the Great Depression, gave needy people meat for free from his butcher shop, so that he ended up broke. However, his son never went broke but shrewdly developed a sound business in parcel delivery that grew to have 175 trucks and 1500 clients – all this, as well as giving millions of dollars away to the impoverished and needy universally, such as American Indians in Colorado, street kids in Bangkok, and for water wells in East Africa. He ran a pastoral business to bolster funds for worthy causes.

As a young fellow he was rendered bald by alopecia. He ended up for life also with a scarred, misshapen nose as the result of a hammered wedge swinging back to chop through his nose as a young fellow. He was a charming man and one felt on first meeting him that he was concerned to help you if needed.

Kerryn and I cannot recall how we first got to know him. It was about a year before Kerryn went to work for Veith Transport that we discovered that Mr Veith had a holiday house down at Cape Schanck. What we had gained financially was not the greatest of gain for a modest house in Warburton, weatherboard and a mere 10 squares. The profit from the sale was reserved or put aside with no assurance that we could buy a place nearer Melbourne where regular emergency teaching was more certain. Day-to-day living was a material struggle, and Mr Veith very kindly and at a modest cost allowed us to have a holiday at the peak time of January 1983 in his holiday house on the Cape Schanck road, close to beautiful places such as Bushranger's Bay, the Pines Picnic Area, Fingal's Beach and the Cape Schanck lighthouse.

As it was then, there were only a few houses on the Cape Schanck road, and the scenery everywhere was breathtaking. Our three children revelled in sleeping in the bungalow behind the house where Kerryn and I slept. Day after day our children grew pleasantly weary early evening from walking to the various beaches surrounding us, and swimming under the warm sun, or sliding in the sand down the slope at Fingal's Beach, then going to sleep under the spell of hearing the enchanting Narnia tales.

In 1984 we returned to the Cape Schanck holiday house, thanks to Mr Veith's generosity. We returned again and again as a family to Cape Schanck until the beginning of the Nineties. Mr Veith also made it possible for Kerryn and I to retreat to his holiday house at times on weekends.

Words fail to tell what those times at Cape Schanck meant to me. Many a time I walked alone, down to Bushrangers Bay, down the road to descend the steps to Pulpit Rock, or closer by the house and up Long Point Road. They were days of a great searching of the soul. I grew dispirited at what appeared to be a vain hope of church ministry but, while the spirit had seemed to be broken, the heart was being mended. Such a state of mind coincided providentially with the possession of some wonderful books.

Colin Shepherd was manager of the Koorong Bookshop at Blackburn. He had begun Koorong as a small business from the garage of his own home in another suburb some years before. I longed to purchase certain books at Blackburn but did not have the means to acquire them. What did Colin do? He allowed me to work in the shop at times in order just to 'earn' the books. Moreover, he allowed me to put the desired books at the back of the shop on shelves reserved for myself and some others until we 'earnt' them. Needless to say, his generous spirit, as well as his happy and carefree nature made him a cherished friend that the Lord brought into my life.

I could tell of so many books that helped mend my heart, but perhaps the choicest book – apart from the Scriptures – was *Keeping the Heart* by the Puritan John Flavel. It cost only 50 cents and was worth far more than its lightweight in gold. It arrested me from its beginning –

> 'The heart of man is his worst part before it is regenerated, and the best afterward; it is the seat of principles, and the

fountain of action. The eye of God is…principally fixed upon it. The greatest difficulty in conversion is to win the heart for God; and the greatest difficulty after conversion is to keep heart with God.'

Although we would spend no more than a fortnight on holidays at Cape Schanck, they were times when I could be alone quite often, and therefore open to what God may say to me as I contemplated on the future. As Flavel puts it, the heart is like a musical instrument that can so easily fall out of tune. The temptation to be bitter was a sore one – the future could look bleak if I fell prey to despair. The swinging moods of a melancholic may make introspection a grave danger, bordering on suicidal tendencies, but I took Flavel's counsel, nonetheless: 'The heart can never be kept until its case be examined and understood,' and 'It is the most important business of a Christian's life.'

I am not sure how many times I read *Keeping the Heart* and turned Flavel's counsel over and over in my soul at Cape Schanck in the summers there but, being also surrounded by the majestic power and beauty of creation down by the sea, my heart began to mend, as it had to, if I were to remain spiritually sane and in satisfying communion with God.

There were any number of places at Cape Schanck to walk and talk to one's self and God. I could be taking the track to Bushrangers Bay, scanning the ocean and watching blue wrens hopping about the tea tree, while pondering about God not patronizing laziness without soul searching and obtaining assurance of His love without it. I could be sweeping my gaze down the long coast of Gunnamatta, Rye and Sorrento from a cliff above and struggle with the view that God had been showing me more of His grace in my affliction than He might have in any prosperity. As I scanned the silvery-blue sea water lazily lapping the shore at Flinders, I knew that fretting about the future was more damaging than any external hardships one may face. I could be lying down on a carpet of brown pine needles in the Pines Picnic Area and looking up at the blue sky, while I mused that I could complain to God but I ought not to complain *of* God. While crunching on the stones of the frequently walked Long Point Road, surrounded by pines, there was the possibility of hastening any of God's promises if I watched my heart more. Indeed, there came a day after four years of holidaying at Cape Schanck, up on Long Point Road, that I believe as I took in the beauty of the pines nearby, God spoke to me and said "As the world is beautiful, so are My plans beautiful." To this was added: "All My promises will come true." I called that sacred spot The Seven Pines.

In that same summer by the sea I realised in a new way that I was loved of God and nothing else mattered. How can we care as to what happens when we know the love of God?

The Unexpected Teacher Again

In 1984, the Rowville Baptist Church had called a pastor, so it compelled us to begin looking for another place to live. Could we afford to buy a house in suburban Melbourne? Or, would we have to rent? Kerryn still had work at Veith transport but finances were shaky when emergency teaching could not guarantee a consistent source of income, particularly in warmer seasons of the year, and certainly none at all during school holidays.

We launched out into the deep and decided to buy a house. Towards the end of the year we saw a house in Knoxfield that we liked, and it was selling for a price that perhaps we could afford since the owners had to sell quickly. But could we actually meet the requirements of a bank loan? We had to get sufficient finance in addition to what we had. An old friend, whose parents had me for holidays while I was at the Sutherland Homes, lent us a considerable sum as a 'gift.' Kerryn's mother lent us a sum until the day of settlement, and Mr Veith lent us a good amount as well.

The bank gave us a loan as a result, and we moved into our new home early in the following year of 1985.

As Providence had it, the Education Department signed me up for permanent teaching within the first few weeks of moving into Knoxfield. I was to be a 'temporary permanent teacher,' or was it 'a permanent temporary teacher?' I was assigned to a special school for mentally challenged children, then after a term to yet another special school, with my hope that I might continue teaching for a longer time in that kind of teaching, as I loved doing it. Yet, I did not have the necessary qualifications.

In the ensuing years I felt I was a permanent teacher, but permanently moving around to temporarily teach in one school or another! I was temporarily permanent in one school until I became permanently temporary in another!

I was to be more settled when in 1987 I secured a position at the Chandler Primary School. However, the same questions dogged my footsteps as they had done at other schools since I had secured permanency in 1985: Why did you leave the Education Department in the first place? Oh, so you became a minister for a time? Why did you leave the ministry? Not every teacher was as deep in prying, for I had learnt to hold my head high without becoming too agitated – you can get it down to a fine art, despite the sorrow within of not being where you would love to be.

My heart was still in the Baptist ministry and I had sought an audience with a new general superintendent. His rise in the denomination had been rapid, bypassing in the first place to the chagrin of not a few people the usual necessity of completing a theological course at Whitley College and being ordained in his local church with the countenance of the Union, instead of Collins Street Baptist where ordinands in number normally were ordained.

After being greeted by the superintendent upon entering the Union office, I paused as he opened up with conversation.

"Well, what can I do for you?"

"I'm here to discuss with you the chance of getting back in the ministry," I replied.

"I have looked at your history in the churches and can see you have had some experience, even in going to Tasmania for a pastorate. Yet, I am afraid there is quite a waiting list of men wanting a church. We can put you on the list."

"The previous superintendent had offered me some hope a year or so ago," I said anxiously.

"I'm sorry. That's the way it is at the moment."

"Well, how many men are on the waiting list?"

"I cannot divulge that. Just to say that there is quite a list, as I have said. Besides, as you probably know: my power is limited in this business. Much lies with churches as to who they want as their pastor."

My audience with the superintendent barely lasted any longer, and I sadly left the office, leaving myself open to being twice bitten with a certain bitterness: bitter at the little effort being made to help me gain a pastorate, and bitter at departing from one who had been ordained without having to attend Whitley College.

The bitterness was fought against, as it had to be, as it could be. It could be because I had learnt to submit to God, Who had mixed any blessing with adversity so that I could still cling to Him with faith.

By my second year of teaching at Chandler, a fuller blessing had blossomed out of what had seemed the barren soil of adversity. The proverbial

'All is grist to his mill' had become true for me. Any pent-up doubt or despair found a considerable outlet in writing voluminously in diaries, as I had given myself over to writing page after page of everyday insights into many passages of God's Word as they arose through discovering the treasures of reading all the Scriptures in one year. As I also reflected on the various churches which we visited and gained insight into how the modern church lacks true power, I wrote copiously about the dire need for revival. Book after book of spiritual truth had been read most fervently and increased my desire for revival. The Lord also answered an agonising prayer of "Jesus, be brother to me" down at Cape Schanck on the Long Point road, and did so by bringing into my life a wonderful friend in Major Howard Davies, whose preaching revived my soul again and again. Need I tell you, as well, of the way Kerryn was a rock in such times of possible overwhelming sorrow?

I kept clinging to the Three Words God gave me under the Seven Pines at Long Point Road at Cape Schanck : "As the world is beautiful, so My plans are beautiful," "All my promises will come true," "I would not deceive you." The achingly lovely music of *The Dance of the Blessed Spirits* would carry me back in my mind's eyes to that spot of The Seven Pines.

Kerryn had started work nearby as a teller at the State Bank in Knox City Shopping Centre in November 1987. In April of 1988 bandits used bolt cutters to cut the padlocks on a roller door before bursting in on the 10 staff members about 9.10am They sprayed red paint over the security camera and told staff to lie on the floor. As two of the bandits attacked the inner safe door with a sledge hammer, one, armed with a silver pistol, stood outside the bank and warned shoppers to keep moving. They opened a compartment and scooped out about $140,000. They sped off in a stolen car which was later dumped in the shopping centre car park. It was one of a number of banks robbed in that year, before they became more impenetrable with pop up protection screens. The raid on the State Bank took a bare two minutes, but the trauma from it had a far-more lasting toll on the staff. They were given counselling and support for some weeks after that.

The discovery of classical music lent itself to soothing Kerryn and me in the night-time, when we had disturbing dreams that doubtlessly arose from the trauma of Ulverstone and then Swan Hill, as well as the bank hold up. Our eldest daughter Belinda was seven when we departed from Swan Hill and of the three children, she was mostly left in a frightening spin at the suddenness of our departure. Kerryn and I felt that we could not tell her why we were leaving at the time for we were too distraught ourselves. As a result, she was haunted by our exit. Then again, all those moves at Swan Hill – four in rapid succession when we first went there – doubtlessly left its scar also.

The heart had to be kept with diligence, as John Flavel's telling book *Keeping the Heart* exhorts us to do, 'for out of it are the issues of life.' Needless to say that with Kerryn and I ensuring that we diligently kept our hearts, out of them were to a degree the issues of the lives of our three children. Belinda and Janine were advanced teenagers by the time I was at Ferntree Gully in 1989, while Stephen was yet to reach teenage years. As many of us learn, teenagers are a breed of their own, old enough to start asking questions but to which they have "the answers", less of your time and more of your money, spending some precious time at home with you so long as you deflate the air out of the tyres! Yet Kerryn and I learnt patience we never knew we had but for the grace of God. One learnt to ride the rough and then see it pay dividends.

While I could not help but to aspire to re-enter the ministry, I thought I had become a better, more equipped teacher than before, able to make learning more 'entertaining'. At my new school near home in Ferntree Gully I memorized classical stories and then gathered the students around me – as at a campfire – and told the stories from memory. Such a story as *The Great Escape* enthralled them. They learnt wisdom in a fun way from exercises in logical thinking. Group singing and learning songs had gone out the window years before, yet the students loved the music I introduced to them. Such a song as *Where Have All the Flowers Gone?* was sung with feeling and with a sense of mystery. Classical music was introduced to counter-balance the prevailing pop music (even heard at school) and opened the students' eyes to new vistas – Villa-Lobos's *The Little Train of Caipira* had them figuring out the varying pace of a Brazillian train, Mozart's Variations of *Twinkle, Twinkle, Little Star* indicating by raised hands when a new variation of the many variations moved in, Hovhaness's *Whales* with the actual song of whales interspersed with orchestra caused wonder. They developed the art of speech in one minute talks through 'mystery cards.' All kinds of language games played a fruitful part. Logic puzzles were attempted as I was seeking to have them achieve the art of learning beyond my time with them.

While changes were ever taking place in teaching method, and one could watch while so-called new methods came around again and again on a merry-go round under new dress, I took some pleasure in knowing the students were being given proper and lasting tools to learn to use. I bucked against the new method of written expression and clung to the tradition of teaching sufficient grammar to enable the students to write fluently and coherently.

Dorothy Sayers (1893-1957) said of her work that *The Lost Tools of Learning* is too radical to implement in modern education. Yet ever with modification on her part, the great Christian English writer thought that theoretically the adopted methods of teaching in the Middle Ages could have definitely succeeded in her time. She, who interestingly enough was probably the most popular writer of detective novels in her life, lamented that the students of her day were being taught 'subjects' but not how to think – "they learnt everything except the art of learning." For her there were three stages for successful learning: the Poll-Parrot stage, the Pert, and the Poetic. The first stage is easy: learning things by heart, history dates, rhymes, etc. The Pert stage is one of 'nuisance value': students learning by 'answering back,' 'catching people out,' learning to reason. As for the Poetic, it is linked to writing, debating and the like, with the desired air of appreciating "the beauty and economy of a fine demonstration or well-turned argument."

Sayers amusingly answers the objection that the Pert Age may encourage young people to correct and argue with their elders and thus become intolerable. She says: "My answer is that children of that age are intolerable anyhow"…!

Sayers never expected that her approach to education would be given a hearing. I never thought it would either, but it influenced me enough to streamline it to some satisfaction in my teaching and to the satisfaction of the students.

After being at the Ferntree Gully school for almost four years, rumours were circulating about some schools being closed down and teachers becoming redundant and therefore dismissed from schools that had a drop in student numbers. It was 1992. The Kennett government was in state power. Thousands of teachers throughout Victoria went out on strike on November 10. About half of my schools' teachers joined the strike. I refused to do so.

After a glorious weekend with Kerryn at Eugene Veith's holiday house at Cape Schanck, I returned to school with a sense of foreboding, shaken by rumours that some of us would lose our positions. Unfortunately the Ferntree Gully school was declining quickly in numbers, one reason being that it was situated in an awkward location due to increasing heavy traffic that put parents off from keeping their children there. I wrote in my diary: "There is some injustice that affects me at work, and I feel that I need to draw attention to it, so that I am not moved elsewhere unreasonably."

Some other teachers had also encountered difficulties at the school, and there was a move afoot to establish 'mystery friends' in the following year. Yet, a number of us feared that we might not be around for 1993 and it remained more of a mystery as to who would have to move on.

In the next week Bill Marsh, the principal, called us to an extraordinary meeting to inform us that while we currently had 17 teachers, in the new year we would only be entitled to 13.3 teachers. We learnt that it lay in his power to select the teachers required. Dismay arose even more because Marsh explained that excess teachers all over the state were to go into a pool for emergency teaching. Was I bound to return to that unsettling work that I managed to shake off eight years before?

In years gone by one had the security of being a regular teacher in the Ministry of Education, never fearing 'the sack,' or being plunged into 'a pool (!) of emergency teachers' in excess. Would it be cheerful for me in the way I had read about recently? I had read that if any patients came to Carl Yung, the psychologist, with news of despair, he would say "Let's celebrate; we'll open a bottle of wine, for this will lead to something challenging."

A few nights on and I had a dream of one of the women teachers leaning on my shoulder and crying over her dismissal at the school, and then stood there amazed to think that I had not been told about my own! She was a teacher in reality, who with another, had had a nervous breakdown, and I thought that she would be one who could well lose a position at Ferntree Gully.

On December 4 the school secretary broke into my classroom and told me Marsh wanted me in his office. Just as I had entered it, dark clouds of a summer storm had gathered and heavy rain began to pelt down on the school roof.

I sat across from his desk.

"Look," he went on, "I'm sorry to have to do this, but I must dispense with three teachers. I'm afraid you're one of them."

He gave me a split second to take in his grim words. "It is not that you are an unsatisfactory teacher. You are a good teacher. It's just…well, that's the way it has to be. And there are two others who are being told of this bad news. Sorry."

I stood up and sullenly made a quick exit from the office.

"I knew it, I knew it," I said to myself.

I knew the true reason for my removal. I had once reprimanded Marsh for his foul language. After enduring the crudity of the teachers in the year before when the staff were holding their Christmas celebration, I had sought recent permission to receive the first present at Christmas time among the teachers and then leave the premises. Marsh conceded that the staff got crude on such occasions, yet it irked him to make a concession for me. Once he appeared when we were alone in my classroom – to echo the words of Ecclesiastes "Do not be over righteous" – Marsh as good as told me that I should 'live it up' and have more fun on weekends. He resented my belief in Christ.

Eagerness to get home quickly at the end of the day overtook me, there to find a card from Howard, my friend, a Major in The Salvation Army, as you may recall. He had enclosed the following words without knowing what I had passed through that afternoon, though he had had a hunch of what was to happen –

> "He that spared not His own Son, but delivered Him up for us all, how shall He not with Him freely give us all things?"

I rang Kerryn but as she was still at work, she could talk little. I wanted to hold her in my arms, to know that she thought I was a person of worth.

It is hard to face rejection, but John, a teacher and a friend at the school, though a worldling, had said a few weeks before my sad news, that "if you get the boot from Marsh, see it as a compliment." In a sense grander than what John meant, I saw my dismissal as a compliment, as arising from my preparedness to stand up for the truth as it is in Christ. Individually, I got along fine with the other staff when it was one-on-one – it was more 'the herd mentality' that tested one's loyalty to the Lord.

Howard, as a true brother in Christ, paid us a visit and confirmed my conviction that I should count myself honoured to have suffered as I did, reminding me of Acts 5:32. This was of a different spirit than that of the brother, who was in my bible class at Boronia Baptist, claiming that Paul's words of "…everyone who wants to live a godly life in Christ Jesus will be persecuted" do not apply to us nowadays because we live in a western civilized country. Beautiful were the words Howard read to me:…" in the shadow of Thy wings will I make my refuge, *until these calamities overpast*," and "He shall send from heaven, and save me from the reproach of him that would swallow me up."

I shrank from returning to teach in the next week. With the oncoming removal from the school, the irony of being a former pastor intensified. It seemed that Marsh looked on me as a failed pastor when he learnt of my history upon first arriving four years before. There was the pang to think ignominy breeds ignominy. 'Give a dog a bad name and you may as well hang it'. I prayed that God would put paid to that proverb.

Kerryn felt too ill to eat.

Before returning to school on the Monday, I was to preach at an unfamiliar church on what I titled ": In the Twinkling of an Eye." I had to hide my broken heart as I preached, yet I could not help but pour out my troubles to some lovely, sympathetic believers after worship.

Our family sat around that evening in the dining room crying. Janine, who had been away for the weekend, was upset to hear of my dismissal and said that on Friday night she had woken up from a bad dream crying, "feeling that someone was hurting you." I wrote in my diary: "Yes, someone was hurting me, my dear daughter."

Little could prevent me from returning to the vortex of dismissal on Monday, and yet I needed to think much on God's burning holiness. There was the temptation to believe that God is lethargically loving and not see Him as burning with jealous love. Was I being self-righteous? Dear reader, think of the Psalmist, who appears self-righteous in the eyes of many, but who saw God as a Being of grace as well as One of burning love. Marsh had greeted me in the office that dark day, while looking out of the window at the darkened sky just before the lashing rain fell, and precisely said "It looks ominous." I prayed that one day in the near future I could say: "It only *looked* ominous."

Dear reader, I could write ever so much about what God taught me in such a short time after my dismissal, but I shall be as brief as possible.

I learnt from a gem of a book *Golden Treasury of the Puritans* about the desperate need of patience, for the morning of my return to face all the teachers and the students. I read that patience shortens our troubles in God's eyes; that those who know not God will not recognize or will not be able to read or see any virtues we believers may have except one, the virtue of godly patience.

Patience was strenuously exercised that morning when I had to confront many a face that almost seemed to signify that all had voted for my dismissal. Almost every other teacher received me with what appeared as coldness. No comfort came forth there except from one fellow-teacher, to whom I had written a letter of encouragement when once he had his nervous breakdown.

I thought "I must not hit out." One teacher in the western suburbs had thrown a chair through the principal's window when he learnt of his dismissal at the time.

Even if everyone was not at home in that week, it was bliss to be at home alone, away from the deafening, shrill silence that I faced three kilometres up the road. The house had a lingering perfume of love in the air.

It cheered me to learn from John, the same fellow-teacher who had reckoned that it was a compliment to 'get the boot' from Marsh, that a parent defended me at a meeting and stated that I should have been one of the first to be kept at the school.

It was in a jaundiced mood that I became tempted to despise modern education. A.W. Pink reckoned that secular education should not go beyond the 3R's! While I happened to be alone in the classroom one day when my class had a specialist subject, I reflected on what good I might have achieved, what influence there had been on the students. For instance, I relished on reflection the thought that during the Easter activities of that year, I told my class what actually and originally caused the festival to be celebrated. I grew bold when concluding about Jesus' resurrection by asking the class, "Who would love to live forever?" Many hands shot up. Needless to say, it was a little short of crossing the line and asking students to "come up to the front to be counselled," yet on reflection it seemed reckless but rewarding to tell them of redemption and resurrection through Christ. To my relief in the following days post-Easter nothing was said about what I had done. I imagined the defence I could have legitimately made for what I did, but there was no need for it.

It heartened me also to learn that many people in the community were surprised to learn that I was leaving and there were those who had hoped that I would be teaching their sons and daughters in the new year. Well, if it had not perhaps been for the dismissal, I would not have learnt how appreciative people had been of my teaching!

On January 25, 1993, all dismissed teachers attended a meeting at Deakin University to learn of our position as excess teachers. We were all to be based at a school regularly teaching something, unless some school somewhere else needed us for emergency teaching – I think that was the expectation. We also heard the Minister of Education hoped "the pool of excess teachers would dry up by July 1." Perhaps being likened to a 'pool' was a gentle way of viewing our situation – in teachers' college days at Coburg we sang our anthem that likened us to 'a single branch of one vast outspreading tree,' sang of a vision splendid that did not foresee some of us as branches being lopped off so that what once had been 'one vast outspreading tree' became cut back and with chopped off branches to arrest the spread. A pool can be defined as a supply of people when *needed*. Yet I guess we were floating in a pool when *needed*, not lopped off!

I could not take my mind off pastoring a church, particularly when an enquirer from a country church rang, two days after the Deakin University meeting, and for some months I hung on in hope. I had been waiting 15 years for a church, and I sought to be patient. The well-respected Baptist minister Alex White had put my name forward to the church. Three proven men had reportedly failed to arrest 'the slide' in the country church in mind, but would I fare any better? Still, I hung on in hope. It was almost four months before Alex was able to inform me further about the church but I learnt through him that the church had at last resorted to the Baptist Union Advisory Board. Alex said to me, "It looks like they have capitulated." Alex had little time for the Advisory Board, needless to say. I still hung in hope, though it had dimmed.

Time at the base school was always short-lived. Doubtless, like many an excess teacher I went from pillar to post under the title of STRT (short term replacement teacher or, if you like Shuffling Troublesomely at Random Teaching). One was not always teaching – there were occasions such as seeking to kill time by asking a librarian "Is there anything I can do?" Going from one school to another, there was the constant pulling out of boxes material as fitting for the grades one would face for often a mere day, returning material home for another lot of materials required on the next day when the phone would ring and you found yourself travelling to a new school for another day – a new school, new teachers, unfamiliar children, to be often at a schoolroom where, irresponsibly, no directions had been given as to what the students were to do. Admittedly, this is painting STRT work at its worst, but I grew frustrated keeping things in case I remained a teacher for the rest of my life, while also anxiously keeping things in case I re-entered the ministry.

I worked as a STRT until 1995, when I was appointed to a school at Clayton West. Although it was to prove a difficult school, day-to-day was gratefully more routine. Over the two years spent at Clayton West copious personal diary writing was more occupied with some momentous and disturbing events with less reference to my dark feelings about teaching as it had been.

I was swept up with the excitement of the publication of my book on biblical meditation – *A Tree By a Stream*, and was busy promoting it. Some domestic affairs were entangling, when Kerryn and I looked anxiously to

God. Sadness too was felt when Howard was compelled to move on from the Salvation Army temple at Glen Waverley according to the customary Army practice, for his preaching had sustained us for quite a number of years.

Because I was seized by anxiety over several things, I sought out a naturopath who happened to be Jewish. I had a battle with her as she probed the past on the first visit and tears welled up in my eyes without us proceeding too far. On the second visit the tears actually flowed as I could not help but spell out the homosexual advances that had been made to me when I was young. Two remedies were recommended : One being the taking of drops of French Violet and Bottlebrush, the other being to write in full what had happened all those years ago and then burn it. Back home with cold comfort I thought: Guilty men do not suffer trauma, only torment.

As for further cleansing through writing, I discovered its worth completing the writing of my life at the Sutherland Homes. People close to me wondered how I was satisfied in handwriting about it, with no thought of publishing the material. Yet, after 10 years a desire arose to put the manuscript up on the computer, with a hope of having it published by a Christian publisher.

Kerryn and I began attending an Independent Bethel Baptist Church in Mulgrave. Graeme, a fairly young pastor, deserved a bigger congregation than what he had, and he was to prove the most hospitable pastor I have ever known. A calm man, an exceptionally good listener, as well as being loyal to God's Word.

Then there were more choice books I found at that time to still my soul, such as the one that contained Thomas Goodwin's *The Heart of Christ In Heaven Unto Sinners on Earth*. I said to the Lord when I had not even finished it : "Lord, this is so rich that I cannot feed on it for a while!"

Alex, faithful retired Baptist pastor who recommended me for the aforementioned country church, was an elder at the Bethel Baptist Church, and still could preach powerfully.

God was working wonderfully and strangely in our three children. Divine providence has been likened to Morse Code, when you find three dots and a dash – ... _____ – for one thing can wonderfully follow one other thing (as in the three dots,) and then there is a considerable pause when nothing seems to happen, a time to test patience. We longed to see all three children come to know the Lord. I remember one night when I challenged all three about the Gospel in a way that spoke of the possibility of exclusion from the Kingdom. Stephen cried out with "Count me in!" It was an unforgettable cry through the Holy Spirit. If ever I had doubted where he stood before the Lord till that time, I felt certain that night about his burning desire to follow Christ.

As for our two girls, there was the time of patience (the long dash,) though one night pointed in a strange way to "pains of childbirth until Christ was formed in them" (Gal 4:19).

It happened one evening that one of our two girls had invited an unbelieving friend to dinner. The young fellow had recommended the book *Narciss and Goldmund*, by Herman Hesse to our daughter. I had read the book earlier in life but needed to refresh my memory of it. After dinner I opened two books – the Scriptures and *Narciss and Goldmund* – on the dining table.

> I began, "You gave my daughter *Narciss and Goldmund* to read. This is my old copy. It is rather foxed, but I have kept it for the sometime purpose of using it in my preaching. I have marked one passage that has remained quite useful for

illustrating what makes for being at peace in an uncertain world."

Our guest responded, "You have obviously read it, so I am interested in what you want to say."

"Thanks," I said.

For the sake of my two daughters, I described as briefly as possible the drift of Hesse's story. I spoke of Narciss being a teacher in a German monastery, who had a favourite pupil in Goldmund, but he knew that Goldmund would never be a scholar or a monk. Goldmund quits the monastery and embarks on a life of blood and lust, as he changes into a fugitive, losing his vision of perfection. Goldmund, unsurprisingly, reflects on the quest of Narciss, who sought to balance a life of sensuality with that of an intellectual satisfaction. In his quest for such, he had made 'a journey within' by making a journey *without* – for instance, he travelled to India for enlightenment.

I read out my underlined passage from *Narciss and Goldmund,* the words near the close of the book, those addressed by Narciss the teacher to Goldmund who says "I envy your peace" :

> "There's nothing to envy, Goldmund. There is no peace, in the sense in which you mean it. No doubt there is a peace, but not the peace which abides, and never forsakes us"… "All you can see is that I am less subject to moods than you, and so you think I must be at peace. But like everything that is not true, it is all battle and sacrifice."

"Well," said the young man, "I cannot see any difference between Christianity and other religions. They are all seeking peace, and none of them find it."

"Yes, well," I answered, "I know that Hesse the author was affected by the horrors of war, horrors that set him off on the journey 'within,' but he never explored Christianity at the core, did he?"

"Maybe he didn't".

"Christianity ought to be given a chance to present what it offers."

"What does it offer?"

"Let me read from one of life's stories of Jesus – the Gospel of John."

We saw together that Jesus is the only way to God. He comes across as a perfectly balanced man but who made astonishing claims, claims that can be verified by having faith in Him for eternal salvation. It is as C.S. Lewis said: "Until you have it, you will not know what you wanted." All believers have a peace that the world cannot give.

Our guest raised questions or made comments that are typically put forward against Christianity and, to my surprise, our two daughters, who had turned their back on the Gospel, were seen arguing the case for Christianity despite what our guest said by way of dispute! At home there had been many a night when devotions after dinner were met with dissent and contradiction. We took heart to know our daughters could not help but confess the truth, albeit demurely that night when their friend was present.

It was a tonic that with the apparent inner cleansing I had gained by writing of my encounters with homosexuality and burning the paper about the horror of it all, my mind was eased. There and then it appeared that the issue concerning two horrid advances and molestation through homosexuality would never erupt again as it did in the presence of the naturopath – that it had been a dormant volcano for so long, but it would never erupt again.

Yet problems with my voice never lay dormant. Time after time I had to take sick leave or, if I returned to school, it meant carrying out limited duties. If limited duties were out of the question, then I recuperated at home. In September, in my first year at Clayton West, I was once at home for four weeks with a lost voice, much to the annoyance of the headmistress.

The new year of 1996 for teaching did not get off to a good start, as I not only had voice problems, but was diagnosed by my doctor as having asthma. I was to begin the new year at school on light duties, which made the principal testy, and which led at least to one teacher insisting I was 'faking it.' I was to do only three hours of class a day, and the principal was adamant that I sip water all day, even including her commandment, and the practice of it, in a work contract! Teaching remained part-time until early March, when I got a few opportunities to preach, particularly in the church we became attracted to – Bethel Baptist Church at Mulgrave. I began dreaming of retiring from teaching at the end of the year.

It irked the principal considerably when I was subjected to an examination by a specialist, and it was recommended that I should be on WorkCare, a government-sponsored program that involved a certain absence from work until healing was completed. I succeeded in coming under WorkCare that was designed for me to do 50 percent teaching, and in the remainder of the work week to pay regular visits to a speech therapist. This was to be for a month at least, just when the school year left only one more term of teaching to go.

At the same time the principal announced that one teacher would have to leave on account of declining enrollments at the school. She declared that it would make matters easier if one of us would voluntarily ask to leave. This served as a contrast with what had happened at Ferntree Gully but, unlike the dismay of being compelled to leave Ferntree Gully, I felt relieved at the chance to depart from Clayton West, because I learnt that if I did volunteer, the Ministry of Education promised to grant me a teaching post nearer home. Besides, I had proved to be an irritant to the principal in more ways than one.

Not only because I was absent from teaching too much in school, but because the principal found my Christian convictions discomfiting.

Early in the year, a certain part of the science syllabus required me to teach the students about the Solar System. I sought to counter the common belief that ancient people regarded the Earth as flat. I spoke of Galileo and the Catholic Church, and how the Bible taught long, long ago that the Earth is round and hangs on nothing. The students listened intently when I felt constrained to tell them the Bible contradicts the scientists' theory that a giant meteorite put an end to the 'terrible lizards.'

Somehow word got out about what I had taught and I was called to the principal's office.

> "Tell me," she said, "about what you were mentioning to the students yesterday in Science."
>
> I told her.
>
> She went on to say, "It is not in the syllabus."

I answered, "Well, there is nothing in the syllabus to prevent me from mentioning what I did."

"It is NOT in the syllabus," she insisted.

I answered, "I see Science as a subject where it is logical to size up all possibilities in order to arrive at a reasonable conclusion."

"It is not right what you did. Everybody knows that evolution is fact."

"I'm sorry to say," I responded, "that as a Christian I do not believe in evolution."

"There are church people who do."

"They are not following the Bible, if they do."

"Whatever, the point is: You are to stay within the syllabus. Do you understand?" she said, as she began to shuffle a pile of papers on her desk, reflecting the very business- like and anxious manner she had adopted in her short experience as a school principal.

I had to promise not to teach anything outside the Science syllabus, and in general to keep my Christian convictions to myself.

An elderly gentleman came to the school once a week to teach religious instruction, which would give me a smile, in days when there were few objections or withdrawals from the religious instruction classes, almost all students being taught the subject. One day a fellow-teacher whose classroom was across the corridor from mine and whose class was being taught by the gentleman, said to me as she walked past: "Is that part of the syllabus?" For the strains of music filled her ears with –

> "Would you be free from your burden of sin?
> There's power in the Blood, power in the Blood.
> Would you over evil a victory to win?
> There's wonderful power in the Blood."

In trying to be as laconic as I could, I simply said, "Yes, I think so."

The speech pathologist under WorkCare asked me if I thought of retiring from teaching, or perhaps doing it part-time. I told him there was no opportunity for part-time, and I intended to continue full-time teaching, for it was better financially to do so. I had put my hand up to leave Clayton West voluntarily on a promise that I would be given a school nearer home for the new year. Hopefully, my voice would not be taxed, as it had been at what proved to be a difficult school. The new school promised to be of a place of more manageable students.

It appeared that the rest of my working life was to be spent teaching. I was getting fairly regular preaching at our new church, but the prospect of a pulpit anywhere appeared to be out of the question. A dear old friend, since passed, had said to me "God will use all that you know." I had taken great heart on first hearing those words, but now they echoed with apparent mockery. Also, Noel Vose's words of long years before rang out in mockery: "It does seem to me that God has given you a significant pastoral teaching ministry." Had I not become better equipped for pastoral work? Had I not become more pure-hearted when, like the great poet George Herbert, I had through trials learnt that only sincerity before God and an open breast in the confession of sins can render ineffectively the pain God brings through those trials? Had I not learnt from trials the empathy needed to comfort those suffering from adversity? Through William Still, a Scottish preacher and author of *The Pastor and His Work*, I discovered the inestimable worth of preaching through whole books of Scripture systematically, as he had done so successfully – and that created a thirst in me to obtain a pulpit.

There were the lines of a song that sprang to mind –

> "I can recall the time when I wasn't afraid to reach out for a friend
> And now I think I have a lot more than a skipping rope to lend."

Said the speech pathologist, "If part-time teaching is out of the question, I guess you have some years left before you retire. Therefore, we need to ensure your voice can cope effectively with the remaining years if you have no choice but to teach."

"Have you been doing the exercises?" he asked.

"Yes, I have," I answered.

"Good. Now I had wanted you for several days to observe your voice. To have worked out when it was best, when it was worse. How it was affected by weather, food, emotions, vocal strain and the like. Have you done that?"

"Yes, I have."

For the remaining sessions he stressed several vital points. Particularly in the light of future teaching, I was to concentrate more on how my voice *felt* when teaching, rather than trying to hear it above any noise, especially when outside with students and engaged in giving orders in sport. I was to slow my speech down and have the students see my face when listening, rather than raise my voice. Use of nonverbal means to gain attention was less taxing. While there was a need to drink water frequently, the therapist also advocated the massaging of the chin to increase saliva flow and keep the larynx and vocal tract moist.

He said that I was not to be too discouraged, as many who use their voice professionally suffer from voice problems.

I returned to 50 per cent teaching at Clayton West. It looked like that there would be little of the year left, even if I were able to return to teach full-time once more at that present school.

I discovered that my chances of getting a retirement package were more hopeful by voluntarily being prepared to leave Clayton West. Still, preliminaries for teaching assessment under the school principal were required. Hope lay in the principal putting aside her prejudice towards me on account of my Christian convictions when assessing me, so that the chance of a retirement package would increase. Things did not go well in the assessment, as her thinking was no doubt coloured by my convictions, and coloured by my all-too-frequent leave on sickness. As it was, the retirement package did not come my way and I received an appointment for the coming year at Wantirna Heights, a mere ten to fifteen minutes from home.

What a joy there was when the holidays came! Bethel's pastor had given me three successive weeks of preaching. My sister lifted my spirits as we walked along the wall of the Cardinia Dam on Christmas Day, when everyone else walked ahead to prepare a somewhat unusual alfresco celebration of Christmas with a picnic on the grass by the dam. I went alone to Cape Schanck once, sank into the pine leaves and thought of our wonderful God Who had showed me while wandering down to Bushrangers Bay a hovering Kestrel directly above, which all of a sudden swooped down within a metre of me and scooped up what seemed to be a mouse! There were also the lovely few days Kerryn and I spent with friends at Longford before travelling on to Lakes Entrance, where the Reeves Channel was emerald, with boats bobbing up and down, and terns diving deep and vertically down for fish.

Thoughts of teaching in the new year perhaps for six months before retiring mid-year drove me on, but Kerryn and I grew increasingly anxious about our three children, who tempted us to think at times that it might have been better not to have taught them too much about the Lord in their younger days. Then again, was it a time when the pangs of spiritual childbirth were being felt by us?

"Oh, my dear children, I feel the pangs of childbirth all over again till Christ be formed within you...! Perhaps I could then alter my tone to suit your mood. As it is, I honestly don't know how to deal with you." (Galatians 4:20, J.B. Phillips translating the words of Paul).

Yet the Lord so arranged matters that when I knew despair, Kerryn would lift me up and, when she knew despair, I lifted her up. We took heart from "Is there anyone in trouble? Let him pray." In their different ways our three children were struggling with knowing full well what the Lord was asking them, and only God in His sovereignty could charm them into yielding peacefully to Him. Our Bethel pastor, Graeme Lowe, proved to be a blessing at such a critical time; he had a rapport with our three that was hard to resist; he proved that he was a counsellor I had not met the likes before and perhaps will not know again.

As for teaching in 1997, all the staff in the new year suffered the tension of working under a permanent principal, who from May was to stay on sick leave for the rest of the year. An acting principal took her place. Certain disenchantment had existed the year before in the school as student numbers had dwindled alarmingly from 221 to 131 students in just 12 months.

Around midyear an innocent enquiry was provoked by a newspaper article that had me wondering if I was a child among many others in institutions across the land, who had been victims of experimentation with vaccines in the 'forties and early fifties'. I had discovered that I could obtain records and reports concerning myself at the Sutherland Homes.

I was to be on WorkCare again for at least two weeks in July of 1997, but my desire to preach at Bethel was such that I went ahead to plan a sermon on 2 Thessalonians, believing that my voice would not be taxed too much when preaching. However, to my detriment I spoke more animatedly than planned. While still on sick leave, it also gave me the liberty to attend a meeting in a section of Parliament House – organised by some people on the issue of compensation for the so-called *Lost Children* who were victims of experimentation with vaccinations – as aforementioned – and allegedly suffered much also by being in an institution.

Joyce and I made arrangements to seek help through Human Services.

Meanwhile, soon after Kerryn had become hospitalised for a brief time, our pastor and his wife visited us, and did not leave our house before our pastor told me that I had "opened up a can of worms" when I preached on 2 Thessalonians, concerning the Man of Lawlessness sitting in Jerusalem's temple in the future.

An elder at the church and who had done a sterling work to resurrect the church after it had been riddled by intolerable legalism and strife for some years, had apparently complained about my interpretation of the Man of Lawlessnes.

On August 15 – on what used to be my birthday at the Sutherland Homes until it surfaced that the date was really June 9 – Kerryn came across a practitioner who looked like helping her avoid any more hospital visits. On the next day we lunched with Pastor Graeme and Wendy, when in the course of conversation, it was hinted that there could well be a ministry for me at Bethel in the new year. I became excited, but I sought to suppress my excitement without being pessimistic. There arose a spectre of one elder, who could prevent me from being accepted in the church, just when some work at Bethel promised something less taxing for my voice.

Two days later at the church's annual meeting Graeme couched his words in a report with an obscure hint of his possible departure from Bethel.

In early September of that year, I had my first meeting with Lisa Gatcliff of Human Services, who, with loving concern broke word about the abandonment by our father when I was four and my sister Joyce was two. (Joyce decided to be counselled by someone other than Lisa and apart from me). The news proved even more shattering when both Kerryn and I learnt of my mother being chronic schizophrenic, and that she may still be alive.

Nine days later Lisa rang to tell me that I had a brother, and then the next we met and she told me that my brother was also chronic schizophrenic. (What Joyce and I discovered in those harrowing days about our past are found in greater detail in *The Silver Poplar*, but it is to be added that our discovery came at the same time that the breaking down of my voice led the specialist to tell me to give up teaching, and that the great desire to return to pastoring was tempered by the lack of complete certainty about Bethel).

Following on from the innocent enquiry into possible experimental vaccinations in institutions in days of childhood, life became rather disturbing. Quite a few meetings with Human Services were to leave both Kerryn and me drained and grief-stricken. Joyce, who once had been such an inspiration when she learnt of the struggles we were encountering in our family – assuring us that God had said "Never will I give you a burden that you cannot carry" – was to fall apart when she attended sessions with Human Services. She would grow angry with Human Services for telling her what they did, though voluntarily seeking to find it out!

Uncertainty also hung over the future of the school where I taught. As early as June the media carried the news that the Education Department was deliberately stalling about keeping the school open, the Department having failed to act promptly after complaints were made against the principal who had to be replaced because she had been a long time on sick leave. A decision was reached to close the school and I was to teach in a neighbouring school in the new year. I could not decline the directive for, despite the advice of the specialist, and with no certainty about future at Bethel, there was some possibility perhaps of my voice lasting out until I was to retire from teaching.

It was a most distressing time in trying to reach another certainty – concerning my mother's existence. On September 8 I had asked Lisa about her: Was she still alive? Lisa could not guarantee it.

Kerryn and I travelled to Brunswick to my sister's place.

> "It is so good to see you!" I exclaimed.
>
> We both gave her a hug.
>
> "I feel so strained," she sighed.
>
> Tears came to my eyes.
>
> She sobbed, "My counsellor told me that our mother was alive only up to four years ago, that for 50 years – from aged 21 to 71 – she was locked away in mental institutions."
>
> "I knew about the mental institutions, but my counsellor is unaware of our mother having died four years ago!"
>
> "Well, that's what mine told me," said Joyce adamantly.

I could not dispute the matter, for Joyce could be dogmatic, not one to dispute with. Besides, her counsellor may have investigated matters more deeply than Lisa did. I was already shocked at having learnt to the contrary from Lisa that our mother was at least alive in 1958, and Joyce's news was an aftershock.

> "And", my sister continued, "our mother fell into post-natal depression when she had me – her third child. It was just like her mother, who also had post-natal depression after her third child – our mother. I fear for myself..."

Joyce was not married and did not look like getting married, but we knew what she was trying to say.

> "So what about our brother Robert? Now that we have found out about him, do you wish to see him?" I asked.

> "I don't know," she moped.

She proceeded to tell us of some things that were new to us concerning Robert, then to conclude that she did want to meet him after all.

> "Have you learnt of anything else from your counsellor?" I said.

> "Yes," she conceded, "our mother had two sisters, one of whom is still alive."

> "Where is she?" I enquired.

> "She lives in Narooma in New South Wales."

> "We ought to contact her."

Joyce became silent.

Something seemed amiss.

"Yes," she said in a rather low voice," I suppose we should arrange to see her."

"Oh!", she exclaimed to change the subject, "remember how I gave you a copy of our father's parents wedding certificate, and that our grandfather's wife was a Marsden?"

"Yes."

"Well, I am not so sure now that we are related to Reverend Samuel Marsden."

Kerryn and I more or less ended the conversation at that and left my sister's house soon after.

When I pressed the point at home over the phone about seeing or getting in touch with Aunt Joan in Narooma, Joyce refused to give me her address and said she would contact Aunt Joan to find out if she wanted to get in touch with me. That aroused my anger. Then after several days, Joyce informed me that Aunt Joan intended to write to me, and Joyce sent a large bunch of flowers to us as reconciliation.

Yet, I had become distraught to hear from Joyce that according to her our mother appeared to have died.

In the meantime, our pastor Graeme had been unsuccessful in securing a church in Queensland, and was waiting to hear news from a church in a suburb of Sydney. He definitely desired to move on from Bethel.

Time ran into late October when Lisa of Human Services rang, she unsure if my mother was alive.

I told her about Joyce's claim, but Lisa said she had found no record of my mother's death – unless she had died interstate or changed her name.

The next morning back at school, and on taking students for an excursion to Jells Park, I was overcome with grief and craved to be alone, so I rang Lisa, who assured me that she would investigate the matter concerning our mother promptly and ring back the following day. When she rang back the next day, it appeared my mother was dead. This seemed to be confirmed when I contacted a second cousin at Benalla that I had somehow tracked down and she, upon answering my phone call, had stated she had a copy of the inquest into my mother's death.

Two days later we learnt that our pastor had secured a church in Sydney. His wife said to me somewhat cryptically that she believed that "you will be a part" of what was to happen at Bethel. We visited 'Dad' and 'Mum' at Diamond Creek, and while I was "cautiously elated" about Bethel, we told them the disquieting news about my mother. I was kept in further suspense, as my second cousin rang to say that in the confusion of conversation the first time with me, it was not a copy of the inquest into my mother's death that she possessed but that of my mother's mother who tragically died at the age of a 35. So, was our mother still alive?

I was still "cautiously elated" for several reasons. Would Bethel's congregation accept me as their pastor? Alex approached me about working with him for the following year as a fellow-elder. He seemed quite confident about me being considered for the pastorate.

Pastor Graeme had been preparing the church for a new constitution but was he departing without an actual constitution speedily being formed, or would it be formed with membership newly defined within the church? Who would or could then decide on a new pastor? To add to the dilemma, I felt unworthy to be a pastor when my three children were not exactly true believers and who – as many other Christian parents whom we knew could testify – were special targets for the Devil.

I wrestled with Paul's words to Titus about qualifications for an elder –

"An elder must be blameless,....a man whose children believe and are not open to the charge of being wild and disobedient..." (Titus 1:6, NIV.)

Now, it would not have mattered in many churches as to whether or not the children of one who proved to be a good pastor were disobedient but, in a church such as Bethel where we were zealous as to be true to the Scripture's directives, I felt it was quite imperative to have my children living in line with what the word of God teaches.

The words of Paul to Titus seem puzzling. The key Greek word is 'pistos': does it mean 'believing' or 'faithful?' Translations vary considerably. The ESV has.."where children are believers" – and so do other translations. Yet, even though a number of scholars agree with translating the word as "believing," or term it "believers," they turn around and interpret it to mean "faithful," as it can occasionally be rendered. J.B. Phillips gives the passage a twist with:....."and with children brought up as Christians." Now, our children were not wayward or disobedient as to be 'wild' but were they 'believing' or even 'faithful?' Some may say : Why fret over just one word, what does it matter? For my part it did matter. God's word ought to be followed to the hilt. Mind you, I took solace in reflecting on the night in the presence of a guest in our home that our two daughters defended the truth of the gospel, though they were not living it. As for our son, he was definitely the believing kind. Still, I prayed fervently for the salvation of our daughters at what I deemed a critical time for their own sake, as well as the sake of our church.

It was only as late as November 12 of the year of 1997 that through Lisa I learnt that my mother had died – not four years before as Joyce believed – but October 1988. It had taken a long two months before we found out with certainty that she had died only nine years before. It was with difficulty that Joyce was convinced by Lisa's discovery. With the certainty of learning that she had died and no longer suffered, I felt a degree of relief.

We felt the pain of never knowing her and had a longing to visit her grave in Ararat – there to weep, not ever having seen her throughout our entire lives.

Four days later saw me meeting Bethel's leaders, who wondered if I intended to have a break after teaching. I wanted a break by being fully committed as the pastor at Bethel! However, they were playing cautious and spoke of sharing the ministry with Alex for six months. After that? Nothing was said of what lay beyond six months, and yet I did not need to be concerned, as four days later Paul, one of the other leaders rang to say that they had accepted me as their full-time pastor, without reference to serving just as a co-pastor for six months.

> "Do you wish to take these records home?" Lisa gently asked on the next visit to Human Services.

Wisely Lisa had not given me too much detail, and left it up to me as whether or not I wished to read of what my mother suffered. With tears I took the envelope with its many pages. I tore up the most disturbing pages at home, and burnt them in a prayerful desire for oblivion. The kept pages were to remind me of some of what she suffered for much of her life. It caused me to wonder if my father caused her insanity, or if she would have recovered from insanity if he had not deserted her. She did speak of cruelty that she suffered at the hands of our father only days before she gave birth prematurely to a baby girl, who had to be transferred to the Children's Hospital, and who died only eight days old. As my emotions seesawed between the desire to delve into the past (and in a way not altogether wanting to) and the bright prospect concerning Bethel, I felt as George Herbert, the devotional poet of the sixteenth century, did – on the rack under the hand of God.

As George Herbert described it, there are times when one is peering over 'fourtie heavens,' then sometimes one is falling to hell. His plea to God was –

> "O rack me not to such a vast extent;
> Those distances belong to thee..."

Yet, although God may stretch or contract us, it is "to make the music better" (Herbert). It is a tightening or the loosening of the strings of a musical instrument in order to improve the melody. If we think truly, then it is "whether I flie with angels, fall with dust, Thy hands made both," and God's love and power can be perceived everywhere.

Finally, my name was put forward at a church meeting on the last day of November. The church formally agreed to call me as their pastor just after I had learnt that the school at which I had been teaching got the news that it was to close down. I was assigned to a neighbouring school for the following year. I had to meet the principal who planned to place me with a taxing grade for 1998. I had yet to receive official acknowledgement of my resignation I had tendered to the Education Department. I 'played the game' with the principal, smiling invisibly to know that his plans for me were not sure to be valid.

Acknowledgement from the Education Department of my desire to resign from teaching came a few days later. My joy knew no bounds at the prospect of being a pastor again at last.

Restoring the Years of the Locusts

It was during January of 1998, before I was inducted as Bethel's new pastor, that there appeared 'contractions' to signify the pains of childbirth in us as parents of our two daughters until Christ was formed in them (Gal. 4:19.) One of them had called it quits over a certain issue and became subject to God in humility and with tears. The other one confessed at last that she had been a rebel. Our son had been hanging on to a hindrance though he had been a believer for some time – no longer hanging on but letting go with grimness. So, on the day of my induction, not only were Kerryn and I rejoicing at the marvel of God's grace in our three children, but I was greatly relieved of the uneasiness of being a pastor whose children did not follow the Lord and who could have threatened to cast a dark shadow on my ministry by bringing discomfort through their abandonment of God.

How perfect is God's timing! God set the alarm on the clock and we did not know the time set for what He had in mind for Kerryn and me; He had our children in view. It seemed the clock had stopped when they were straying from Him. To us it was as if He shook the clock and got it ticking again, each of our children woke up and began in earnest to look to God out of questing hearts. One of the girls confessed that God in His marvellous grace had taken her by the hand and made her look back on the futility of the world, but then made her turn back and keep walking. She had been "playing on the road and God grabbed me by the hand and pulled me away." As the three of them became fully committed, were we seeing right and were we hearing it right? Kerryn and I had hearts full of thanks to our God, as we could only ascribe the changes in all three to His sovereign grace. Yes, we had reared them on the knowledge of the Lord that ironically had increased the yearning to rebel, as has been the way in many a Christian home. God is good!

After my induction, the church leaders encouraged me to attend a Banner of Truth conference in New South Wales, and then to share with Kerryn in her annual holiday from work before I returned to Bethel as their pastor.

I set out on a course to draw up a new constitution for the church. Graeme had done some spade work in the sense that he preached a series from the Scriptures on the nature of the church and its government, but no move had been made to begin setting down a new constitution.

Why a new constitution? Things had changed considerably since Bethel had been established by an American Independent Baptist missionary called Burl Nelson in 1970, and the church had done a radical turnabout when a young Chris Bowen in 1980 became the pastor and embraced what is superficially known as Calvinism. A new constitution was formed under Chris but, while I concurred wholeheartedly with "We believe in God's electing grace," members under the existing constitution had to adhere for one thing to the belief that "Christ shall reign a thousand years in righteousness until He hath put all enemies under His feet."

Alex had made it clear to me that he did not believe there was a millennium to come and disagreed where the constitution also stated that "God shall give to Jesus the throne of his father David." Yet he was not only a member of the church but an elder as previously stated, who held the church together with sound leadership until the arrival of my predecessor, Graeme Lowe, in 1992. Graeme himself did not hold to the Article of Faith under question. Doubtless, if Graeme had continued at Bethel beyond 1997, he would have deleted that article concerning the millennium.

Although I held to the doctrine of the One Thousand Years and believe that Jesus will inherit David's Kingdom in the future, I did not wish to include in a new constitution such an Article on the Last Things as a bar to membership. In fact, it was not my wish to prevent anyone from being a member of Bethel if they did not heed to *all* that I considered a Basis of Belief – that included disagreement with the doctrine of election, the very doctrine that was responsible for the great turnaround in the church that took place under Chris Bowen.

My desire was that membership to the church would be open to any who showed the evidence of God's regenerating grace and who had been baptised by immersion, but other persons not baptised by immersion could be considered for membership under special circumstances. This concession was coloured by my experience as a young believer, when baptised in the Anglican Church through sprinkling – considering it valid in my own eyes because I went forward to the font as a regenerated believer.

The office of eldership, as apart from a diaconate, would be introduced.

Only elders and deacons would be expected to submit strictly to the churches' new doctrinal basis, whereas other members would only have to be in substantial accord with the basis of faith.

It was the hope that the new constitution would be far less wordy than the old one, which included matters quite minor as: "the abstinence from the sale and use of intoxicating drinks as a beverage," and a warning "to avoid all tattling, backbiting and excessive anger." (Had the old one allowed for taking a *little* wine for the stomach's sake and frequent ailments, as the apostle advised Timothy?) The Bible would be respected as the only infallible rule for faith and practice, without making it essential in the style of the old constitution to include many so-called proof texts to endorse many an article (under "Of the Scriptures" there were 24 proof texts; under "Of the true God" 26"; "Of the Devil 27; and so on.)

The new constitution was mainly of my making and I was proud that it was approved of without much fuss. Of course, in practice there was no guarantee that it would lock out all theological problems that would doubtlessly arise from time to time.

In a short time in my new ministry there were things in the world which strengthened my faith and in turn that of the congregation. The Port Arthur massacre, with the killing of 35 people, shocked us all in Australia so that the Prime Minister was moved to confiscate to a large-scale any guns of the nation's citizens. I read *"To Have and to Hold,"* Walter Mikac's story of grief and questioning after his wife and two little girls were callously gunned down by the crazed killer, Martin Bryant. Walter asked: "What I really need to know is whether there is an afterlife." He also said: "But there is no punishment on earth that fits the crime – capital punishment, gouging his eyes out, ripping him apart, whatever, cannot be adequate." As I saw it, it was a case for the justification for hell. *"To Have and to Hold"* was a sad book – Walter was somewhat moved to believe in heaven but doubted that it existed.

There was another notable thing in the world which also strengthened my faith and in turn that of the congregation. One lady, who used to attend Bethel in past years, returned to church after she claimed that the book *The Murder of Sheree* convicted her of sin, then later in the year showing her that she was no better than the murderer of the little girl at Rosebud. Kerryn and I could understand how such a conviction may happen, strange though it may seem, though a book that was not explicitly out to convict anyone of sin.

According to Wayne Miller's *The Murder of Sheree*, a police investigator concluded that the killer of the little girl had used "goodness to mask evil deeds." The killer was in a league of his own – he had been a church elder of a spiritually sound and respected denomination – and one whom people could accept and trust, "but (in the events of the investigation) there was no good in him at all." It should be an easy step for all to see mirrored in the universal man the mask of 'goodness' we all wear to cover up our evil, and how we may seek to manipulate God, as the killer did. If I remember rightly, a psychiatrist on the case of Sheree's murder felt compelled to read the Bible. For the police investigator, he saw that *"(evil) exists but it's like trying to visualise the universe."* A skilled apologist says: "When you assert that there is such a thing as evil, you must assume there is such a thing as good." Such a sound assumption proves the existence of God and shows that He is good despite evil's existence.

The lady of recent conversion joined our congregation of approximately forty people, who formed an interesting gathering of people, with only a few who could be regarded of a professional kind. All the same, with the new constitution the way it was, we could feel we were all equal in Christ, even though Bethel overall still held a solid stand on the sovereignty of God in salvation. One member, Mary, would walk down to the front and to the pulpit, almost as soon as worship was over, and begin debating with me whenever I touched on the theme of sovereign grace, but she felt at home in our church, appreciating sound teaching. Mary, along with a dear lady called Alice, were kindly brought to church each Sunday morning by Paul from as far as Carnegie and Bentleigh, and taken home by him as well. Paul was a prominent member of the church – quietly spoken but a diligent church secretary and a generous man, having in the early days a young family that was trained to sit through the sermon each Sunday morning with the innovative practice of ticking off key words that they would hear in the sermon.

Early in the piece at Bethel I began a series on Matthew's gospel, as part of the object of preaching through the whole Bible, as far as possible while I was the pastor. William Still (previously mentioned), a Scottish Presbyterian pastor in his *The Work of a Pastor* tells of how he came under the conviction of preaching through the whole of the Scriptures, book by book, in his parish. He met a bad reaction from the people, particularly from those who only wanted "the simple gospel" preached each Sunday. Numbers dropped off, but there were those who remained in the congregation to be well nurtured in the Word. Still was left with smaller numbers to preach to, but many among them became believers of great calibre, as seen in not a few of them becoming missionaries the world over.

I began preaching on Matthew with some apprehension, believing some fellow-elders would object to some points I hoped to make.

It is never exceptional, of course, for pastors to find among their people those who will contend with dissenting views to do with the church's doctrine, but to vocalise some of my views at Bethel left me wondering about certain ones who, while conservative, held to some odd beliefs, such as believing in Christ does not necessarily mean that one possess the Holy Spirit. Another person believed he was perfect, free of sin! Still another maintained he was "pan-millennial" – not interested in what is said about the future in the Word, for *"all will pan out"* without us getting tangles up into knots about it.

The matter of coping with any inevitable dissension at Bethel after the "honeymoon" followed with a visit to a newly found cousin. Bertie

Charles Lancet Smith lived in Mooroolbark. He was 82. He had no sleep the first night I rang him. The trauma of his early life with his wretched father awoke in him memories so that he wondered if he could face another Smith. Bert (as he preferred to be called) was relieved to discover that I was not like the kind he knew. He said that he was glad when his father died. His stepmother was cruel, and his three stepsisters would not talk to him. Bert claimed his father was a womanizer and an alcoholic. He recalls seeing my father only once. It was on a memorable day up at Silvan when our two fathers met for the first time in 25 years!

Bert was likable and quite refined, and I found that what he said about the past was believable, and it squared up with other things I had heard elsewhere. I came home from seeing him, saying, "Ah, Lord God, You preserved me from a similar wretched life!" Meeting Bert gave rise to being thankful for God's providence that existed even before He called me to be in Christ, but at the same time meeting Bert gave rise to much reflection on what was missed by way of a normal life. There had been a subconscious hatred of my father at Sutherland where I entered at the age of six. As previously stated, I was branded backward by the authorities because I appeared to have a contempt for company, had a longing so often to be alone and seldom spoke. Much of my 11 years at Sutherland were marked by what was not exactly a sound beginning for one who was to become a teacher and a preacher tested often by inevitable dissension.

Regarding preaching and the pulpit, it was supposed to mean I could be seen *at the pulpit*. My predecessor, being a tall man, had a pulpit made according to his stature. We were blessed with the arrival at Bethel of a Spanish-speaking family from Paraquay. Vincent and his wife Juliana spoke reasonable English. They had been converted through a Baptist pastor in South America. Vincent was a skilled cabinetmaker and he offered to cut the pulpit down to suit my smaller stature. For them it was a struggle financially as a family in Australia but they proved to be a blessing to Bethel – through hospitality and music. Their son, Vincent Jnr., was an accomplished harpist, with his father making harps to suit Vincent's stature as well – this as Vincent grew taller from the age of four, when he first began playing the beautiful instrument.

Things were going well in my first year at Bethel. Midweek studies were well attended. My own written course of *Christianity Made Clear* met with considerable opportunities to reach people outside the church. Afternoon discussions after our weekly church lunch comprised follow-up questions of a pragmatic nature to reinforce what was preached, with men of the church helping to form panels for the occasion. We began a series of Men's Breakfast on a Saturday morning at a McDonald's restaurant first of all with the infectious style of Bill Medley as he proclaimed the gospel, with several unbelievers present. Bill is author of the well-known little book *Religion is for Fools,* and became a beloved friend of mine.

Near the end of the year several people were baptised, but we were to miss on Sundays an elderly lady in Alice, one of the two ladies whom Paul, our church secretary, brought to church from afar. Despite her age, Alice was a great inspiration. She was an intelligent lady, quite well acquainted with New Testament Greek, and who absorbed scholarly books on science that were linked with creationism. She said that she was diagnosed with lung cancer but, when she was operated on, no trace of cancer was found. Yet, into the new year of 1999, she was obviously quite unwell. She expressed the wish to have her ashes scattered in the grounds of Bethel.

I wrote my sermons out word for word, not only as an aid to support what was actually said from the pulpit, but simply to avoid repetition. To avoid sermons sounding too formal or too impersonal, I would read them so many times in my study during the week that what I had written in preparation before entering the pulpit did not find me burying my head in the words when preaching, but looking up to have eye contact with the congregation, preaching without making it too obvious I was merely reading notes.

In early 1999 Kerryn and I flew to New Zealand for a holiday soon after our daughter Janine had started her first job there as a speech therapist. At Janine's church I preached in Dunedin on the day the new pastor was being commissioned.

I had great admiration for Paul. He was quite young in my early days at Bethel. He and his wife and three children, who, as said previously, were trained to sit in for the sermon. He was extremely generous and although he was a travelling salesman he gave much time to church activities, as well as helping our disadvantaged people.

In 1999 my preaching was greatly shaped by deep contemplation of the meaning behind by the constant name Jesus gave Himself – that of "the Son of Man." I recall a day when I was the pastor of Ulverstone, that a church leader left me somewhat groping for a satisfying answer when he asked me, "What did Jesus mean when He called Himself the Son of Man?" Yet, after spending a delightful retreat with Kerryn in a modest holiday house in the beauty of the rugged Grampian mountains, I returned to Bethel loving Jesus all the more through grasping insights into Jesus' humanity, thanks to Godet, an orthodox German scholar of the nineteenth century.

What insights did Godet give me? Largely basing his insights on what Luke tells us, Godet says that from His miraculous birth, Jesus began on "the pathway of progress from innocence (lost through Adam) up to holiness *which had been the course originally opened to man*" (italics mine)... Jesus followed the normal development of mankind. Adam was of a miraculous birth too, except that Jesus got back the power not to sin, which Adam had possessed before the Fall. Yes, even as a child He not only grew physically but spiritually as well – possessing a sound body, and a sound soul as drawing from God ever-increasing wisdom. He was the ideal Man. He was what you and I should have been, ought to be, and will be by God's grace."

It was wonderful and unbearably sweet to read Luke from this point of view.

I had been fostered on the importance of acknowledging that Jesus is the Son of God, yet, without decrying such an emphasis, I arrived at the conclusion that many of we believers do not appreciate as much as we should Jesus' humanity. After our retreat in the Grampians, I felt much closer to Jesus, as well as seeking more to be an ideal man myself.

Godet says so much about Jesus being the Son of Man, but suffice to say that I gained enough from him to equip me more to love Jesus, to examine myself in the light of His humanity, and it found me more concerned about the humanity of the people that God entrusted me with.

Godet's insights magnetized me into reading him more than once after our Grampians' stay, for I craved to have the teaching of Jesus as the Son of Man an abiding part of me.

Our stay at the Grampians had also lent the chance to visit Ararat and see my mother's grave once again, and to visit my brother Robert. I was to write later that "it was the best visit we had with Robert." We took him to a Chinese restaurant in Ararat.

> "What would you like to eat, Robert?" I asked him.
>
> "Not much," he answered softly, looking at me intently for a quick second and then looking away to stare into empty space.
>
> "We'd like you to eat something," said Kerryn, and read out some suggestions.

After we left the restaurant, we drove Robert home. We entered his lounge room, where the carpet was noticeably punctuated more by holes from cigarette butts and ash. Even along the window sill there were similar reminders of Robert's smoking habit. He looked at me, offered me a cigarette and, when I declined, he lit up one for himself. Silence fell on our presence momentarily, and then I broke the silence by giving him the Christmas present we brought with us.

"Happy Christmas!" we both wished him.

The parcel comprised a summer shirt, some socks and a CD of Fifties music, and that opened up the conversation more on his part, as he displayed a staggering memory of movie stars of the Fifties, and cricket and football heroes.

We left his home and wondered as we returned to Melbourne about his ill-dress, searching for a reason for him having few and well-worn clothes. Why did the State Trustees not show greater care? Did no-one of health care services seek to redress (excuse the pun) the problem? Then again, it could have been that Robert had little money in savings.

In late May we had another of our men's church breakfasts on a Saturday. Twenty-nine were present, including perhaps nine unbelievers. Alex had been a RAAF wireless operator and air gunner in the Second World War, serving on Beaufort Bombers and Dakota transport aircraft. We advertised as widely as possible with leaflets that carried Alex's title for the occasion: "Wartime Experiences and Peacetime Conversion." It promised to draw men to hear Alex speak.

Rather than the quieter Notting Hill McDonalds where we usually met, on this occasion I reluctantly decided on the busier food court at Waverley Gardens Shopping Centre where we would have a larger audience. Unfortunately, amid the shopping centre's loud music, and general noise surrounding us made it difficult to concentrate fully on listening to Alex, despite the clear voice he possessed.

God indeed showed signs of coming to my aid. For instance, I preached a sermon one Sunday morning with the title 'Rift and Rescue'. A stranger from New South Wales was present. He was divinely led to visit. After the sermon he was in tears over the sermon about worldly believers. Yes, preaching can 'come home' to the heart, for the Spirit knows what any listener truly needs to hear.

I became increasingly conscious of the fact that it is easier to be bold in the pulpit than beyond it. Dear old Alice died, many of her relatives were unbelievers and it gave me opportunity to be bold in the pulpit, but then I felt also constrained to talk openly to some of them after the funeral, proving it is possible to be of courage and unafraid outside the pulpit, to show how precious and unashamed it ought to be in believing in Jesus for eternal salvation. We planted a tree where Alice's ashes were laid near the entrance of the church.

When I daily prayed for my congregation, praying specifically that quite a number of them would change their ways and habits, and overcome natural tendencies. I regarded it a sign of devotion to Christ in doing things contrary to our nature or temperament. If I looked at the most spiritual of Bethel's people, I could see it was true. For instance, while there were those who oddly hinted that visitors to the church may not visit us more than once, and who had no wish to go out of the way to encourage visitors to pass through our doors once more, others, contrary to the tendency to be coy, out of a greater love for Christ did their best to make new people welcome.

The pastorate was made more difficult because we were an independent Baptist church. Moreover, we were independent of the other independent Baptist churches! We stood alone on what we regarded as the foundational truth of God's sovereignty of salvation. When Bethel made it foundational, other independent Baptist churches had ceased to have any ties with us. There were times when I sighed at the best of memories that I had of my earliest church life in the Baptist Union – that wonderful sense of fellowship with other pastors and churches. Times of loneliness tempted me to approach the Union for acceptance of Bethel into the Union, so long as Bethel could keep its doctrinal stance, but I never said a word to anyone at Bethel about it, for I would have been well and truly cried down. Indeed, to express such as wish could have hastened on an attempt to have me removed from the scene.

In the year 2000, Berry Street, which had been caring for children since 1877, organized a Sutherland Homes Reunion and Farewell. The welfare group had taken charge of the Sutherland Homes in 1994 and decided to stage a farewell as the doors closed on the old Sutherland Homes site in Diamond Creek before the property was subject to a possible sale. The farewell and reunion came with very wide publicity. Peter Brock, renowned racing car driver, was to be the main speaker on the Sunday afternoon of February 27, the date of Kerryn's and my wedding anniversary. On the Saturday we travelled to the reunion with considerable excitement.

So many of the inmates that I had known and shared childhood years with were there, also some staff and my Grades two and four teachers. Quite a few, who had been children there, were barely recognizable of course, but once we learnt of each other's names, we fell into conversation – some of it animated out of happy memories, some clogged by bitterness.

> "Did you know that Dennis and Norman wished that they hadn't come today?" someone said.
>
> "Is that so?" I queried.

"You know who I am talking about? So, I caught up with Dennis and Norman," it was whispered.

"Yes, but why did they come today?"

"It beats me, because they complained about the bad treatment they got here."

"Well," I said in return, "we had our tough times, but I have good memories too."

"Weren't you an orphan?"

"Yes."

"Well, it must have been sad."

"Yes, it was. I often longed for my mother to appear out of nowhere on Visitors' Day."

"Mm, at least I saw my mother fairly often."

"Well, when one is a child," I philosophised, "one is quite resilient. And I am thankful that there were things hidden from me – that was a blessing."

I found myself drinking deeply from the past as we were walked around with many people and looked at all of the Homes' property inside and outside as it was, and as it would soon not be, since the property was said to have been privately sold.

At that time of the reunion, I had completed the manuscript for the autobiography of my life at the Homes – *The Silver Poplar*. I thought that since Peter Brock and I knew each other well at school, I could in the course of conversation open up about the possibility of Peter writing a foreword for the book. Would the book not be a best-seller with his illustrious name emblazoned on the cover? As it stood then, the autobiography would hardly offend because the story of my conversion to Christ was still somewhat cryptically told in passing, so that Peter even as an unbeliever could possibly endorse the book. In truth, I thought that he might look on me as an object of pity when memories of Sutherland were at their height in the reunion and farewell, but I sensed that he showed little interest in my memoirs, and the matter was not pursued.

That was the year when my father in the Faith, Cyril Smith, died. Even though we did not see as much of him as we used to, until late in life in steady correspondence by letter he would sign off affectionately 'Dad'. Our children knew him as 'Grandad'. I was privileged in the last few months of his life to visit him and comfort him with the Scriptures. I well remember – when he was aged close to 90 – how I was reading Psalm 121 when he could barely speak and I read out the words "…He who watches over Israel will neither slumber nor…" Was he asleep? I hesitated to proceed, only to hear him softly say "sleep." I cried a little as he finished off the Psalmists words.

I was privileged to join several others – mostly of 'Dad's' family – in the eulogies in the "toy church" of St Katherine's, St Helena. I finished my eulogy by paraphrasing the words of Apostle John –

> "My father in the Faith, I have loved you in the truth, because of the truth, which lives in us and will be with us forever."

Nothing prepared me for what was to occur in September. I came through an operation at The Valley Hospital in North Dandenong when, just as suddenly I fell into deep depression for days after the operation, far deeper than anything I had known before.

Is there any human explanation as to why on earth it happened? I do not know. It seemed that the anchor of strong faith had been pulled up fiendishly and I was being swept away into the wild waves and depth of despair. I felt I was fast losing my mind despite my attempt to reason my way out of darkness. God had deserted me. I feared that I would become as William Cowper – consigned for the rest of life to abject despair.

Yes, I had read of great saints of old who had been 'jealous' of what has been called *The Dark Night of the Soul*. Yet it was far from my thoughts that I was a great saint and who would bravely pass through such a 'night'. In gloom I did not see it as a badge of honour. It was not to be wished upon anyone.

What could I do to climb out of such despair? How could I break its shackles? It seemed that my *reason* caused me to believe I was God's child, but I was overwhelmed by beastly *emotion*. I took to reading some lovely Keswick hymns that I knew as a young fervent believer but the memories only made me sadder and full of misery.

I attempted to go it alone, in the belief that no one could help. A song haunted me –

> "I could not do without Thee,
> For years are fleeting fast."
> Then God's word was a slim shaft of light –
> "Cast your cares on the Lord
> And He will sustain you;
> He will never let the righteous fall."

Two more days went by and even deeper darkness had fallen on me. I prayed, "Ah, Lord, this depression has to be muscled out of mind" but it seemed nothing in this life was of any moment, that all I could do was to mope and wait until life ends, when such sorrow would be over.

I was hiding my feelings from the one I love. I asked myself: Should I tell her? Yet I did not want her to be downcast. I did not want her to think she was the cause in any way of the despair – for she was not. I wanted her to be happy. Indeed, I wanted to crown her life with far more happiness than was in my power to give.

I kept hanging on to the words of "He will never let the righteous fall" – hanging on ever so grimly. I even threw up the question: Was it the anaesthetic drug that produced the despair?

The darkness lingered: I had to tell the one I dearly love. Besides, there seemed no wise fellow-pastor I could talk to.

September 13 was a sunny day, promising 20 degrees Celsius, and after taking a slow walk out in the sun, I reached out to a volume of the life of Dr Martyn Lloyd Jones, for I suddenly remembered that he had also gone through "the dark night of the soul". A little light shone on me as I read of his despair. It was only a little light but I thanked my God for it, as on that day I had felt the spite of Satan in a way I had never known, felt God's hatred of him, felt God's hatred of sin, causing me to crave for a purer walk with God.

Returning from work, Kerryn brought me a little bottle of Bach's Rescue Remedy, a naturopathic liquid to calm one's mind. It seemed to do a little to lift my spirits but any greater reason for beginning to feel better lay in the beginning of Paul's letter to the Galatians, where in the benediction that many of us may glide over, my eyes lit on "*Grace and peace* to you from God our Father and the Lord Jesus Christ..."

Peace! How sweet it was at last to have it descend on me. It began to banish my fears. I felt that no matter what was going on around me, so long as I had the peace of Jesus all was well. I recalled the song I used to sing down on my knees in the bungalow as a young believer when I lived with 'Dad' –

> "Wonderful peace, wonderful peace!
> Wonderful gift from above!
> O wonderful, wonderful peace!
> Sweet peace, the gift of God's love."

On the next day I was still exclaiming: O peace of Jesus! How sweet it is!

Only days before peace flowed over me, the threat of death saddened me. At 17 I seemed so far from death but, as I was ageing and drawing closer to that great Enemy, I had trembled with fear, yet in rising out of despair I was quivering with joy to think of passing on. As I contemplated the future redemption of this world, my senses were also sharpened to know Jesus is the coming King. I had been through an anaesthetic at the Valley Hospital, and it seemed that I had come out of another one, but out of one that caused me to be as alive to God in the way I was when first He made me His child.

I lost confidence in myself – God be thanked!

And now that my sense of salvation and eternity had proved to be far more heightened than for many years, I reconsidered my autobiography – in-the-making. I had hoped to impress the secular world with it, but I decided to rewrite it and make central the unexpected revelation of Christ that I encountered while still at Sutherland. How foolish just to make a casual, somewhat cryptic allusion to the most momentous thing that is ever bound to happen to me! Why, at the Sutherland Reunion in February

I had written in the Memories Book on display that the greatest memory at Sutherland was in 1958 when I came to know the Lord!

I am sure that my people at Bethel sensed more urgency and earnestness in my preaching after the Dark Night...

In three years of preaching we had covered: Genesis 1-16, 1 and 2 Samuel, Proverbs, Ecclesiastes, Hosea, Jonah, Matthew, Romans, Philippians, James and 1-3 John. Into the new year of 2001 we ventured, covering more books of Scripture through mid-week meetings, Sunday morning worship and Sunday afternoon discussions and panels. Alex described Bethel as "a peaceful church"...

Still, some grew uncomfortable at times with the preaching whenever Israel was the subject. I attempted to be sensitive to belief about the meaning of 'Israel' in Scripture, but it was difficult to avoid a fairly open disagreement now and then.

On September 11, 2001, our focus at Bethel, along with the rest of the world, was on the terrorist attack on the United States. I took to reading the Koran, when suddenly it had seemed that the whole world was a tinder box. For me, the Islamic threat had nothing to do with the prophecy of Revelation, but it could be viewed perhaps as playing a leading part in the prediction to do with all the nations warring against Israel. Psalm 65 proved to be assuring –

> "You answer (we of Israel) with awesome deeds righteousness
> O God our Saviour,
> the hope of all the ends of the earth
> and of the farthest seas,
> who formed the mountains by your power,
> having armed yourself with strength,
> who stilled the roaring of the seas,

> the rearing of their waves,
> and the turmoil of the nations."

Yet, on the Christian front, pressure was being applied to be interfaith and accept all religions as of equal standing.

The Americans turned to fight terrorism in Afghanistan just when the calendar passage in the One Year Bible read –

> "Do not learn the ways of the nations
> or be terrified by the signs in the sky,
> though the nations are terrified by them."

Inspired by such Scriptures, and having been exhilarated by the opportunities that had come my way from the early days as Bethel's pastor in regular door-to-door visitation, I seized the moment to persuade the church people to purchase multiple copies of John Blanchard's telling booklet *Where was God on September 11?* I then went door-to-door with a short, enclosed note about the offer of the booklet in an envelope. The booklet was on loan and the note said that in a fortnight I would call again. I hoped it would generate discussion on the second visit. It did, and though we saw no new people at Bethel, I met with many good responses that led to fruitful talk of salvation in Christ.

Of course, the newspapers were full of viewpoints after the terrorist attack on the U.S. – Philip Adams, a renowned columnist being one of them. Adams conceded he is awed by the majesty and the mystery of the cosmos but claims it is meaningless. He said we all are at liberty "to formulate one's own philosophy, one's own morality, value and ethics." He sought to convince us that in adopting his concept of meaninglessness one "hates less." I felt that he ought not to be offended if we called him a fool, since all is meaninglessness!

Some people from a considerable distance away began to attend our fellowship, when many of a fellowship of Brethren, whose church was split by division, came to Bethel on recommendation because our name was "on top of the list" for inspection. Even the pastor was in the number who attended. Not all remained, but enough solid believers among them decided to stay on at Bethel. A friend from U.S.A. was visiting Australia his homeland at the time and he inspired me to regard the pastor of the split church as being on trial at Bethel – and not me. Still, nervousness about holding on to the new people had to be fought – I wishing that I had the enviable hide of a hippo as my U.S.A. friend had.

It was in October of 2002 that Kerryn and I attended a wonderful reunion of the Marsden family, whose clan I belonged to through my great-great-great grandfather, John Marsden, who was transported for life as a convict to Tasmania. (Details of the reunion can be found in *The Silver Poplar*).

The stranded pastor of the split church thought that the doctrinal difference between some of those from Bethel and me could have led to a church's demise, but I maintained that it is not so much doctrinal differences that create division in a church, but the way differences are managed.

Unexpectedly, I became the Australian representative of The Society for Distributing Hebrew Scriptures when I sought the Lord for a way to witness to Jewish people. The society's mission is to give Jewish people free copies of Scriptures that have the English text on one side of a page, and on the corresponding side the text in Hebrew. Both the Old Testament copies and the New Testaments are beautifully bound and many Jews are surprised to learn that they are given out free. A friend of the society, Amy, and I began week by week on a certain day to walk the streets of St Kilda,

Caulfield and Bentleigh to offer the Hebrew Scriptures to Jews we met. Before the end of the year we had been greatly blessed through the work so that I wrote in my diary that "I could easily go full time for SDHS if there were an opening."

My desire to freely speak, albeit out on the streets, satisfied my strong conviction about taking the Gospel to "the original messengers." At first I combined such work while still serving our church at Mulgrave.

With respect to the subject of preaching about Israel, one elder felt that all the leaders of Bethel ought to have a meeting one evening to decide what he deemed a difficulty in preaching about Israel. Some of the other leaders believed that Israel was receiving too much precedence in my preaching.

Preaching was supposed to be more occupied with such subjects as evangelism and sanctification. At the meeting the question was asked: What does Bethel have to do with Israel?

As a reader, who perhaps may not be familiar with the issue entailed for several reasons, outlined here is the issue in question.

David Pawson, a noted English bible teacher, once wrote –

> "Alas, Christian opinions about (the future) are now so confused and convictions so divided that there is an unspoken agreement not to talk about the subject at all, lest the fragile unity of Christians, particularly those calling themselves 'evangelicals', and believing the whole Bible to be the Word and the words of God, be further imperilled."

Back in 1989, when I had grown bamboozled by the many options held by Christians in our time concerning Revelation 20 in particular, but believing that God would not leave us baffled about the Last Things. I took up only the NIV translation of the Bible and my Greek New Testament for enlightenment – I was determined not to be swayed by the many interpretations of men.

Actually, I decided to begin investigation by looking at Revelation 19, where we read of One, who by name is called Faithful and True, Who rides in triumph on a white horse. Despite some shifts of belief about the Last Things, I have always thought that the rider on the white horse depicts Jesus on His descent at His Second Coming. It is natural to believe it is so.

To put it briefly, I became amazed at what is the continuity behind seven visual revelations John received. Seven things are said to be *seen* by John, whereas the revelations immediately beforehand were the things *heard*. (Revelation 19:11-21:4).

Note the sequence of things John saw –

1. The rider on a white horse at heaven's open door.
2. An angel invites birds to the 'last supper' of human flesh.
3. The battle with all anti-God forces at Armageddon, as the rider on the white horse makes war.
4. An angel binds and imprisons the devil.
5. The saints reign with Christ for a thousand years, at the end of which Satan is released, defeated and thrown into the lake of fire, where the Beast and the False Prophet had already been cast.
6. The resurrection of the dead and the final day of judgement.
7. The creation of a new heaven and a new earth; and descent of the new Jerusalem.

More detail than the above is revealed to John through the seven things he saw, but further detail confirms all the more the definite continuity that can be observed – seven visions, each relating to the preceding one.

How did such revelation lead me to the question of Israel? I noticed that after Satan is released from prison once the 1000 years arrive at an end, he seeks to destroy "the camp of God's people, the city He loves" – the city of earthly Jerusalem. Then, when there is the creation of a new heaven and a new earth, it is a heavenly Jerusalem that descends. Much of Old Testament prophecy is full of "the city God loves", and Revelation builds on that truth.

I say that my aim was "to put it briefly" but it also is to make the issue at stake as clear as possible, in order to understand the nature of the meeting held with the leaders.

I also thought that quoting Charles Spurgeon was valid, since the elder, who convened the meeting, held Spurgeon in high esteem. There is no doubt Spurgeon believed that Israel will come to faith in the End Times, and that Israel will reclaim the Promised Land. He regretted he spoke too little rather than too much about Israel and her future.

The upshot of our meeting was that I was permitted by all to preach about Israel as any occasion or text required it in the pulpit, except that I had to put a rider on whatever I preached on Israel – the rider being "It is my opinion…".

Still, I continued to have a full and free voice out of a strong conviction about God's ancient people, through the street work, alongside two assistants of a similar conviction.

Waterloo Bay

In the new year of 2003 who would have thought that something that can only be described as 'volcanic' would occur to me? In late January, our family of seven adults plus a friend decided to spend two days hiking at Wilson's Promontory because our daughter Janine and her husband – who were married two years before – were soon off to England for a working holiday. Prior to making off for Wilson's Promontory I wrote in my diary: "I wonder what the next three days will bring," and "What will the next three days reveal of one another?" Also, "Will the days reveal some things that never had been unearthed? Doubtless they will. To our joy? To our dismay?" Little did I realise that I alone was to be greatly shaken at what took place.

The temperature had already risen to more than 40 degrees Celsius early morning when we packed into a supplied vehicle which wound its way up a steep hill. We stopped at a spot and heaved our camping gear onto our backs and set off tramping on a beaten track, downwards in the direction of Waterloo Bay for the first of our two night's stay in tents. People looked at us all with bewilderment as we, despite the temperature threatening to rise, climbed into the vehicle to take us to our starting point for hiking. In the intense heat it became obvious that it was a long way down to the coastline. On the way down any trickling cool water on the side of the walking track in among ferns and rocks was greeted eagerly.

Most of us were inexperienced for such a three-day hike. Kerryn and I, our eldest daughter Belinda and friend, Chris and Janine, our son Stephen and his wife Freya (who were married the year before), soon felt the scorching heat and welcomed any shade as we made our way.

When we finally came close to Sealers Cove, we hugged the coast until we arrived at Waterloo Bay, a beautiful spot with the whitest of sand, emerald water and large red coloured rocks. We ate cold canned food, for a ranger came by and told us there were fire restrictions.

The brightest of stars became bewitching when night fell and we all settled down to sleep in our tents.

Suddenly terror seized me in the dark. I was whisked away to the night of 43 years before, when in an identical situation – that of a hot night at Sorrento in a tent, on a stretcher beside the man called Ken, him with outstretched hand to molest me. People have admired me for possessing a good memory for it provides me with vivid recollection of things past, but on that night at Waterloo Bay it was a curse. Tears trickled down my face as I lay there in the dark, recalling years before of being shell-shocked the next morning down at Sorrento, lying on the beach, aching to be alone, sitting there stunned on the sand after fleeing from the house at the sight of my molester.

The night was long at Waterloo Bay as I longed to tell Kerryn what I "saw" to my horror. The memory of Sorrento clung like a leech even when morning broke. I ate little for breakfast, longing to be alone. I thought no-one bar Kerryn would understand; it would seem ludicrous to the others to learn that night of 43 years before had tormented me still. Yet, it was volcanic in nature. The nightmare of 43 years before had laid dormant down all those years and showed no signs of eruption. The suddenness of it shocked me. Oh, the beauty of the bay! And yet, its beauty deepened the sadness that swept over me, as I walked slowly about on the stretch of sand alone.

When we moved on from that bay, we had to climb some steep slopes as we hugged the coast. At some point I was seized with fright at the closeness of the cliff to the walking track and I burst out that I was unable to go any further. The others looked at me as I broke out in tears. I felt a fool but rage and grief had overwhelmed me. It was not the most fitting place to make known why rage and grief troubled me. Kerryn came to my aid as best she could, telling the rest tersely what had happened in the night. I was led like a little child to the top of the climb.

I stumbled away on my own at the top as the others surveyed the sight of the ocean. I sat on a large rock removed from them all.

They appeared stunned and at a loss to know what to do to help. Then Janine collected herself and she came over, put her arm around me.

"It's not your fault, Dad," she said.

To this day I do not understand fully what she meant. I did not seek an explanation. I only know that to this day I recall her words of unspeakable comfort to my soul. Then, there was Stephen, who in the presence of all of us prayed for me. Belinda prayed as well.

Back home I asked myself: Will that dark act of bygone years now haunt me for the rest of my days? As already mentioned, I had visited a Jewish naturopath some years before when, in the course of seeking to locate the source of an ailment I had then, the matter of that dark act had risen. She told me to write about it – the 'volcano' had rumbled in her presence. Remember that I was to write all that had happened at Sorrento and then burn the evidence to erase it from my mind forever. Waterloo Bay proved that such advice had failed me.

Kerryn wisely advised me at home to calm myself with music. I took to listening over and over Satie's 'Gymnopedie'. Each time I played it, I was carried back to Waterloo Bay just to recall thankfully the beauty of its beach. 'Gymnopedic' had some power even to carry me down to Williamstown, where as a seven year old I was 'adrift' from the other children of Sutherland's institution on Williamstown's foreshore, alone, but innocent of perversion and lust and shame.

The shock and its ensuing distress of that first night at Wilson's Prom threatened to continue to haunt, – a month later I decided to contact a Christian counsellor.

She proved to be very understanding, and she sought to show that I would become a stronger person for all that had taken place in my life. She suspected that the sexual abuse at Sorrento was even to be bundled up with what took place before I was 19 – to do with my early life at the Homes. I began to see I was easy prey for my predator, fragile before I was 19. I felt foolish for visiting her for counsel at 61 years of age, but she said most poignantly that although the Sorrento abuse occurred 43 years before; "At Wilson's Promontory you were 19!" Back home I broke down and cried at the words... "you were 19!" Yes, it was a kind of levitation in being caught up at Waterloo Bay and then taken back to Sorrento, – a kind of time warp whereby I was whisked back to that cursed night more than four decades previous.

After a soothing holiday at Lakes Entrance, I saw my counsellor for a second time. She got me thinking about the longing for a father when I was young, which surprised me as I often felt a longing for my mother at the Homes. She also got me thinking of my wariness of men, of the wariness I had for a particular man who had become quite recently one of the closest friends I had ever known.

Did I gain much from the counselling? I was hopeful that God had tied up the wild dog well and truly.

Bethel life was proving to be a trying year when there was a certain coming and going taking place – some key members were having to leave us because of circumstances related to careers. Some senior folk of the split church thankfully decided to become members – reliable believers with a wealth of experience. There was even Alex and his wife, who in their declining years had decided to move out further east from where they lived to be closer to their family. Alex and his wife had proved to be a blessing right to the end – particularly in helping some believers who were living shattered lives. Only one family was leaving discontented – the father was such a contentious fellow to the extent that I fell out of his favour only because I claimed that Christianity is a religion, just as James 1:26 says.

While there was the threat of numbers dwindling at Bethel, the spiritual temperature pointed to good health, if good attendances at our midweek meetings were a guide.

And the spiritual health of a number of Bethel's people were all the better for attending the South Yarra Presbyterian Church Sunday evenings. We at Bethel had no Sunday evening service. The fellowship at South Yarra was very sweet. It felt like a revival, with many adults creating a buzz through their excitement at knowing Christ. They sang and talked much about the Lord, before and after the service of lively preaching by Professor Milne. It was heaven on earth.

One couple, who had come from the split church, wondered if Bethel should explore the possibility of joining a good number of those who had broken away from their pastor of old, and had formed a new fellowship further east of us. As we were losing key people at Bethel in the new year of 2004, I made plans to visit the new church for evening worship to see if we may find it of benefit to join them as a fixed fellowship, in order for we of Bethel to survive more comfortably.

On the upside, the new church attracted me, since doctrinally they had much in common with Bethel, as well as being a fellowship that seemed to follow the type of ministry that John MacArthur exercised. I had great admiration for the famed American pastor.

The vicissitudes of life at Bethel caused me to ponder about what happened at Waterloo Bay, though not in a way that haunted. It had nothing to do with sexual abuse, though stemming from it, I suppose. It was another issue that made me mindful of my vulnerability and sensitivity that threatened to work as a curse in the church. It compelled me with resolve to help form a sound shield for my defencelessness. Yes, a shield to protect me, a shield as a trustworthy weapon. Understanding my vulnerability and sensitivity was therefore a shield used offensively in the light of any weakness I possessed, and was to drive me to see in my helplessness the need to trust in the sovereign power of God. As I wrote in my diary in December: "The weaker part of me says 'Give in.' The stronger part: 'No, endure, though the likes of some people tell me with antagonism what to do.'"

That December also gave rise to disturbing news concerning my sister Joyce.

She had had an operation for a cancerous tumour. This was followed up with a scan, the news of such results that Joyce did not want to know as to have a happy Christmas.

Thoughts of Joyce possibly dying caused me to soliloquise on the times we had together since we first learnt of one another when I was 15 and she was 13 –

> "Remember how I met you first? I am not sure if I ever told you about your name swimming around in my head at high school when I first learnt of you and your name. Remember, Sis, those early days when I stayed on weekends with you

in your tiny terrace house in Victoria St? Remember when your 'Dad' got free tickets for the musical *The Pyjama Game?* The fun we often had in you trying to sing with a male voice operatically and I joined you in with falsetto? The joy you had, Sis, in seeing Kerryn's and my three little children in their early days? You were so kind when our family was left devastated at leaving Swan Hill. You have been a strange sister in many ways, but I love you."

After Christmas Joyce learnt that no more cancer had been discovered but she had to begin chemotherapy. Under that treatment she was in relatively good spirits. When we saw her, she seemed to be her own self. Yet, by early February it was discovered that the chemotherapy had failed to keep any possible cancer at bay – it was spreading in her stomach. Another type of chemotherapy was to be tried.

Meanwhile, there were testing times at Bethel. Two key couples had to depart in connection with their careers. Kerryn and I would be overseas in March to visit Chris and Janine, during their working holiday there. My diary recorded at the time that one key fellow "is flitting around like a butterfly this summer" – meaning that he had often been absent from worship with us. (A.W. Tozer lamented the season of summer for church life, as many go missing too often for worship then. It becomes a shut-down season, just when the pastor would like to see the church life not suffering from lethargy.) As well as others of long-standing in the fellowship needing help of all kinds when our numbers were decreasing – our new folk hankered for the joyful past that they knew before their former church had split.

Still, what I had learnt years before from Merlin Carothers about praising God in all circumstances stayed with me, therefore I was able to praise

God for the privileges I had, while seeing the likelihood also of a wider ministry in getting a book about the Gospel of Mark published, and perhaps the possibility of my autobiography being published also, once it was reworked to highlight my miraculous conversion to Christ.

With Joyce having the dreaded, untreatable ovarian cancer – a cancer that moves oh so swiftly and without warning – Kerryn and I wondered about going overseas to England, yet Joyce encouraged us to go.

For other reasons I was most apprehensive about going away. There was my fear of heights to be considered – particularly heights of unfamiliar places in England. As I did not wish to cloud the holiday so as to spoil the time away for Kerryn's sake, it was suggested that I try hypnosis to overcome such a phobia that seemed to be going from bad to worse as I grew older. I went "under" several times with a local doctor and tried out the lifts in multi-story places at Knox City Shopping Centre in order to experience looking out of windows from great heights, but all to no avail. Then, there was the feeling of homesickness that crept on me as the time drew near for the day to leave Australia.

As it was, my anxiety grew acute, mostly at leaving Joyce and perhaps never seeing her again. We had only been in England for one week when she told me over the phone that the doctor at the clinic seemed reluctant to tell her that the new radiotherapy was not having an effect. Her anxiety led me to think that I should leave for home. I flew home and found her gravely ill. She consoled me with: "I am honoured that you have come home. I am glad you are here." Yet I grieved that Kerryn could not share such an anxious time when she was oceans away.

Was I right in coming back home after only a week? Just when days found Joyce in good spirits, doubt crept in. Joyce said that my decision to cut short the holiday was "my problem." I had to restrain myself from being overwhelmed by regret.

Perhaps the specialist, who told me over the phone when he felt pressed for an answer before we left for England, was right in saying that Joyce may live until August. Yet in early April we spent time visiting Joyce after Kerryn returned from abroad and Joyce would receive us favourably. Once she asked me to read something from the Scriptures. I chose Luke 12 and assured her that despite what lay ahead, in God's eyes she was worth far more than many sparrows, and she gave me a big hug before we left the hospital ward.

By the end of July 2004, however, it seemed that Joyce sensed the end was near. She was put on morphine, and she was transferred to a hospice in Broadmeadows. Sweet but sad memories flooded my soul of the times that Joyce and I had down the years.

Church work was hard to cope with, but thoughts of future glory for Joyce were enhanced by listening often to Elgar's most beautiful *Serenade On Strings*.

Kerryn and I visited Joyce one night and we took hymn books with us:

"Would you like us to sing a hymn?" I asked.

"Yes, sing that one for me."

Joyce came to some life as we sang.

"And what about *And Can It Be?*"

"Yes, please," she answered. "I remember it from the Billy Graham Crusade."

Brightening up a little more as she reminisced, she said, "I was only 15, and I should have been at least 17 to be in the Crusade Choir."

"That was cheeky," I commented.

Over the next few days Joyce was hanging on for life, but I felt concerned about her striving to hang on in the evening of August 2, when Kerryn, our eldest daughter Belinda and I were present beside Joyce, and I felt constrained to whisper to her, "Let go, Sis. Fall back in the arms of God." She fell back and died peacefully in Jesus.

In truth my relationship with Joyce was a roller-coaster ride over some years, so that the words "She loves me...she loves me not" would come to mind, and yet I could not help but love her.

Three days after Joyce's funeral Kerryn and I visited brother Robert up at Ararat on what was a good and worthwhile visit. Recall that some visits would seem fruitless because of his chronic schizophrenia. We told him of Joyce's death but we were not surprised that Robert was unable to understand in full the loss of our sister.

We became grandparents for the first time in November 2004, when Janine gave birth to a boy, Calvin, in England, after Janine was perilously close to losing her life when she contracted septicaemia. Kerryn had quickly booked a flight to England when we learnt about Janine's recovery, and assisted Chris and Janine with their newborn. What joy to be grandparents.

Bethel was proving to be more trying as time went by with numbers diminishing, but God is One of all comfort, the Father of mercies, as Paul the apostle reminds us. Thankfully we were still "a peaceful church," just as Alex used to say, and there came into my sights very providentially the writings of A.W. Tozer. Tozer has been considered a prophet of God in the 1950's, his writings reflecting his astute reflection on the state of the church. He arrested me with an essay titled *Faith Dares to Fail*, declaring "No man is worthy to succeed until he is willing to fail." This word came at a time when I grew tempted to hand in my resignation to Bethel, lamenting at what appeared as a deadness in lack of true worship of God among the people, as well as the depressing decrease in numbers. Was I willing to weather what was happening to Bethel, and willing to fail? Could it be that in being willing to fail, God may bless us with success when I learnt that I was not less dear to God because of apparent failure?

It heartened me, if you know what I mean, to read Tozer about how crowds and new converts "can be accomplished without help of the Holy Spirit." One only needed "a good personality and a shrewd knowledge of human nature...to be a success in religious circles." This Tozer tonic compelled me to wait on the Holy Spirit, Who appeared so much in the man's thinking. Ah, I was not aware of the Spirit as I should have been! Tozer says that longing for an awareness of the deity of the Holy Spirit can rightly become an "obsession". And so it was, as I became wonderfully aware of the Spirit's presence to the degree that I ceased to be shaken by what was happening at Bethel – or what was not happening!

A key family with two children were leaving the church on account of too few children being in our congregation. If it had happened before I experienced a greater fullness of the Spirit, I would have been king-hit.

Therefore, much changed at Bethel, or more to the point with me. My preaching on the Spirit in the book of Acts hushed the congregation more than once. My fervency bred contagion of a sweet kind among a number of people. Then, when the Lord's Supper was celebrated with all its simplicity, I believed I saw Jesus in His presence several times over the congregation that took my breath away and left me in wonder at His love. Even our studies in the book of Joshua mid-week throbbed with pulsation at the thought of pursuing God as we ought. In November I wrote in my diary: "Never known a time when You have spoken so much to me through Your word. Then again, never known a time when I have spoken so much to You, my great God." The year of 2005 seemed to have been outwardly a blighted year at Bethel, and yet it had been the most blessed since I first knew the Lord.

The following year was marked by Bethel allowing me to take two months leave in order to do some intensive work as Australian representative for the Society of the Distribution of Hebrew Scriptures (SDHS). I was still to preach at Bethel Sunday by Sunday, but to repeat a series on Romans that I had done six years before. Paul encouraged me to do Romans again – not only to free me up more for SDHS, but because he believed the former series was worth repeating.

Time for SDHS was well spent. Street distribution of hardback copies of both Old and New Testaments was carried out where Jews live in preponderant numbers. Libraries were sought for lodgement of the Testaments for public use. The Testaments were also posted Australia-wide for those desiring to give them free of charge to any Jews. Testaments were sent to prisons with permission as well.

The lady called Amy, was one who loved God's ancient people, and often accompanied me in distribution. She was quite elderly, a little hampered by a limp, but keen to walk the considerable distance required in shopping areas.

Actually, three of us – Amy, a man called Graeme, and I – found street distribution quite absorbing. Once Graeme and I entered a travel agency where a young Jewish lady was approached.

I introduced ourselves and asked her if she would like to take Hebrew Scriptures free of charge.

> "Yes, I'll take a Tenach (Old Testament)."
> "Would you like a New Testament as well?" I asked
> "No, thanks. We don't believe in the New Testament."
> "Whose 'we'?" I enquired.

Brief silence elapsed, and then I told her that the New Testament was written by Jewish people. She took a New Testament, but suddenly a lady colleague broke in to prevent the younger lady from further conversation, except that the younger lady softly slipped in a word as we turned to leave the agency: "It is good to have an open mind".

The Ultra-Orthodox men with big black beards and high black hats looked forbidding, and proved to be difficult to convince. One appeared quite friendly one day in Balaclava Road but gave us little time, insisting we go farther east to St Kilda, to visit prostitutes who he reckoned needed more help than he did. Another one rigidly expressed his belief in the Tenach (Old Testament) as God's final revelation, and that animal sacrifices will be carried out again, once the Temple in Jerusalem is rebuilt. Another, who threatened to call on 30 of his Orthodox colleagues to grab me and frogmarch me out of the street, stood over me and shouted: "Jesus is burning in hell!"

Yet, many Old and New Testaments were given out over the two months, with joy found in giving God's life-giving word to His ancient people.

Katerina was born in September 2006, the second child for Chris and Janine and our second grandchild. Kerryn and I often looked after Calvin who was 22 months at the time.

So, 2006 passed by with a certain contentment in ministry at Bethel, and continued that way until the year's end with street distribution of Hebrew Scriptures carried out regularly. I was certainly buoyed up by reading more of Tozer's counsel; I could not get enough of the man. If ever I felt that there was a lack of fervour in the church, I thanked God it was so, as it meant that I was being compelled to lean heavily on the Holy Spirit. I learnt to adore the attributes of God far more. Tozer arrested me with: "If God is the Supreme God, then our highest blessedness on earth must lie in knowing Him as perfectly as possible."

I kept "seeing" Jesus rapturously every time we had the Lord's Supper, at one time close to laughing with joy! At times I felt an unusual nearness of one of God's angels at my right side whenever I was alone.

Of course, Satan was ever seeking to gain a foothold on me, even using believers. One church member said she read the Word and did not need men to get in the way with their comments. Then there was the fellow who wondered why it took so long to prepare a sermon. In addition, a new believer to our congregation was upsetting quite a few with his hard line about remarriage, so that there sprang up some evil things being said against him, when we should have been more compassionate and sought to understand him.

One of our prized communion chairs went missing, and then it appeared the next morning (Monday) at the church's front door! It was around the time when the middle-aged man, who frequented Bethel from time to time gave me a purse that he had made. He insisted that I have it. On the Sunday night when Kerryn opened the purse, there inside was $500! Was it a set-up? He had been recommended as a good Christian man years before my time, to a lady of Bethel who had been a Middle Eastern missionary and sought a marriage partner here in faraway Australia. She admitted to being deceived: the fellow was far from being a Christian. There was tension between the two of them at home, and in church they sat apart from one another whenever the husband attended Bethel. He still warmed to me a little because I had a love for Bach's music, still teasing me about my inability to pronounce Bach's name as gutturally as they do in Germany. Yet I was wary of him. Had I been set up by him with the $500? Needless to say, we returned the money to him.

The year of 2007 saw us pressing on at Bethel with what can be common ups and downs in a fellowship, with some people leaving our small number, and some new faces bringing hope of greater fervency amongst us for the Faith.

My brother Robert was admitted to the Ararat hospital on quite a few occasions, as he kept falling over at home. If Robert's deteriorating health was not enough of a concern, something at Bethel was soon to reveal how some could say that they would not want to be in my shoes because I was a pastor but the same people could give you the most trouble. Brother Paul knew the struggles I had and, even though he seldom said anything by way of encouragement, he made it plain a few times in writing that he prized my friendship and ministry, believing that encouragement expressed too often can be "habitual and insincere." Genuine encouragement is often rare in many churches, and a pastor may conclude that he is being taken for granted. However, a crisis often reveals who can be counted for support of the pastor, though some may have said little to urge you on previously.

It was a certain crisis that caused me to write in my diary: "I must act quickly to secure Bethel's future: Perhaps we shall unite with another church." We had a good number of people who remained with us after the split in the Glen Waverley Gospel Chapel, and who still had links with the people of the newly formed congregation east of us.

Brother Ron was wary of us merging with another fellowship, even though we had much in common with them.

Although I admired John MacArthur, the renowned American Evangelical and Reformed pastor, who appeared to be the inspiration behind the other church, I had to think hard about Bethel uniting with that fellowship when, with some faith we could perhaps ride out the severe trial we knew, and pray fervently, just as Alex, a leading elder, had experienced years before, and who saw Bethel revived in numbers and fervour over time.

When you have a diminishing congregation, as the pastor you ponder much on the possibilities that tempt you to merge with a stronger fellowship, for quite a number of considerations must be calmy weighed out. The Bethel folk were wary of the other fellowship, with its strength perhaps depriving me of what gifted ministry I possessed. Indeed, they were fearful of not being able to use the gifts any of them had. Did not the other church already have sufficiently gifted members, so that we of little Bethel could be railroaded and our gifts would fall into disuse? Was it wise for us to merge?

A night came when in sleeplessness I got out of bed, crept to the back room to look at the stars, but I found it hard to pray. Kerryn sleepily came into the room, and sought to comfort me, telling me to remain strong and wait on the Lord, this while knowing it was in the days when her father was dying. Our church secretary's exodus with his family had been spiritually like losing a loved one to dying. I rang my friend in U.S.A. who said yet again that he had gone through a similar crisis once and told me to 'tough it out' – not to be tempted to merge with the other fellowship and wait patiently on God.

It seemed all right for my U.S.A. friend to tell me to 'tough it out', he was unaware of my different temperament – sensitive, given to fear and uncertainty, hesitant to grasp firmly the nettle, him failing to see that I was not exactly a man of mettle as he was.

On Sunday, August 26, I preached to a mere ten people. Only two days before that worship service, I attended the funeral for Brother Roy who, with his wife, had attended the church faithfully and enthusiastically over many years, and whose shouts in the midst of sermons of "Hallelujah!" "Praise the Lord!" "Amen, brother" were to be missed. The lady the church secretary used to provide transport to Bethel from some distance each Sunday for many years, had left us too.

At the same time that Kerryn and I learnt that her father had died, I was informed that my brother Robert was ill, and I visited him several hours away at a place of care in Willaura, where he was staying until he was able to return to Ararat and his own home. Kerryn and I had our personal trials to contend with, as well "the pressure of my concern" for Bethel (2 Cor 11:28). Still, the beauty of Willaura gave me heart – after seeing Robert, to look at the lovely lake, the golden sun going down, swans swimming across the water...God could be counted on, despite any frailty, and faltering, or failure.

I wrote around that time in a diary drenched with page after page of whirling words –

"You are forcing me, Father, to lean on you so much. Dark thoughts threaten to rush in as soon as I drop my guard. I need to dwell on Your sovereignty and believe all is well when it seems not."

Anyone Can Know

While trials threatened to overtake me, there was great relief in devoting time to editing a manuscript I had written up years before, often submitting it in vain to a number of publishers, just to meet rejection, so that I eagerly took to reworking it with new hope. The overriding reason for reworking the manuscript lay in my change of purpose for the story of my boyhood life in the Sutherland Homes for neglected children: I was still uncomfortably convicted about success through a secular press by playing down or omitting altogether an account of the great event of the Lord saving me by His grace for eternal salvation at the age of 17. It had been difficult to write cryptically and skimpily about my conversion as the manuscript stood originally, fearing the story of my conversion would be too jarring to be considered for publication by any unchristian publisher. The manuscript had to be changed radically – almost like a complete overhaul of the work.

Yes, it was a blessing that the manuscript had been rejected by secular publishers.

Why need I play down the one event that dramatically changed me from being a sinner under the wrath of God to one who, in joy that could not be contained at the time, had found planted in his heart a living hope of eternal life through His mercy? It required many new pages and more – as the manuscript would be more satisfying by the story of new life and its marvellous aftermath, when I ceased to be the same person I was before 17.

Therefore, the manuscript underwent sweeping changes, making central to my story a chapter known as *Crossing from Death to Life*. It was to also have questions about my parentage solved, and to include a Tasmanian reunion with many discovered relatives who all heard me preach at the reunion in a little church up beyond Burnie on *For Me to Live is Christ*.

I was becoming far less sensitive also about my under-privileged background as a child. Several factors played a part. Kerryn believed that I had a story worth telling widely – about life at Sutherland and the astonishing way the Lord graciously saved me there. When I also began delving into my family history, I felt more fulfilled, as there was an ancestral past that left me less puzzled and perplexed about my early childhood.

In fact, in growing less ashamed, there was the contrasting tendency to become too proud and to see my past as more unique than the history of other people, particularly after successful publication, when the likes of one person thought upon reading *The Silver Poplar* that I had "an incredibly strong spirit to have endured all that life had presented." An ex-high school contemporary was to think it had been written to set myself up as having had a more unique boyhood than the likes of him. It was never written with that in mind for, had I succumbed to such an ulterior motive, it should have been plain to see that only by the grace of God did I come through all of what I experienced.

The next move for a possible merge was to discuss the issue with our own church members. Of the leaders, Brother Ron was not opposed to further discussion with the larger church, but he was cautious. For one thing, he thought highly of my ministry and wondered if I would have any ministry at all in the merge of the two fellowships.

When our church members gathered to consider a possible merge, some other members, like Brother Ron, were concerned about my future role if a merge was to take place.

Another meeting with the pastor suggested some promise of good things to come, if we at Bethel were willing to contemplate our building being enlarged in the near future to accommodate his large numbers, since his church was only renting on Sundays from a school that hardly contained them. There was talk of an enlargement of our building, maybe to establish a Bible college – similar to John MacArthur-style.

At such a time one of our members, Brother Neil, was close to death. He and I had become close friends since his arrival at Bethel. I visited him in hospital –

> "You can still smile, Neil," I commented.
>
> "Yes," he said feebly, "it is because I know the Lord."
>
> He added, "You know…you are almost the closest friend I have ever had."
>
> All I could do was to clasp his hands.
>
> "I am so glad," I responded.
>
> "Stay sound and strong," he advised.

He was shaking, for it appeared that the chill of death was closing in. We clasped hands again.

A week later Neil died. His desire had been for me to take his funeral, at which I preached on a matter that had come to Neil as a great revelation through conversation I once had with him – I spoke on "Jesus still is a man," as based on Acts 17.

A real joy in June 2008, our third grandchild was born. He was named Charlie, the first child for Stephen and Freya, they were immensely proud parents.

Sadness fell on us as we had our last worship service at Bethel. I had been there 11 years as their pastor. I preached a farewell sermon to do with what forms a model church – Ephesians beautifully describes what any church should be. We lunched together for the last time.

Several spoke about the way they saw our future, a little uncertain of being in a larger congregation and becoming "lost." Still, most felt we had little choice but to merge.

Had we at Bethel made a mistake? When meeting with the other church's elders, our small flock of Bethel pressed to have me made an elder without the need for probation. Was I to be an elder over the two merged congregations as well? No, but to be over Bethel's people only! In defence it was said that their own elders were ready to recognize me as an elder, but allegedly their people were not.

All the same, I was invited to attend the weekly meetings with their pastor's fellow elders at his office. A month or two passed by, without any indication of the appointment of me as an elder. It looked like there was a hesitancy about having me to preach, though it is true that only one elder preached from time to time, apart from the pastor.

I dearly missed preaching and carrying out pastoral work in visiting Bethel's people, as well as doing street work for evangelism. Martyn Lloyd Jones said of preaching that it is the highest vocation any Christian can have. How true! How true it sorely felt after I had discovered the writings of A. W. Tozer. He was a man full of the Holy Spirit's power, ruthless with himself as well of certain preachers, whose lives did not match their words behind the pulpit.

Once he said –

> "There is today no lack of Bible teachers to set forth the principles of the doctrines of Christ, but too many of these seem satisfied to teach the fundamentals of the faith year after year, strangely unaware that there is in their ministry no manifest Presence, nor anything unusual in their personal lives. They minister constantly to believers who feel within their breasts a longing which their teaching simply does not satisfy."

Tozer penned these words in a work he called *The Pursuit of God*, a classic that proved to be "a masterly study of the inner life by a heart thirsting after God." Tozer was a farm boy with only a one-room country school education, but he became a giant of Christian scholarly. His thirst for education was such that as a young man he even got down on his knees to pray for the understanding of Shakespeare's works. He was all for orthodoxy but wanted it with power, the power of the Holy Spirit. He figured that many of us as believers are afraid to seek the Spirit's power less the Spirit prompts us for courage that we do not dare to possess. Yet the Spirit seeks the best for us.

> "It will be a new day for us when we put away false notions and foolish fears and allow the Holy Spirit to fellowship with us as He wants to do, to talk to us as Christ talked to His disciples by the Sea of Galilee. After that there can be no more loneliness, only the glory of the never-failing Presence."

A friend of mine took offence at my admiration of Tozer, saying that he was a 'heretic', for he believed in the autonomy of the human will when it comes to salvation. Yet, I read enough of Tozer to know that he spoke eloquently – as if he could not help himself – in favour of the sovereignty of God in salvation; what many regard as solely a human response to God when it comes to repentance and faith are an act of God.

The great man was not faultless, as none of us are. However, I for one found he hit the mark about both "doctrine and life…bring a strong regard and awe" (George Herbert). I strove to be exemplary in life as well as in doctrine, though there seemed little opportunity to use the gifts God gave me.

Then after some months, to my surprise the pastor included me among his elders to do an evening series in the rented school hall, on what he called "theology on legs" – a quaint way to describe a series on practical theology. I chose the subject of Humility as it appears in Paul's letter to the Philippians. Paul writes of thinking less about ourselves and more of the interest of others, with Jesus being our model of humility. Interestingly, the original language speaks of Jesus being obedient to even death on the cross, with no definite article before the word cross, in order to lay great emphasis on the character of His death – the shame and degradation of it. In other words, He dared to be branded and die a criminal. To think that a death measured out for criminals should be such that leads to Him ultimately being the One to whom every knee in heaven and on earth and under the earth should bow!

A.W. Tozer inspired me when for the first time I had the chance to preach in the morning. Our new church seemed to be a victim of what Tozer called 'textualism', that is, "simply orthodoxy without the Holy Ghost." John Macarthur's doctrine had been regarded as the hallmark of orthodoxy, correct belief. Indeed, it may well be, but our new church was seen by me as Bible-taught rather than Spirit-taught. I had felt the power of the Spirit in my final months at Bethel and I desired for everyone to know the exhilaration of knowing the indwelling Spirit as well.

I made up a story about three brothers to hold the interest of the large morning congregation, from the very beginning of the sermon. Three brothers wish to stay with you for some time, as they are related to you. They want to tell you that you have fallen into a fortune.

The first brother is to hand over to you your fortune eventually. The second one has worked hard to become the inheritor, and you are enjoined to carry out whatever he tells you to do, though you cannot see him for a while.

The fortune is tied up with the ways and the language of the land to which they belong. As for the third brother, he is to bring to life the words of the second brother, so that you understand the way to possess with assurance your inheritance – yes, the third one translates for you what the second one is commending you to do. However, his instructions are a dead letter unless the third one translates, unless you also carry out more than mere snippets of the second brother's commands.

The three brothers are an analogy of the Trinity. The Father has promised an inheritance. The Son laboured and gave His life to save us, but not without leaving instructions or commands to obey. The Holy Spirit brings what may be a dead letter of instruction unless we pay heed to Him the Spirit of Truth. He is the Spirit of Truth to ensure we do not escape notice of what Jesus commands and claims of us. The words of Jesus, as in the Scriptures, are paper and ink, but through the fulness of the Spirit we can get His personal attention.

Jesus also refers to the Spirit as the Spirit of Truth when speaking of witnessing to unbelievers. Apologetics may play a part in our assurance of eternal life, but without the Spirit of Truth we may as well address dead people in a cemetery, as to address people walking our streets. You can be sure that you are not eclipsing the glory of Christ by paying close attention to the Holy Spirit. He has come to glorify Christ. You cannot know Christ and His love unless the Spirit speaks to you about Him.

Other things were preached to endear the hearers' hearts to the Spirit, so that a considerable number of people expressed warmly their appreciation of the attention drawn to Him whom Tozer called "The Forgotten One".

I never became an elder at the new church. I preached twice in a year and a half. I was given visiting to do, but it was restricted. A request to lead evening bible study was reluctantly granted, but promoted formally and briefly to be run by "Mr Smith". The long and the short of it lay in my decision to retire from the ministry altogether. Bethel retained our prized property, with the pastor and his elders desiring to acquire it. Instead, we of the little band of Bethelites decided to sell it to people of another denomination with the purpose of establishing a home church for needy and believing Christian Sudanese. Any profits from the sale being donated to missions.

A hot summer followed, and on several occasions the sun would rise 'innocently' with the morning air being cool until the sun would finally reveal its menace with searing heat of more than 40c mid-afternoon. Relief at times would follow after a day or two. Once as I sat to read the whole letter of Romans, our windows began to rattle, forked lightning ran across the sky and thunder rumbled. It was so awe-inspiring and a reminder of what a young man formerly of the large church said about God's sovereign power, that I merely sat at my desk and watched long the lightning lead the way for the roar of the thunder.

Then came February with the tragedy of the widespread fires of Black Saturday. One hundred and seventy-three lives were lost in our state of Victoria. The Prime Minister said that "the fury of hell" had come down on the state and on "good people." There was a deafening silence about God, but we were still urged to remember the fire victims in "prayers."

In the new year of 2009, time moved on quickly as I became absorbed with the writing of all kinds for the sake of publishing. Chief among the various things I had in eagerness of mind was the submission of my autobiography.

On April 1st news was received that a publisher in Sydney expressed the wish to publish *The Silver Poplar*. I already had a book published on biblical meditation several years before by a Scottish publisher, but *The Silver Poplar* promised to be a more satisfying accomplishment. I began dreaming and imaging various people reading it, their eyes being opened to what had remained a secret for many of them over the years. It was strange that whereas once I was sensitive to the point of shame about having been raised in an institution for neglected children, I still felt tempted with pride of having been raised in a life of neglect. Was not such a life unique? Had I not made good despite the disadvantages I had been under? Yet, to curb any enticement to pride, God humbled me as I reminded myself that I was what I was by the sheer sovereign grace of God. For that reason, anyone could know about my boyhood past. I dreamt most of all about many people reading of the miraculous way Christ saved me for eternal life; I dreamt of readers then believing in Jesus for the first time and crossing over from death to life too.

My years as a pastor had come to a close 'in ministry at the large church that we at Bethel had merged with but not merged with'. I sought the Lord for guidance about what to do in my retiring years. It seemed there was an opening to write books. *A Tree By a Stream* had been reviewed favourably some years before, overseas and here in Australia. I thought of writing short stories and begun one called *The Way Out*. I had a manuscript for what I called *The Tapestry of Mark*, and used some of its material when I preached occasionally, now beyond my end of ministry.

As well as the story of my life at the Sutherland Homes, *The Silver Poplar* was to refer to the discovery my sister Joyce and I made about our infant days, about our father and mother, and about the discovery of a brother we had known nothing about. *The Silver Poplar* was to refer to our visits to our brother in Ararat, but through lack of knowledge there could only be scant references to Aradale, at Ararat the mental institution that Robert and our mother had lived in.

When I rang Kerryn with the news of *'The Silver Poplar'*, I cried so much that I could barely speak. To hear her say "I'm proud of you," to learn of our three children being happy, helped me cry all the more, "Oh, thank you, Father."

In May 2009 Kerryn and I visited Ararat for the first time to see Aradale and were to become far more acquainted with the history of the mental asylum of Aradale through a 90-minute tour. Perched on a hill outside the town of Ararat, the asylum is still said to be the largest abandoned building in Victoria, taking almost two hours to walk intently around it. It comprises 63 buildings. It was a town in years gone by within a town, the town of Ararat – having had its own market gardens, orchard, vineyard, pigs and other livestock. At its peak it had 2000 patients and staff. It sat on 240 acres and was built in 1863.

I told the tourist guide at the outset that both my mother and brother had been inmates in the asylum, so he seemed to take us a little more slowly around the place, painting an informative but sometimes grim picture of what took place there at Aradale in over more than 100 years of existence. We passed the chapel that was converted from a fire pump station. Did my mother and brother enter it? Surrounding the whole asylum was what was known as the Ha-Ha-Wall, which from the inside presented an unscalable forbidding face to patients, should they have ever contemplated escape. On the outside of the Ha-Ha wall lay a sloping trench. There was a large hall used for dancing and showing films. Did my mother and brother enter there? Dance? See films?

The grimmest of places were pointed out. There was the pharmacy, where heavier and heavier doses were made up as patients grew used to milder ones. We passed by the wings where the patients were cooped up at night under the fearful eye of ever vigilant staff. We passed by small dark rooms, where patients were kept in solitary confinement until they were ready to return to their compound. There was the extra-large kitchen seen before we walked outside to the morgue. It is believed around 13,000 people died in Aradale over the years.

A particular sadness fell on me the next day when we eventually arrived home, until I started feeling grateful I had an understanding soulmate in Kerryn, and a sound mind, together with a well-grounded hope in God, all to be thankful for.

On the brighter and also lighter side of things related to Aradale, there was what had to do in bygone years with the ministry that Gordon Moyes – best known later as General Superintendent of the Wesleyan Mission of Australia – exercised at the mental hospital, when he was the pastor of the Ararat Church of Christ in the Fifties.

On his first visit to the asylum one Sunday morning, Gordon approached the guarded front gates with his pass. He walked then towards a huge building, presuming that it held the chapel, where uniformed warders were seen herding a long line of people through the door.

> "Good morning, I'm the new chaplain and I have come to conduct the service here," said Gordon. Answered a certain warden that he had approached, "So you're the new chaplain, are you? Nice to have you. Just get into line with the other people and you'll be inside in no time."

"But I'm the new chaplain," said Gordon emphatically, "and I have to take the service!"

"Still, stay in line with the others, there's a good lad."

Attending the chapel was compulsory for every inmate if they were physically able to be there.

On the first service there, Gordon stepped down from the pulpit in order to be closer to the strange people, who had "no light of sanity in their eyes," in order to speak simple-like to them of the life of Christ. Suddenly, in the middle of his sermon a lady got up from the back row, walked quietly down to the front, drew closer and closer to him until she leant forward and kissed him full on the lips, before quietly wandering back to her seat!

On Gordon's next occasion to visit Aradale, a fellow introduced himself to Gordon as Colonel James Rosmussen, Deputy Superintendent of the hospital, and kindly offered to give Gordon a guided tour. In the second week he met the Superintendent and mentioned that he had already met the Deputy Superintendent the week before.

The Deputy stared at him and then burst out laughing.

"Oh, that's who he was last Sunday? I'm surprised that he didn't introduce himself as Beethoven or Napoleon! Actually, he's quite a harmless fellow, and he knows much about the place."

Gordon said of Aradale's inmates that there was "no light of sanity in their eyes" upon seeing them at his first service in the chapel, but did their eyes deceive him?

After brooding over comments made by Aradale's psychiatrist that many of the patients at Aradale were quite sane if they kept on their medication, Gordon conceived a plan to hold a mid-week Bible class in which any interested and voluntary patients would study Matthew's Gospel verse by verse.

What response had he envisaged?

Awaiting him for the first session were 200 patients! Through one means or another every patient of the 200 were given a copy of Matthew's Gospel.

He divided the patients into discussion groups and appointed a leader for each group, so that they could also meet between classes during the week to learn verses or passages from the Gospel, and to discuss what was set out for the next Wednesday. One leader was "a highly intelligent man, well-educated," who had been cured of alcoholism and of the danger he caused through it, losing his family and friends but, of his own volition, did not wish to leave the mental asylum for fear of giving way to the old temptation. For sanity's sake he worked in the hospital's library.

After six months Gordon's Bible classes had gone through Matthew's Gospel to the very end. He decided to have a competition based on what had been learnt. Twenty competitors were chosen by chance to answer 100 questions. Until the day of the competition no-one knew who a competitor would be. To his amazement 18 of the chosen 20 competitors answered every question fired at them.

How as he desired was he to get one winner?

His church's ladies' group had donated a silver cup in the hope of one winner. Gordon prepared 150 new questions based on Matthew's Gospel. Even some quite exacting questions would be asked of the 18, such as: "What was the 5th name given in the list of the genealogy in Matthew 1?"

Came the eager day with the 200 patients buzzing with excitement. One by one the final 18 were quizzed, until 5 of the 18 remained unbeaten. Yet there was only one silver cup! "In a flash of Solomonic wisdom" Gordon announced that the cup would be put on display as the property of all the patients, and that the five winners would each be given "a bag of confectionery."

Our man carried out an effective ministry at Aradale that included appreciative social activities as well.

Naturally to hear of Gordon's ministry got me imagining my mother and brother attending the chapel, but I was never sure if they were mentally sound enough for the Bible class. Yet, at least there was that constant image of my brother Robert, after leaving Aradale and living in Ararat's community in his own home, carrying his Bible into town in the morning and sitting on the steps of Ararat's hotel in the main street to read it as people walked by. In a photo exhibition held in Ararat's town hall we were to see a lovely photo of Robert sitting on the hotel's steps with sunken eyes and his Bible lying open on his knees. Who knows what he knew of God's word?

How I ever had a sound mind and escaped anything like the schizophrenia of two generations before me, one never knows, except that the mercy of God endowed me with a mind fit for an insatiable thirst for reading and for knowledge from a very early age, and gave me a sound and retentive memory that proved to be an even greater blessing when Jesus revealed Himself to me.

That Jesus revealed Himself to me in the way He did was what I considered pivotal for two reasons in my autobiography *The Silver Poplar*. I hoped and prayed that it would dawn on believers in Christ that it was God's sovereign power that charmed me into His Kingdom; and for any others to consider their need to come to faith for eternal salvation.

Late that year, our eldest daughter Belinda did much to help promote the book. She arranged for a book launch at her church, and she enabled me to get the opportunity to give my testimony at the forthcoming Belgrave Heights Christian Convention that several thousand attends at Christmastime.

The book launch at the Donvale Presbyterian Church occurred on December 12 of that year of 2009. It was well attended by family and friends, among whom was Thomas, who had been born to Chris and Janine in November 2009, so that he was merely six weeks at the time. Little did we all realise the anxiety that lay ahead over Tom's first few years.

Prior to the Belgrave Heights Convention *The Silver Poplar* received favourable reviews, and had people saying one after the other that they could not put the book down. All the same, I remained still a little too self-conscious about my institutional life but fought against that dread by the desire ANYONE CAN KNOW, for I had a story that was to give God glory. Some praised the book for its ability to capture the times of the Fifties, others saw it as a Boy's Own Adventure. Even if some thought the book "sad," it heartened me to think that they sensed the pain of living in the institution.

One friend, who I always found compassionate, said in an email that it was "quite a task to write about your experiences in the Home, coming to terms with the past and seeing God's fingerprints in the journey." Another friend said that it must have taken courage to write *The Silver Poplar*. Indeed, the whirling emotion since its publication had made me wonder if I had done myself any good, but it was then that I had to look away from myself yet again and think of what God achieved all those years ago.

At the Belgrave Convention at the end of 2009 the *chairman* told me only to tell my testimony on the platform and not refer to *The Silver Poplar*! I followed his wish and in giving my testimony provoked the audience's thoughts first by answering a question that I myself had composed and which the interviewer on the stage asked: *What did the Prime Minister Kevin Rudd say to you just a few months ago?*

Facetiously I replied, "He did not tell me this thing personally, but he publicly apologised to all Australians who had lost their childhood in institutions and orphanages. I am to be numbered amongst them, and as a consequence he has promised me preferential entry to a nursing home in the future! To make up for a missing childhood, I can get ahead of others in applying for entry into a nursing home!"

Further questions led me to explain why I was in the institution in the first place, what life was like in it, what Christian influence ever existed in Sutherland, and when and how I was saved. I sneakily finished answering the set of questions in the interview with "I have had the privilege of two books published."

In the year of 2010 my brother Robert turned 70 and I drove up alone to celebrate his birthday with him. His health was declining considerably. Six months before my visit saw him allegedly falling off his bed at the nursing home while tying up his shoe laces, Robert ending up with 15 stitches in his head. Sometime after his health had so deteriorated that he had to go into the new nursing home in Ararat, his house was put up for auction.

As Robert's health declined, my foster-mother – dear Beryl – celebrated her 100th birthday in September with more than 300 people filling out the rearranged area of St John's church at Diamond Creek for the occasion. She looked extremely well for her age. It was only a week later that Kerryn and I heard Beryl's grandson, Jonathan, preach at Doncaster. In preaching he was far ahead of me at his age. His was one of the most telling sermons I have ever heard.

Kerryn and I paid Robert a visit a month later, travelling by train to Ararat. It began amusingly in the train from Melbourne before changing over to the country one: Kerryn and I watched with absorbing interest a nearby passenger who showed himself to be a young chef, folding his gear carefully and applying deodorant under his arms as the train powered on. At Ararat we took Robert, as arranged, by taxi to the RSL Club. He was weighed down with care, said little, often lowering his eyes as we spoke to him. I took him alone to the Sports Bar for a drink and, amid the noise of men who were watching horse races on two screens, Robert put his hands together with the tips of his fingers and silently said Grace before downing the shandy in his glass. When the three of us ordered lunch, once again Robert put his hands together and said Grace. Then, returning to the nursing home he placed his hands together to say Grace once more as he sipped at a small bottle of Coke. In the light of Gordon Moyes' ministry at Aradale, I wondered at what might have remained spiritual in Robert's poor mind, but we shall never know this side of eternity.

Life began busily in the new year of 2011. Chris and Janine's son was only fifteen months of age, Thomas was fighting for his life at the Monash Children's Hospital when his body was not producing bone marrow, thus in a quite pronounced way his fight for life in late February overshadowed the celebrating of our ruby wedding anniversary. Our anniversary occurred also as Belinda was preparing to marry Brent her fiancée. Chris' parents visited from Queensland to relieve Kerryn and me of helping Chris and Janine during baby Tom's fight for survival, enabling us to have a few days away. The holiday was cut short; things were too desperate regarding Tom. Chris's parents stayed on, as we all grew anxious about our grandson, our fourth grandchild. People everywhere were praying for his survival. It was hard not to cry.

Tom became subject to drug treatment and to very many blood transfusions time after time, all with no certainty of eventual survival for him. Months went by, but Tom's platelet levels began to rise, with some people who thought they were well-meaning by literally crossing their fingers for Tom.

Then, in the first weekend of early July 2011, as Kerryn and I were staying overnight at a country cottage in Healesville, Kerryn's mobile phone rang early next morning and cut out just as a lady we knew at Robert's nursing home rang to say merely: "I have some sad news." Kerryn left the cottage we were in to use the owner's phone to contact Ararat. Even before Kerryn returned to the cottage with the news, I sensed that Robert had died and I broke down in the cottage with loud uncontrollable grief. Sister Joyce had gone, now Robert. All those of my own blood, I was alone. Although he had been a chronic schizophrenic, spoke little, recalled little, and knew little, I loved him dearly. So too did Kerryn.

His was a sad life. We never knew how much he had suffered as a child, no more than the one grim thing he told us. It was just as well we did not know anymore. It would have deepened the sadness of his passing. For many of us it is just as well that we do not always know too much. And the beauty of our weekend retreat was lost in the sadness: the beauty of "White Rose Cottage" with its forty acres set in a valley surrounded by enchanted mountains. Back home I spent several days in tears.

We buried Robert in Ararat on July 9, five days after he died. Although only a few of Ararat attended the funeral, Robert had been well known in the town, where they all affectionately called him "Bobbie." My son put it so well when he said of Robert that he was "the last connection." For a moment of meditation at the funeral I had chosen Bach's *Capriccio on the Departure of a Beloved Brother* – it was a moving way of saying "Farewell, brother, farewell."

My faithfulness was to be tested sorely in a way that I had not dreamt of. Not long after my blood brother Robert died, the State Trustees, who had been the guardian of Robert's financial affairs, sent out a representative who informed me that I was entitled to claim an inheritance of Robert's estate, being his natural brother, with no other person entitled to it. Robert did not have a will. The representative had me sign for the "Grant of Letters of Administration of the Estate." To my amazement Robert's estate amounted to more than $1,150,000! This staggered Kerryn and me, who always had the impression that Robert had little to live on. We frequently bought him new clothes and other things to make life more comfortable for him.

Then came the bombshell. The State Trustees went on the hunt and discovered that Robert had an adoptive sister who was still alive in Bendigo. The State Trustees stated that according to law, his adoptive sister had the sole right to the estate. We did not know Robert had an adoptive sister. She had never been seen. When my sister and I first learnt of Robert, State Trustees began to rely on me for help; I became Robert's medical attorney. They sought my advice on his welfare, about Robert's house and his move to Ararat's nursing home. They leant on me concerning funeral arrangements. It rocked us that State Trustees had never sought to track the adoptive sister down earlier in order to assist them in care for Robert.

Fast forward – it is the year 2012. In late June we learnt that "a good gift was coming our way." It was in providence to come from our Father Who thought it best not to give us too much, and enough "to prevent us from being above ourselves." Exactly a year after Robert died what tiny proportion we gained from Robert's inheritance arrived in the mail. I well know why my eyes just happened to light on Paul's words to Timothy on that very day, but God through His word timed it so that He took away some pain at the injustice that had been done, cheering me by His Spirit to know I had borne the injustice well.

Paul's advice to Timothy and also to me was –

> "But godliness with contentment is great gain. For we brought nothing into this world, and we can take nothing out of it. But if we have food and clothing, we will be content with that. People who want to get rich fall into temptation and a trap, and into many foolish and harmful desires that plunge men into ruin and destruction. For the

love of money is a root of all kinds of evil. Some people, eager for money, have wandered away from the faith and pierced themselves with many griefs."

I knew firsthand that all that Jeremiah Burroughs, the Puritan, wrote in *The Rare Jewel of Christian Contentment* was true. I had read the book as a young theological student but read it as a distant observer of the certain contentment he had in mind, but now I came face to face with the worth of such a jewel when sorely tested.

Of the many facets of the jewel that Burroughs wrote about, he tells us –

"God is contented, He is in eternal contentment in Himself. Now if you have God as your portion, why should you not be contented with God alone?"

To believe that such contentment is a jewel is to regard it as the first thing. The second is to count it as rare. The third is to wear it well.

As well as grandchildren, there are many other things money could not buy. In mid-July 2012 Stephen and Freya welcomed their second child into the world, giving her the name of Audrey, she being our fifth grandchild.

There were the cherished days of yesteryear when my father in the Faith, Cyril, and his wife Beryl took me in after I left the Sutherland Homes at 18. As aforementioned, Cyril had died years earlier, and now Beryl was approaching death. She turned 101 in the Epworth Hospital of Box Hill but, before she went to be with the Lord, she was delighted to see our little grandson Tom, who had begun life with a struggle but was improving. Beryl was buried after 15 days at the beautiful little chapel of St Katherine's in St Helena at a private funeral, after which there was a public thanksgiving at St John's Anglican church in Diamond Creek. The celebration of her life was protracted and so magnified her as to detract from the grace of God. Jonathan, a grandson and a gifted preacher, subtly "put the brakes on" in a superb sermon, showing that his grandmother shone only or essentially because of Christ's transforming power. Still, for me gratitude to God would remain while honouring the way Cyril and Beryl took me under their spiritual wings to shield me when I was young in the faith, and needed protection when going out into the world after leaving the institution. Money could not buy such things.

It would be foolish to deny that there were times in the new year of 2013 when Satan still took me to brink of imagination to ponder and "see" what might have been had we gained the inheritance, how it took some strength of mind to resist what I "saw," but I asked myself, "Did Jesus possess great wealth? Did Paul? Have Two made a greater impression on the world as they?"

> I shared the possession of Tasso's spirit –
> "I long for much, I hope for little, I ask for nothing."
>
> I learn from Henry Vaughn –
> "God dwells in dazzling darkness".

All kinds of blessings actually came tripping along to keep me rejoicing in God the Father. One of the blessings was winning the Caleb Prize for Non-fiction Biography, awarded by Omega Writers Inc 2010. This no doubt helped boost the sales of my autobiography and its presence in a number of municipal libraries throughout Victoria. Contentment was clouded by someone's change of mind concerning an appearance on Channel 9 of Sydney for an interview about the book – the lady in question by phone promised an interview, but one week later sent an email saying "my heart tells me" the interview was to be cancelled.

Around that time Kerryn's mother died. We drew comfort from knowing she loved the Lord. Her courage upon being converted during Melbourne's Billy Graham Crusade of 1959 was to be admired: She left the Seventh Day Adventist Church in Warburton, a town with a dominant population of SDA people employed largely by the Sanitarium factory and Signs Publishing Company. On her own with four young children all under 12 to raise, she could go on to tell of the wonderful way God provided for the family in a time of no recourse to a government pension. I had the privilege of conducting the funeral service for her.

On the heels of the sadness of Kerryn's mother's death, we had to fight back tears on what looked like our last visit to Ararat, which included a free tour of Aradale and a visit to Robert's and my mother's grave. Our Aradale tour leader had read *The Silver Poplar* – that was cheering. He told us how the mentally ill were divided into "moron, imbecilic, Chinese (!) idiot" – that was not cheering to know.

Little Benjamin became Chris and Janine's fourth child, as well as our sixth grandchild when he was born in August 2013.

The past was pushing itself into prominence that year, what with an Eltham high school reunion, Kerryn's mother's death, the visit to Ararat and Aradale, the possible last look at Robert's and my mother's grave, a visit to the Sutherland Homes and seeing remnants of Sutherland's past becoming lost to quick evolving changes, plus the centenary of the nearby town to the Homes of Plenty. Time was quickly passing by – one could not help but think, far more than one did once, of one's own mortality and how fleeting life on earth is.

In 2014, despite getting older and having to adjust to more medical appointments, life had its surprises, as one expects when being God's child. On seeing old friends, memories of past times washed over me refreshingly. New insights into God's Word generated the desire to use them in what preaching opportunities arose, or set me thinking of writing new books. Grandchildren had increased in number to six and added new colour to life and its purpose as grandparents, in the ambit of what God designs one to do as life draws nearer to a close. Places one knew in bygone years became sacred whenever revisited. There was the lady at the card shop where I bought nine cards marked "Thinking of You" and who said "Do you have some friends who are not well?" There was the classical music leaving me in raptures but left me gasping that there is too much to listen to, but too much, too late. There was the surprise of the unexpected phone call from a man who as a boy remembered my first day as a six-year-old at the Sutherland Homes!

I had become a seasoned soldier for Christ, so I could cross over to enemy territory and fight them on their own ground. This may not be good advice for young, or immature believers (who may be immature despite their many years), but it lends confidence as one nears the end of his life and seeks to muster as much hope as possible, particularly when one has already spied out considerable weaknesses of the stratagems of the enemy through keen observation. Not only is there the need to be more armed by the Word of God itself, but we can take the wisdom of some fellow soldiers, such as C.S. Lewis, Pawson, Calvin and Tozer, to name a few, and so press on to enemy territory. In doing this, I gained inspiration for a title of this book – John Carey had titled a book of his called *The Unexpected Professor* – but spied a chink in his armour when he mocked Christian belief and stated that humans are insignificant beings in a vast universe. Well, he is insignificant enough to want masses to read his book and share in his life!

Although retired from the ministry, there was still much to do each day. The manuscript for *Mirrors in Mark* occupied much time. There was the lingering enjoyment of reading and re-reading of many good books; an hour's walking around a delightful lake that is encompassed by bushland; surprise invitations to share in friends' celebrations; chances to speak to historical groups or libraries about *The Silver Poplar;* enough preaching to please my desire to expound God's Word to hungry congregations; awakening each morning to another enchanting poem of George Herbert; wrestling with Randy Alcorn in his *God is Good* when he strangely says that sexual abuse is "a gift of God;" and looking at other possible places in order to live more simply by downsizing.

Lily was born to Belinda and Brent late June 2015 to become our seventh grandchild. What a blessing to be grandparents!

"Children's children are a crown to the aged, and parents are the pride of their children" (Proverbs 17:6).

Towards the end of 2015, after my book *Mirrors in Mark* had been published in the U.S.A., in one way, life came full circle, when to my surprise a lecturer at Whitley College of Melbourne (the Baptist College where I trained for the ministry), invited me to give a lecture on the book of Revelation, as based on the way I saw Revelation structured in *Mirrors in Mark*. It appeared that the lecturer was intrigued with the use of what is technically known as chiasmi, a mnemonic device evident in Revelation.

In *Mirrors in Mark* it would have been obvious to anyone acquainted with my comments hinged on the chiasmi, which I had discovered in the Johannine book of Revelation that I took seriously and regarded it as inspired by God. For this reason I entered Whitley nervously, knowing that it was even more liberal in its teaching than in my days at Whitley in the Sixties. Still, I grasped the nettle. The class I faced was quite small, but technological advances since the Sixties made the class even larger – some students were watching and listening on Skype, one student being in Korea, and one being a Jetstar pilot. With such technology I felt therefore I had come from outer space myself, being away on leave from Earth since the Sixties.

The lecturer appeared pleased with the lecture. I too was pleased to be at Whitley, even though I am of what I think is called the "conservative evangelical" persuasion. I was on the premises of the place where I strangely wondered now at the presence of female students being resident, when in my days at Whitley females were supposedly forbidden to be in the College, casual visits by any of that sex viewed with suspicion.

Certain things pointed to a reluctance by Whitley to see me again so that it was viewed humorously by me as a victory – a raid into the citadel of liberal learning and then out again!

What matters most to me is honouring God. We who seek to honour God and respect what He says in His word may feel at times in certain circumstances like Orlando of Shakespeare's *As You Like It*. Orlando was despised by his brother, being deprived by his older brother of education and training and society. He dares to wrestle a formidable wrestler, not caring if he dies as other opponents of the champion have done –

"If I'm beaten, the shame is all mine, and I wasn't in anyone's good graces to begin with. I won't wrong any of my friends, because I don't have any to mourn for me, and I won't have wronged the world, because I don't have anything in the world. In this world, I'm only taking up space. If I leave, maybe someone more worldly may fill it" (modern translation in Spark Notes.)

Some may seem to oppose us – such as Orlanda sensed not aggressively, but in deafening silence. Yet, un-like Orlando, we discover that there are those who will cherish us. I like to think I shall be missed in this world, that I was not merely taking up space. God did not choose me in sovereign grace in vain. So, in the present and to the very end of my time here, I can continue to live in the present, certain that there remains still the all-surpassing power of God to be seen in me, as it reflects life as it is in Jesus.

Abdul Abul Abul Amir

Life not only came full circle, so to speak, when I lectured at Whitley College late 2015, but it also came full circle as well, early in the following year.

John Osborne said of some, "They spend their time mostly looking forward to the past." While I have sought to live in the present, I confess that perhaps too often I 'look forward to the past,' as there are many sweet memories I cherish and mull on, and sometimes for me a memory among past surprises takes me captive for days, with a joy that I found it hard to express in words.

On one February day a certain song, I know not how, led me to urge Kerryn to locate it on Google. The song? A 1927 ballad called *"Abdul Abul Abul Amir."* Through Google and on old soundwaves there came springing out from an old phonograph an old-time voice of a Frank Crumit. It was a song written in 1877 during the Russian-Turkish War, composed by a Percy French, and tells the story of a Russian and a Turk embroiled in a fight with the intent to kill each other. It is a long song of 24 stanzas.

Why did it enthral me to hear it, more than any other I had known? I can recollect many songs because of a fond love for music. Yet, just one song in 2016, perhaps only heard once decades before, came springing up as a beautiful, bewitching memory of being a small boy at Sutherland Homes. Sometimes I had sung snatches of "Abdul..." over the years without emotion, yet suddenly nostalgia showered me with charm at the old-time voice of Frank Crumit.

I saw the scene as if it were yesterday. I was sitting on a hard-wooden chair with a high back, along with the other inmates in the dining room in Sutherland, all chairs rearranged in rows as we sat and focussed on a man visitor and an acoustic guitar. The song went on and on, verse upon verse, telling of the bold Mameluke (the Turk) drawing his trusty skibouk (whatever that was) and singing "Allah! Allah! Akbar!" as "with murderous intent he ferociously went for Ivan Skavinsky Skavar." Were all other children as spellbound as I was then? I only know that as a born lover of stories, I at least sat transfixed until we heard that a stone where the Dunabe rolled had an inscription placed on it: "Stranger, remember to pray for the soul of Abdulah Bul Bul Amur," and yet a Muscovite maiden ended up weeping for his opponent – for Ivan Skavinsky Skavar.

Just a song? Maybe it has been well and truly forgotten or scarcely remembered by those who were the other neglected children of the time, but it filled my life with joy for days without end that February of 2016, to think that even though I was locked up in that institution in a sense, I felt ever so free when I heard our visitor sing of those foes with the exotic names of Abdul Bul Bul Amur and Ivan Skavinsky Skavar.

Then down in the depression I went as the days passed. The song began to unsettle me, saddened me as the bewilderment of being at the institution sunk in. Something had been amiss at Sutherland. I cried. I feared the song was working against me.

Then the song caused happiness to arise in me once more. Yes, I had been privileged to be in the institution, and recalled the joy of a resilient kind that every child knows, no matter what hard times they are passing through.

Shakespeare knew the melancholy mind well. You see his insight into it in 'As You Like It', in Jaques. Jaques is willing to go into exile with Duke Senior, who had been robbed of his right to rule in his dukedom and Jacques also flees to the forest – Jaques is faithful. Jaques loves music, is attracted to songs that make him sad. When cautioned against hearing that a certain song will make him sad, he says, "I'm glad about it. More, please. I can suck sadness out of a song the way a weasel sucks eggs." When dubbed a melancholy fellow, his answer is: "I am. I like it better than laughing." It is suggested that Jaques may be too serious, but says "Well, I think it's good to be serious and keep quiet." He is curious and claims that he is serious because he has travelled "so much;" knows too much to be frivolous and gullible about what is only froth and bubble in society. You will notice that Shakespeare is shrewd and does not have Jaques in the limelight, and as a central figure, and yet he is one that people are intrigued with, just as Jaques himself is intrigued at the end of the story to depart from view in order to seek out the repentant Duke who had ruthlessly taken over the throne but on repenting had "put on a religious life" – Jaques says "There is much to be learned from these converts."

Just like Jaques there is much about the past and its experience for a melancholic to give thought to so often. People of other temperaments do not find that regret is so sore a temptation. I am tempted to regret with considerable pain for instance, choices made about the ministry, with respect to turning my back on certain churches without good reasons. One ponders what might have been if I perhaps had been more open or sensitive to the will of God.

I ponder much on my journey of life, ponder as I wonder much about moves of all kinds I made. I have noticed that Moses wrote down all the starting places, stage by stage, of the journey Israel made from Egypt all the way to the border of the land they were to occupy. Why did he bother to write them down with so much detail, detail that I am sure that has bored many bible students to read? Yet we are to observe that Moses wrote down all that detail *by command of the Lord.*

Instead of being bored by Numbers 33, we do well to ponder on why the Lord commanded Moses to record all the stations of Israel's journey, and importantly what it means for us in our time. It serves well as an obituary to Moses' great achievements (Gordon Wenham), it was a reminder of the obstacles Israel faced on the way, and how God helped them to get to the journey's end. I am sure God would have we believers in these times to look back on our journey through life, recalling the obstacles faced and how He has brought us thus far.

Now, in early days when young I loved to sing along with fellow saints the song "Have I Done My Best for Jesus?" –

> "I wonder have I done my best for Jesus,
> Who died upon the cruel tree?
> To think of His great sacrifice at Calvary!
> I know the Lord expects the best of me.
> The hours I've spent for Christ are few;
> Because of all my lack of love for Jesus,
> I wonder if His heart is breaking too."

It is a disturbing song. It is meant to be. Yet self-lashing as depicted in this song can shatter a soul so. It is true that some of we believers are not serving the Lord as we ought but, for those of us who are striving to do our best for Him, any anxiety can be allayed by remembering that whatever we do for our Lord, it cannot measure up to what He has done.

The problem entailed can be a more vexing one as the years go by: Yes, He died for me but, on my journey, has not my life been riddled by too much of myself and not enough of Him? In reflecting, however, we may be draining ourselves of *thankfulness*.

George Herbert, who in the minds of many is the greatest English devotional poet we have known, composed a poem '*The Thanksgiving*'. In it he wrestles with how he repays Christ for what He did by way of dying for us. Despite what some critics have said, George Herbert is dealing with the issue rather playfully, serious though the question can prove to be –

"But how then shall I imitate thee, and
Copy thy fair, though bloudie hand?"

In what may pass as daring language our poet challenges Christ to a contest. He calls Christ "King of grief" and entertains the question of being able to weep sufficiently as Christ did in His grief, but quickly concludes that when Christ was forsaken by the Father on the cross "Was such grief as cannot be (equalled)."

Should our poet then leave himself to sing and skip to triumph Christ gained? Yet he says –

"But how then shall I *imitate thee*, and
Copy thy fair, though bloudie hand?"

At this point of "taking revenge on Christ's love, and trie who shall victorious prove," George Herbert ponders on giving away his wealth to the poor, not marrying to avoid being diverted from devotion of more than equal worth, prepared to turn on a friend if he should despise Jesus' name, to build a hospital, to live as least as possible in involvement in the world so that people scarcely know "that I am here, to devote utmost energy to divine music and the reading of God's book until I'le turn back on thee, O my dear Saviour, Victorie!"

Yet what of Christ's passion? It is an afterthought of a kind; our poet being too lost in what he could do to outdo Christ? He is lost for words. As one critic has said: "(Our poet) himself realizes that no action of his can ever adequately render thanks (for what Christ has done)." He ends up with a godly gasp – that's all.

Ours is not to mourn or regret what is past. Says Paul : "Forgetting what is behind and straining towards what is ahead, I press onward the goal to win the prize for which God has called me heavenward in Christ Jesus."

As I seek to imitate Paul, I hope that in pressing on, friends and acquaintances will see that I know far more of the things of God than I did years ago –

> "I can recall the time when I reached out for a friend,
> And now I think I have
> a lot more than a skipping rope to lend."

Naturally, by 2016 I had a smaller ministry than what I possessed when I retired as a pastor – that is, in terms of ministry through preaching and in counselling – but I saw a wider ministry in being an author of several books, though there is nothing that replaces the thrill of preaching, nor carrying out visitation to needy people, as built on the belief of a certain pastor-friend who says of me that I am "pastorally sensitive."

There are certain friends who have persuaded me that "I think I have a lot more than a skipping rope to lend."

I shall tell you of these friends. They are an odd collection, some of whom have aged with me over many years now. Some of them I only see from time to time but my heart warms to them whenever I visit them and recall when we first met. A number of them have opened wide my eyes to this big world of ours, having seen so much of the world themselves, many of them wiser than me. Mind you, some of them baffle me at times. I "slow dance with some, others I ride like breaking waves." Many people have acquaintances that simply say, for instance, "He did this good thing", without explanation – many of mine, I am happy to say, will say in appreciation of my motives "He did this because..." It has come at great cost to me to have some of them, but they are cherished because they have proven to be long-time friends. As I age, I am pleased to say that they do not joke or ridicule me for having mottled skin on account of psoriasis, or for fumbling to hold things with my arthritic hands, or for losing some memory at times.

I have pages upon pages of these friends. Many of them are upright but, if they are not, they are still valued. I can speak volumes for them. If they read me like a book, it does not trouble me, because with their barely visible art – often without me knowing it – they make me a better person. I only wish that I could revisit some of them, but life is growing shorter and I may not have time to call on many of them ever again.

I am thankful for the varied insights they have given me. The way one friend tells it : "I feel what it must have been like to drift down the Mississippi River as Huckleberry Fin did..." Another causes me to be breathless in learning that George Muller waited in prayer on God to move someone to knock on the door with food when the orphaned children sat at the breakfast table with nothing to eat... Another friend has caused horror creep over me to learn Dante descended through the circles of hell and suddenly his eyes fall on the gigantic figure of hell's monarch in Lucifer... I have been held spellbound to know Dorian Gray, upon seeing his likeness in a mirror, falls in love with its beauty and craves that the portrait might age instead of him, with a wish that is granted... Time could tell of more, but I must list the suspense I felt on learning when the little dynamo in

Gladys Aylward, serving God in China, is called on to quell a riot in a prison because the governor maintains that she was always telling people about the living God and therefore he says, "So how could the prisoners kill you?" (I remember asking myself, "Do I truly believe God is a living God?") The best of friends are those acquainted with the Bible.

Yes, I have wonderful friends in *books*.

There are friends too of flesh and blood, thankfully. In early days as Kerryn and I moved about in the ministry, we found good friends who we warmed to very much but, as we passed on from one congregation to another, distance and new situations made it hard to know the intimacy we once knew in various places. Still, we have been grateful to have known many people, especially those with whom we have kept up friendships from quite some years ago.

I would like to meet some writers of great spiritual standing in eternal glory: George Peters who wrote The Theocratic Kingdom, C.S. Lewis, John Calvin, David Pawson, Pascal, A.W. Tozer. They provide fellowship in lean times, especially when one seeks anxiously to find satisfaction in the churches of our day. As for David Pawson, I have not always agreed with some things that he has written, but one always hopes to have a catholic spirit (in the proper sense of the word "catholic") and be as tolerant as possible. A dear friend (who is now with the Lord) wrote something that is wise: "Go to the local...church...If you find that they are not perfect, then help them to reach that standard. If you find that they are perfect, they'll help you to reach it."

Even as one is not spiritually perfect, so one is not physically perfect. This becomes increasingly obvious, and the point to be made is that the ageing process plays a challenging part in trying to grow more spiritually perfect and gracious. In the family circle there is a grandfather who has self-styled himself with the name Grumps. He is good-natured about it, with a name reminding us of the proverbial "grumpy old man" tag. As we age, we all may well grow grumpy, for we are found battling against the falling away of the body to death with all the discomforts that lead to it. Scientists can tell you there is no reason whatever within our frame why we should die. The cells of our body die every day and are replaced through food and fresh air and rest by new cells, but we grow old just the same and are set to grow old and die.

Still, many of us fight to live and live well while we can. Ironically, I know far more about what constitutes good health than I did when I was young. In other words, though in a sense I enjoy better health in old age, it could appear to be too late to arrest any early abuse that has left me paying the price.

Sound physical health plays and promotes sound spiritual health. It is not to say, for instance, that we can blame grumpiness, irritation and graciousness entirely on bad diet. I am conscious of Jesus having said the following –

> "Nothing outside a man can make him 'clean' by going into him.
>
> What comes out of a man is what makes him unclean.
>
> For from within, out of men's hearts, come evil thoughts, sexual immorality, theft, murder, adultery, greed, malice, deceit, lewdness, envy, slander, arrogance and folly. All these evils come from inside and make a man 'unclean' ".

We all know such evils as Jesus describes come from our hearts. We may not like anyone outside ourselves accusing us of such things but we, if honest, admit them as applying to ourselves. I can call myself 'grumpy' but don't *you* dare!

To catch some warmer weather in September in 2016 Kerryn and I flew to Hamilton Island for five nights. The warm weather of a regular 23 degrees Celsius was cheering, and to add to the cheer was the chance to read David Pawson's autobiography with the intriguing title *Not as Bad as the Truth*.

How did he arrive at such a title? Once David Pawson became the target of rumours. He was able to quash them, finding out the culprit in Wales, where he had been scheduled to preach. Three elders from Cardiff drove all the way to Surrey, where David was, in order to find out if the rumours had any substance. In his defence he said that if anybody ever had an accusation against a Christian leader, they should have the testimony of two or three witnesses of the offence. He assured them that there was no truth behind the rumours. David turned to the Lord with the bitter complaint of personal pain and damage to his ministry. He recalls: "I have rarely known God speak to me as clearly as He did then."

God's reply was: "The worst they can say about you is not as bad as the truth." David burst out laughing. His enemies did not know as much as the Lord did! It cured him of any sensitivity to hostile criticism.

The fact should cure us all of what people cruelly say or spread about us.

Not as Bad as the Truth was an intriguing book in other ways too. Our author once ran a non-stop public reading of all the Scripture, each reader reading for 15 minutes. The venture proved to be a great success, and one would like to think that some believers in our time were excited about organizing such a thing. Even just to read the whole gospel of Mark non-stop in a small group to one another would be a great blessing. Our author suggests reversing the order of public worship too, for it is contended that true worship should begin by focussing on the Word of God read and preached, with all the music at the end proving to be a stimulated response to what God reveals to us through His Word. One would like to think that some churches would be daring enough to reverse the worship service, and follow such an ancient practice as the Early Church document 'Didache' makes clear.

The memory is fading to some degree, but a secular book *The Memory Code* by Lynne Kelly inspired me all the more to rehearse daily much of what I know of the Scriptures, and also cling to what she calls "the journey method." Her interest includes the subject of birds and she has memorised the names of 408 birds, together with the names of their families, classification, distribution and the like!

Her memory device for recalling the line of English Kings to a certain point interested me –

> "Willie, Willie, Harry, Stee,
> Harry, Dick, John, Henry three;
> One two, three Neds, Richard two
> Harrys four, five, six...then who?
> Edwards four, five, Dick the bad.
> Harrys VII and VIII, then Ned the lad..."

(Mind you, to master the above rhyme it helps to know the more formal names of those monarchs and history associated with them.)

Some of us may not want to memorise facts of ancient history, but certainly it does the soul good if one who has known quite a long life, considers "the journey method" and "the landscape method." These two methods fit in for what will prove vital, as we Christians contemplate how we are travelling according to God's will, and it will prove subsequently to our own ultimate satisfaction.

Even in a secular journal I once read, it had been stated that we are "deafened to our spiritual selves," needing to give time and place to sit in "silent solitude." If this is advice for the secular man, how much more essential it is for the spiritual person? If we hold to belief in the providence of God, we can link places and occasions to embrace "the journey method" and "the landscape method" in the quietness of our hearts. Lynne Kelly speaks of one becoming "emotional" when taking such a journey through our past life.

My melancholic nature makes it easy to make use of "the journey method" and "the landscape journey," even though it can be to my undoing at times, occasionally bringing about sadness over the same things that on other days can bring gladness, and I have to pull myself out of such misery by counteracting it with a strong endeavour to praise God for all I can think of. Most times, however, it warms my heart to reflect on many things that have happened along life's way.

So far, I have a good memory, and I am still able to retain much of what I have collected on the way and what has been passed through. Life is railway stations passed through. Quite a number of stations have been where I have got out of the carriage and stayed for a time: Carlton was where I began my journey – being born there – and then in the distant past I have arrived and got off life's train at: Camberwell, Royal Park, Sutherland Homes at Diamond Creek until aged 18, elsewhere in Diamond Creek until I went to Bullumwaal, then to Wal Wal and Sunbury, and the Baptist theological college at Parkville, then to West Coburg, followed by East Malvern, Ulverstone in Tasmania, then Warburton, Swan Hill, Rowville before settling down in Knoxfield ever since 1985. Stations and places where I alighted on the journey are well remembered – things well past but things quite present.

My heart goes out to friends whose minds have deteriorated. It is characteristic for some of them now to recall only the early stations on the rail of life's journey. The present is more or less becoming lost to them, this in an age or generation when we are all being overloaded with too much luggage by the way of information as we travel – much of it is trivial and could well be cast off. Sadly, there are even friends who scarcely know your name because they are victims of what John Salisbury of ancient times called "the stepmother to memory" : oblivion. Yes, not all of today's information speaks wisdom. T.S. Eliot succinctly asked –

"Where is the wisdom we have lost in knowledge?
Where is the knowledge we have lost in information?"

To have a good memory is of benefit to me, but wisdom is also a precious gift from God, that which lifts the spirit. Some of us are occupied too much with what is sombre and depressing. One day I put Chekov down – a brilliant writer – and I had to take up something that did not drown me in wretchedness but what is noble: I found it in Pascal who, while he speaks of man's wretchedness, tells us also that our wretchedness is paradoxically a sign that we were born as people for greatness. In our right mind it causes us to realise in misery that we are born for something noble.

Wisdom is a precious gift from God, and so is time. Yet time is such that once lost, we cannot cry out with effect as Shakespeare has Richard II saying: "Call back yesterday, bid time return." Although I had well and truly retired as a pastor, I still found opportunities when 2017 came about to preach and visit needy contacts pastorally. Time itself pressed upon me to meet a certain deadline for the publication of a new book called *The Scandal of God's Forgiveness*. When we holidayed at Lakes Entrance, Kerryn and I had a most memorable day when we strolled around the Entrance itself, for in the sea a seal was frolicking and tossing itself up into the air time after time and then swooping down into the swirling water to seize fish at lightning speed. We were spellbound, not tied by workaday things that time holds us to. Time speeds in its own way and we are to quickly grab those opportunities time affords. What more can I do to serve Christ, and be faithful to the end?

Ageing tempts one to give up "contending for the faith of the gospel" (Philippians 1:27.) I had learned of a man of similar age to mine who left a church because he openly confessed to me that he had grown too old to engage in fighting for the truth. He had served his time well as a soldier for Christ. He departed for a more peaceful fellowship. It is a crying shame that there is such contention to drive out from a congregation one man I still view as a godly man. We are meant to be "contending as one man for the faith of the gospel" (Phil 1:27 again) – not against one another in the church itself. It can be vexing: does one stay and fight for the truth in a church when it seems it cannot be done as one man?

Somehow, we must be concerned about our own sanity and spirituality while attempting to help fellow-believers. Shallow believers may be more dangerous than unbelievers in the sense that they cause the temperature to drop within a congregation by not being as fervent for the faith as they should be. We live in difficult days but, irrespective of our age, we are to "contend as one man for the faith of the gospel, without being frightened in any way by those who oppose (us)."

Providentially I picked up a book of more than 660 pages from a Christian bookshop for a mere five dollars, an omnibus of three original books in one, and called *This Little Church...* Well, I do like a bargain, but I found through experience with fruitfulness that quite a number of Christian books are promoted under "Quick Sale." For example, I once purchased a book at the same shop for only ten dollars, mainly because its title captivated me: *Original Sin*. Had its subject held no interest for many buyers? Was it part of a "Quick Sale" because it had been among those of the "Slow Sale?" That book about the originality of sin is one of the best books I have ever read. It furnishes concrete proof in the way that history discloses why we all are "bad to the bone." Ought not we be lamenting that a poor sale of such a book means that contemporary Christians show appallingly little interest in such a doctrine as original sin, and are content to be ignorant of solid truth? Is it not a sign of the kind of superficiality that Gary Gilley, the author of *This Little Church...*, groans over?

Even some people who are not exactly evangelically orthodox, as far as evangelicalism is concerned, are disturbed at the way Christianity is losing ground in our time. Rod Dreher, a Roman Catholic and author of *The Benedict Option,* suggests the way forward for Christians is to go back – all the way to certain principles behind the monastic life of old, and adapting those principles to build for ourselves, if we are Christian, resilient Christian communities, instead of remaining under siege from the world elsewhere. In concluding *The Benedict Option,* I warmed to the concept of Christian villages, where Christians live near one another in a close-knit way. Yes, our faith life would be more robust in our time as we practised life nearer one another in the warmth and spiritual glow of "order, hospitality, stability and prayer."

My foster father, Cyril, always maintained that we should never drive past the nearest church for us to worship; in his case that was understood to mean an Anglican Church. When I became a Baptist, I drove for fellowship from Diamond Creek to Greensborough, and there was my nearest church. Since the days of Cyril, I have had slight pangs of guilt at times because I have passed closer churches in my retirement, even knowing the sound principle of not merely worshipping with fellow-believers nearby, but living nearby them as Dreher advocates – though such is the spiritual disparity between us in these days that it can prove difficult to form geographically a close-knit community with those of like mind. Still, it is good to dream, and even pray, for something akin to what our author of *The Benedict Option* longs for, what indeed can be a part of such a soul-satisfied community.

I had said that "providentially" I picked up in mid-winter of 2017 the omnibus *This Little Church*, for at the time I had such a heavy heart before the Lord that it relieved me of it through the book. At the time there was little encouragement for Kerryn and me when we sought a kindred spirit or two in our pursuit of total surrender to "the faith once delivered to the saints."

Tozer lightened the heavy load for both of us. The problem of finding kindred spirits may not have been solved, but how the heart leapt to read him saying "As I pursue the Scriptures, I discover, much to my delight, that God thinks the world of me!" "Wow!" I responded. I mean, we knew God loved us.... but to that degree?

Our son-in-law Chris celebrated his 40th in a Fitzroy restaurant, where we caught up with Christian friends who we had not seen for some years, who we once knew in the halcyon time of attending the South Yarra Presbyterian Church on Sunday nights. It cheered me also around that time when someone said that hope was evident in the way I was growing old gracefully, as I told her of the physical problems I had to endure. It was certainly a cheering word, reminding one of Paul the apostle, who said –

"Therefore, we do not lose heart. Although outwardly we are wasting away, yet inwardly we are being renewed day by day. For our light and momentary troubles are achieving for us an eternal glory that far outweighs them all. So, we fix our eyes not on what is unseen, but what is seen. For what is seen is temporary, but what is unseen is eternal."

There are people who regularly walk around a lake that is near us, people who have much in common with me – simply because they are growing old. We converse about aches and pains, how much of our life is taken up with medical appointments, how there are certain ailments we just have to live with, how we try to console ourselves by saying there are some who are worse off physically than we are. There is an affinity among us that the young do not know. It is like a secret we all have, for the young have yet to know what we the aged are passing through.

Yet, in another way there is no affinity between us all. We all are wasting away, but not all of us are fixing our eyes on what is unseen. One or two are fellow believers in Christ as I am, but others who are walking around the lake, are yet to be convinced of the truth of the gospel. One very sociable fellow, for instance, has on quite a number of occasions turned our conversation into something spiritual, or made it easy for me to broach the subject of the gospel. On one occasion we fell into conversation about the politics of the day.

> "Aw, with this merry-go-round of Prime Ministers, in a short time what's Australian politics coming to?" my friend said.

> "Well, it is not just the Labour Party that is in disarray. There is scratching and biting of one another in the Liberal Party," I replied.

> "Yet, you would vote for the Liberals at the next election, wouldn't you?" he asked.

"No government is destined to be perfect. As I have told you on a number of times, there is something that is causing the political strife and turmoil we know now."

"What is it?"

"You don't remember?"

"No."

"Come on," I smiled and became relaxed (as we had become good friends)," you should know me by now, and know what I am getting at."

"Go on, tell me again," he said.

There we stood on the rise of the paved path by the pond by the lake with its thick infesting rushes that hide the moorhens swimming in and out of them.

"You agree that there is such a thing as evil – right?" I said.

"You can't trust any politicians, really," he responded.

"Well, we are all evil," I replied. "That is why the world is as it is. There is no government that can straighten out everything. Never has been."

"Jesus proved to be the perfect person and He is the only right ruler for this world. One day He is coming back to this earth and will rule over it to do away with sin and the sorrow it brings."

"I only wish it were true," my friend said.

The conversation continued but I could tell that my friend was not willing to investigate further the matter of Jesus' future coming being true, and somehow he turned the subject around to something of less consequence. He could not see – as C.S. Lewis points out – that if we have such a longing or wish in our heart for something better than what this world offers, a desire which no experience in this world can satisfy, "the most probable explanation is that I was made for another world."

Yet, I knew also being intellectually convinced about Jesus is more than having set before us the validity of the Argument from Desire (as I call it). One needs the Holy Spirit to convince us of what seems reasonable or logical. For we are naturally blind to reason.

C.S. Lewis once made this epigrammatic remark: "Until you have it, you will not know what you wanted." My friend did not "have it." Only the Holy Spirit can give him what he really wants. When witnessing to others, as a witness, one appeals to what the enlightened mind already knows to be true, and what makes sense of this world in which we live, but in my witnessing, I must leave the final work of conviction to the Holy Spirit.

Any Christian parents may have to learn through what may be a bewildering experience what exactly brings their children around to possessing genuine faith in Christ for salvation. Children may show considerable interest in spiritual things so that we may rush in, or they rush in, upon a desire to be baptized. (I speak here, of course, of denominations that practise what is known as "believers' baptism".) Then there is the dismay when parents, in seeking for signs of regeneration, find little or anything of such signs, particularly when the children are in what often proves to be the volatile years of their teens. We as parents, I confess, had desired their salvation with such intensity that we made the mistake of not taking "our hands off" and with patience watch for the work of the Holy Spirit.

Thankfully, the Holy Spirit became evident eventually in our three children – Belinda, Janine and Stephen – to their salvation, as already written about. We have become a little self-conscious at times upon seeing Christian parents who raised their children to love the Lord, but sadly have seen them turn away from placing faith in Christ. Kerryn and I taught our children well, but the fact that all three of them know the Lord is the work of the Holy Spirit.

And now all three have children of their own. It is the hope that we shall establish Christian families, while aware that – as Cyril used to say – "God has no grandchildren." Although privileged to have Christian parents, individually their children need to make a profession of Christ as well.

As for the parents – any Christian parents in fact – A.W. Tozer's searching words concerning possession must be considered if we truly desire to follow Christ and deny the self-life. He writes in his classic *The Pursuit of God* about Abraham, who appeared to have become "an eager love slave of his son." Indeed, God was testing out the strength of Abraham's affection for Isaac. Abraham's relationship to Isaac "bordered on the perilous" as he saw Isaac grow into a young man. Imagine the agony of following God's command to plunge the knife into his son, the darling of his heart! God would have Abraham to go through the suffering "up to the point where (God) knew there would be no retreat, and then forbade him to lay a hand on (Isaac)."

Tozer's insight into the angst Abraham passed through, when torn between affection for his son and becoming obedient to God, grew out of the personal experience of Tozer doting on his daughter when she was a little girl, so that she threatened to take first place in Tozer's affections in preference to God. He learnt, as Abraham did, to surrender his girl to the will of God, traumatic though it was.

Do we dread God's will? Are we afraid to dedicate our child to God lest...?

After his wife had given birth to six boys, Tozer's wife gave birth to a girl, who of her he said: "She and I became sweethearts." He and his wife had the baby girl dedicated formally in church, "but she was still mine." Let him tell us in his own words what happened –

"Then the day came when I had to die to my Becky, my little Rebecca. I had to give her up and turn her over to God to take her if He wanted to at any time. When I made that awful, terrible dedication I didn't know if God would take her from me. But He didn't. She was safer after I gave her up than she had ever been before. If I had clung to her, I would have jeopardized her; but when I opened my hands and said with tears, "You can have her, God, the dearest thing I have," she became perfectly safe."

If Tozer lived in our time – he died in 1960s – he doubtlessly would have perceived an even more widespread possessiveness among Christian parents of their children, yet there was consolation of a sort as far as Tozer was concerned; he held that God will move in to save ourselves from ourselves so that we let go and let God be the first in our lives.

> "...we will be brought one by one to the testing place (as Abraham was), and we may never know when we are there...our whole future will be conditioned by the choice we make."

What a blessing is in store when we surrender our children to God! Even more so, is the blessing for we parents when children do not merely taste a thinning run of joy through being under the roof of believing parents, but when the joy runs thick with mirth and knows the exhilarating love of Jesus for themselves, when of their own volition the door of faith is opened for salvation, as aided by the Holy Spirit.

There are those who make the great sacrifice of having to say farewell as parents when a child of theirs leaves home to serve God abroad. Among these we saw this in those dear friends in the late Elton and Dot Short of Whittington, east of Geelong. Their son Philip has served the Lord for more than 50 years, many of those in earlier days when Elton and Dot were alive. Most of Philip's life in those early days were spent in what has been described as the most inhospitable country in the world, living among the largest nomadic pastoral people of the world. Elton and Dot were phlegmatic people and displayed little emotion, but I am sure there was a wrench in their heart whenever Philip was returning to Niger after what seemed too brief a time at home, as well as a wrench in Philip's own heart.

The Christlikeness that shines through Philip and his wife Carol has been gained to a considerable degree through doing God's will abroad, as well as through the sacrifice of both Philip and Carol's parents of their own son to God's call. It has been seen as a gain to those who are privileged to know the charming couple.

It could be argued that Philip, for example, merely brings out to the full good traits of one who is phlegmatic in temperament – of someone who carries the natural tendency to be good-natured, easy to get along with, calm, dependable, with a practical mind. Yet, it is when the phlegmatic person is Spirit-filled that such traits radiate in the way God intended him to be.

As we consider the nine fruits of the Spirit – as spelt out by Apostle Paul – we know that anyone of any temperament who is filled with the Spirit will manifest the nine fruits, seeing weaknesses of his or her temperament transformed. A phlegmatic person is open to being slow and lazy, stubborn and indecisive, but through the Holy Spirit what a change there will be, as to bring forth the fruit of love, joy, peace, long-suffering, gentleness, goodness, faith, meekness, temperance (Galatians 5:22-23)!

It was in early October of 2017 that Phil and Carol stayed overnight with us before they were to return to Niger, soon after the time when Kerryn and I received an invitation to attend the 150th anniversary of Aradale's opening at Ararat, late in the month when I would be one of three speakers at Aradale on account of my poor mother and brother having lived in "the lunatic asylum" there.

As someone near and dear to me said, "It will be an emotional time for you." On one hand I saw the invitation to the anniversary as a privilege, but would I cope with returning to Aradale?

Aradale

It was Ron Roberts of Ararat who was influential in inviting Kerryn and me to the 150th anniversary at the opening of Aradale Mental Hospital. Ron and his wife Pauline had allowed us to stay overnight in their beautiful home over a number of years whenever we were visiting my brother Robert. Ron had discovered that he had a sister at the time we had first met Robert my brother – as well as that in common, he too had been a primary school teacher and was only a year younger than me. He is a jovial fellow, often causing much laughter at the breakfast table.

He informed me that I had been invited to speak at Aradale on the Saturday afternoon, when a good crowd was expected for a formal welcome for the celebrations.

There were to be three speakers in all: first to speak would be a Dr Blair Currie, who was to revive memories of his time at Aradale as the former psychiatrist superintendent; he was to be followed by a local historian named Graeme Burgin who naturally enough would relate to the crowd a history of the mental hospital; last of all, I would be called on to speak of "My Family and Me" out of my connection to Aradale through my mother and brother having spent considerable years there. The afternoon saw in attendance a large crowd of us seated and facing what used to be known simply as "The Building." Aradale arguably had sixty-three buildings in all, but "The Building" was a standout with its towering height – erected originally as the administration block, with the topmost level having had initially the quarters for the medical superintendent. The towers of "The Building," even from one's entrance from the back gate of the institution, were immediately visible and an imposing site.

Kerryn and I felt most honoured to be invited. Not only was I to speak, but we were to have free admission to a $60 a head dinner on Saturday evening at "J Ward" (the prison situated in Ararat itself for what historically had been the prison for "the criminally insane"), and we were also to enjoy two nights of complimentary accommodation at Ron and Pauline's house. We had not been back to Ararat since Robert's funeral.

The Ararat Advertiser carried news about the celebration beforehand, letting the public know that the celebration was to include "a spectacular sound and light show projected onto J Ward's blue stone wall at the southern end on Saturday night," which would be open for all the public to see. A group called Friends of J Ward was organizing the weekend. We three speakers were to follow one another on the platform after a welcome to all was extended, and some formal speeches were made in appreciation of the organising of the event. Aradale, which was first known simply as the Ararat Lunatic Asylum, saw its first patients admitted on October 19, 1867, so that it was almost to the day that the celebrations were to be held.

Ron and Pauline warmly welcomed us on Friday night. We settled our belongings in the bedroom down the hallway overlooking the little lake and then enjoyed an evening meal with them.

Next morning saw Ron kindly take Kerryn and me for a tour of J Ward, which we often had driven by in past years, but never visited. It was a network of grim bluestone buildings that originally took in men deemed criminals on the goldfields from 1859 on, until it was acquired by what was known as the Lunacy Department in 1886 through the Victoria Government and became Aradale's maximum security ward for those classed as "criminally insane" till its closure in 1991.

As Ron led us through the entrance of J Ward, the green lawn and lovely rose garden that greeted us belied the horror once hidden behind the main cell block and the West Wing of the place, Ron making it clear that a certain fluidity ran between J Ward and Aradale in the old days, contrary perhaps to what many have surmised – there were those who as inmates came and went between J Ward and Aradale as hinged on the possible change in the gravity of their mental illness. If the story of the confinement in Ararat of Thomas Varney is any guide, it illustrates well what Ron meant.

In 1965 Thomas set fire to the Bairnsdale police station as a young man, struggling for some years with resentment for authority. He was arrested and taken to Pentridge Prison, to the maximum-security section. He became subject to psychiatric treatment. Then he was moved to J Ward in Ararat as "criminally insane." Yet he began to attempt overcoming the mental disorder that dogged his life. Men with more severe cases of insanity had surrounded him each day and Tom became depressed. Still, he built up a will to survive, after feeling the weight of agonising months. Tom learnt that he was to be transferred to the less harsh life at Aradale.

Although restricted to the mental hospital's grounds, and bound by the surrounding red brick Ha Ha Wall, Tom was soon deemed sound enough even to be employed in manual work around the place. While many inmates at Aradale had given up hope – finding Aradale was a way of life and the chance of being released as a threat, since no possibility of holding down a job outside Aradale was likely – Tom eagerly sought Trial Leave and outside society from the mental hospital. In the end he got it.

It is unsure as to how many experiences were similar to Tom's, but his published memoirs in *From Gutter to Glory* tell us of the fluidity that could certainly run between the two mental institutions of Ararat.

Soon we returned to Ron's house where I scanned through the notes for my speech. Both nervousness and an excitement ran through me.

Before we knew it, 2.00pm came around and 200 people or more had seated themselves under a leaden sky, facing a bracing cold wind, and in front of us was a raised platform erected for the momentous occasion. The president of Friends of J Ward extended a welcome to the crowd, and then he introduced someone to give the Mayoral address, but had we heard right, or was someone else coming forward to adjust the microphone for the Mayor before His Worship spoke? No, it was His Worship himself. Only the mayoral gown gave his identity away, as he stepped forward in a casual shirt, denim jeans and stockyard boots. He spoke and then unveiled a plaque to commemorate the occasion.

As anticipated, Dr Blair Currie, who had been the former psychiatric superintendent of Aradale, and a local historian in Graeme Burgin spoke before me. Dr Currie spoke somewhat quietly but with feeling about the unfortunate lives that Aradale's inmates led in his time. Graeme spoke for 20 minutes about the establishment of Aradale. It was a simpler rundown of Aradale's history than that found in his tightly-packed account of two volumes about the places of Aradale and J Ward. It looked like hope was placed on me to put a human face to the institution's history. It had been decided by somebody unknown to me to name my speech "My Family and Me."

Kerryn squeezed my hand as I rose to ascend the platform.

I had written my notes out in full but had gone over them many a time so that I could follow them but make as much eye contact with the people as possible while I spoke.

UNEXPECTED

I started off –

> "It all began 20 years ago. An innocent enquiry led me to have a meeting with a counsellor of Human Services in the city of Melbourne.
>
> I was to find out as far as possible about why I ended up as a six year old in the Sutherland Homes for Neglected Children in Diamond Creek.
>
> The lady (Lisa by name) told me that my father had worked as a gardener at the Presbyterian Babies' Home in Camberwell. After three weeks there he must have taken time off, and he asked the Matron to take care of my sister Joyce and me, until he returned from whatever he was doing. Joyce was two, and I was four. Our father never returned.
>
> Lisa informed Kerryn and me in counselling that my mother had ended up here at Aradale in 1980, after being in the Mont Park Mental Institution in Melbourne. She was a victim of chronic schizophrenia and my father had deserted her, confining her to Mont Park.
>
> Lisa stunned my wife Kerryn (here with me today) and me with the news that my mother may still be alive.
>
> As it turned out, my mother had died, and was buried here in the town's cemetery, aged 67.
>
> I have often thought about how I used to drive regularly through here in Ararat in the years of 1963-4 as a teacher at a school north of Stawell while my mother was alive here at

Aradale. Yet it is a mercy that we never met, for her sake and mine.

On September 17 of 1997, while recovering from the news about my mother, Lisa of Human Services rang to say that I had a brother! I visited Lisa the next day. I discovered that Robert, like our mother, was chronic schizophrenic and had been here in Aradale too, both unaware of each other's existence, though, as you can imagine, it may have led to confusion and puzzlement to their disordered minds if they had been told about each other. They were the times when treatment for chronic schizophrenia was probably not advanced enough to settle the inmates' minds sufficiently to think all that rationally. Certainly, it was the case with my mother.

The medical reports would claim over the years that there was "a slight improvement," but at the same time she was regularly described as "hypomanic," incapable of discussion, etc.

I still have copies of medical reports which, on reading only last Tuesday, I found distressing.

At least on re-reading the medical reports related to my mother, to some degree it was cheering to realise that her two sisters would enquire of her welfare from time to time, and up to the year of her death.

You may get the impression that it was only my wife who accompanied me when I visited Human Services in that bewildering year of 1997, and that my sister Joyce was not present. The truth is that Joyce wanted to find out things very *cautiously on her own. It was always a roller coaster ride with my sister in our relationship to each other, though I loved her.*

Joyce was a troubled soul. Thankfully, her Christian convictions helped her much in her single state, but she was quite independent. Both Joyce and I wanted to know about our past, about our mother, but to a greater degree than me she did not want to know all that much. In fact, she was to later blame Human Services for telling her too much.

As for our brother Robert, we both wanted to meet him, though with mixed feelings.

Yes, Joyce wanted to meet him on her own, which she did in Ballarat.

Almost three months after learning about Robert, Kerryn and I drove up here to Ararat to meet him. By this time, he, like others who had been here in Aradale, had moved out to live in a house in town. Robert lived in Eucalyptus Court.

He was 15 months older than me.

The mother of the three of us – Robert, Joyce and me – in 1945 was said to be pregnant with her third child. Actually, it was to be her fourth child. The baby died when eight days old. Here at Aradale it was not known in 1980 that Robert, the eldest of us, had been born out of wedlock and adopted as a baby down in Melbourne by written consent. As I said, our mother was admitted here in the beginning of 1980, and at the time the powers that were in existence did not know of him except as Robert Murton, not knowing that he was Barbara Smith's son.

Joyce never married and she carried her adoptive name of "Forde," so there we were – Robert Merton, Eddie Smith and an unmarried sister Joyce Forde – all born of the same mother! And had the same father!

What was Kerryn's and my reaction to meeting Robert for the first time? It was difficult to converse with him, until we discovered that he loved to talk of the 'Fifties. We found out that he had an amazing memory about the VFL footballers of the time, and the singers and the actors of the era. As for times beyond the 'Fifties, all was a blank.

Next day on that first trip we paid him another visit before setting off for home, after staying with the Roberts overnight. He had a Bible open on the couch. When asked why he read the Bible, he told us that he wanted to be wise, as wise as Solomon.

We learnt that Robert was accustomed to taking his Bible down to the local hotel, to sit on the step to the entrance and read it.

What was Robert's past? He claimed that as a boy his adoptive father would hit him with a poker. His adoptive parents were in their fifties when they adopted him, though we did not learn that from Robert. He said that he used to live in Bendigo and played football as a rover for Eaglehawk. On future visits his blue eyes would light up when I called him 'a nuggetty little rover.'

What a strange time for our early lives! Firstly, Robert, first-born; born out of wedlock; adopted out supposedly with our mother's consent to British migrants of Swan Hill; but with much of his life spent in shadowy, vague years here at Aradale.

Secondly, myself, born 15 months after Robert; deserted by our father; left reluctantly with a matron in a babies' home and remaining there in the babies' home until I was actually six. The matron became alarmed to see me grow babyish in my ways; but then finally dispatched to a home for neglected children in the country at Diamond Creek after being briefly at what was known as the Royal Park "depot;" being placed at Diamond Creek so long as I did not prove "sub-normal;" not deemed available for adoption because "mother inmate of a mental institution;" remaining at the Diamond Creek institution until I was the age of 18.

Thirdly, Joyce, the youngest of us and deserted with me by our father when two years old; also goes to the Royal Park "depot;" then independent of me is taken away to Brunswick to be fostered by a childless couple; discovers she has a 15 year old brother when she is 13; finally adopted and carries the name 'Forde;' then to learn of the existence of another brother 41 years on.

As for our mother, she was here at Aradale for nine years.... To die here after 43 years of mental torment, not knowing her children."

I went on to tell the people in attendance of a number of other visits paid to Robert. How on our second visit, we saw him in the morning before we headed home, with Robert in all seriousness telling us that he had slept for four years in the night! There was only one time that we drove up to see Robert with my sister. Eventually, our three children joined us in visiting him and he enjoyed meeting the whole family. The visit of the whole family coincided soon after his fortnightly injection, making our visit easier and finding Robert chuckling over things that amused him.

I mentioned also about my brother's closing years. His house fell into disrepair – termites were taking over, the pergola was unsteady, the air conditioner was broken, and Robert was keeping the door to his fridge open to save electricity! At such a stage in his life, visits were not always fruitful, like the time in 2007 when he was admitted to hospital, and as Kerryn and I stood beside his bed, he kept his head under the blankets the whole time we were there. In the same year he entered Lowe Street's new nursing home, where he lived until the day of his death on July 4, 2011.

Our three children joined us in attending Robert's funeral! I told my listeners that although only a small number of the town were in attendance, he had been well known around the town, with many affectionately calling him "Bobbie."

I included some other memories of Robert, as I sensed there were those in the audience who had been staff and cared for him, had either known him at Aradale or in his own home. The audience showed they were clearly interested also to learn how I viewed my brother's life. I told them how he was not always home when we had spent two to three hours driving up from home to see him, and yet it often took little guessing to work out where he was – down the main street at McDonald's bakery, or in Safeway...

Since I was conscious of the need to slip in something in defence of belief in God, I related to the attentive audience about Robert's custom of saying grace on a certain occasion when we were at the RSL club for lunch. We were at the bar where several men were drinking and had their eyes glued on the horse racing on either one of two TV screens. He wanted a shandy. Yet before he downed it, he put his hands together, bowed his head and quietly said Grace amid the din made by the men who were watching the races. I made the point that in saying Grace, Robert showed "a certain soundness of mind" in expressing thanks for God's provision.

I moved on to finish my speech within the allowed fifteen minutes –

> Someone here at Ararat once said to me, 'Robert has had a sad live.' His face often suggested he was oppressed. We shall never know how he suffered. As I said: he could not tell us.

> We do not always know what passes on as mental illness from one generation to the next. It appears that mental illness passed on at least for three generations in our family. Our maternal grandmother is said to have been 'a little strange for a while' when she gave birth to our mother's eldest sister. It is said that six weeks after the birth 'her mind went blank and that was that.' Our grandmother was gifted – had studied to be a concert pianist – but she succumbed to depression (lingering post-natal depression perhaps) and died at the Mont Park Mental Hospital at the age of only 35.

> Then our mother lost her mind, supposedly suffering from the delusion that our father wanted to poison her, and as well lost her three children, believing that the neighbours were talking about our father not wanting her anymore. Perhaps our father played a part in our mother losing her mind. Who knows?

It causes us to reflect on the possibility of people perhaps of a somewhat sound mind being the cause of another's mental illness.

Mental illness is a complex issue, is it not?

Was my dear brother Robert, a victim of chronic schizophrenia and vulnerable because of our mother's condition?

Now, mental issues have not gone away with Aradale closing. If anything, they have increased alarmingly in our society, and for some reason or other than those known as well in the days of Aradale.

There are many incidences occurring in our time that beg the question: Why are there some people out and about, inflicting pain and cruelty on innocent ones, without being put in isolation, away from the public?

I am no expert on such matters. All I know is that mental illness is not treated seriously as it ought to be. It is never an electioneering issue in our materialistic world. Electioneering is chiefly aimed at the hip pocket – issues of the budget, superannuation, taxes and allied matters.

Money comes before the mind, it seems.

Yet there are those who show public concern. Why, only this week was the news about a group of motor cyclists who have gone on a journey for what they call an "Extra Dollop tour to raise funds for mental illness."

In the conclusion of my address, I thanked all the people for listening, and expressed the hope that I had provided an insight into the way Aradale touched my life through my mother and brother having lived there. I said that there is "a sad history about this deserted place," but appreciated being there to commemorate Aradale for the weekend.

Mine was a gentle rebuke of the chosen word of 'celebration' to mark Aradale's anniversary, as a *celebration* may mark a significant occasion, but as a word it stands for doing it with "an enjoyable time of activity." To *commemorate* is to honour the memory of something as a mark of respect.

Was not the weekend to remember with respect the sterling work done by many staff who cared for the unfortunate inmates, with them caring, we trust, out of respect for such inmates in the knowledge they were fellow human beings despite their mental illness? Or, was it a weekend to mark Aradale's significance in the course of our state's history and to do with enjoyment?

On reflection I realise that it would not have done to completely call the anniversary a commemoration. It would have suggested a sombre occasion altogether, whereas there was the promise of enjoyment – or perhaps 'satisfaction', more to the point. For that Saturday was to see the staging of the light show to illuminate J Ward's bluestone walls from 9pm on, for modified tours of Aradale's buildings, together with joy of a reunion for a number of former staff over afternoon tea, and the grand Formal Dinner in the West Wing of J Ward.

I came to see that we could celebrate and commemorate that day. After the speeches were over, and the crowd were free to wander around. Staff over many years spent time renewing acquaintances. Many took to seizing the opportunity to speak to we three speakers. I found such a time intoxicating.

My address had left me drained, but still highly charged with emotion. A lady with eagerness came up to me and said, "You ought to tell your story elsewhere." After that weekend I was to put on paper that I would find it hard to have such a captivating audience than the one on that day at Ararat, as many attending had been workers at the mental asylum. While I had spoken to all the people by keeping to my prepared notes, which notes were wrung out by me with sadness at what might have been and what had been, yet after my address I found myself with a full heart of love and appreciation of the people saying that I was brave to speak as I did. They knew that I was understandably emotional, particularly if they had known my mother.

One lady, who began work at Aradale aged 17 years, told me that she had looked after my mother and that Robert had the same eyes as our mother. People milled around me even as late as the Formal Dinner that night, and it warmed my heart to think they knew and understood why I could speak the way I did.

Words fail to express on paper the emotion that surfaced as I spoke in the afternoon. There were times when I sobbed and thought I could not continue speaking. I would look at Kerryn there in the front row, then wait until I could pull myself together and continue with my address.

I came home exhausted but felt warm inside for knowing the Aradale anniversary was the nearest to my mother I could ever get.

On the Monday it was with eagerness that I rang a lady at Ararat, who had asked me to call. She described my mother as having brown hair, of 5 foot 2 inches in height, one of a few words, "unassuming," "a little stocky in build," but she could not recall the colour of her eyes. I came even nearer to my deceased mother through hearing those things.

Our friend Ron of Ararat had a good idea: He suggested that the Friends of J Ward may wish to have copies of my autobiographical *The Silver Poplar* on sale whenever tours are conducted through J Ward. If a letter from the secretary of Friends of J Ward was any barometer as to being receptive to the idea, then the book was bound to be readily available for visitors to J Ward.

For the secretary wrote –

> "Your speech was a very emotional one and undoubtedly moved the audience on the day. We believe it was a story that had to be told."

Aradale Revisited

Aradale is now regarded by some as 'the most haunted building in Victoria'. In the minds of many it lends itself to the perfect Creep Show. Its cold, bleak, desolate cells arrived at by long concrete corridors, its morgues and wards, all may close in out of discomfiture on you as the guide for the two-hour tour in the night-time air tells you about 13,000 people that are believed to have died in the hospital – not just your ordinary people, but 13,000 lost souls to madness of one kind or another. The Creep Show has a further macabre touch, for the guide does not hold back on telling of the painful and even experimental treatments many of the inmates received.

While one may well become entranced but horrified of what you hear during the Creep Show, it is easy to forget that mental illness still defies modernity, with the claim that at least 25% of our Western population will report psychological illness. Its defiance is symbolized in Aradale itself – its huge array of buildings standing solid and still on a high hill, with the town in the distance, lying flat around it. Some concede that while Aradale is in strident disrepair, it is beyond any cost of restoring it to some respectability. Yet, even if it were restored, what use can be made of the former mental institution beside titillating people's minds with the Creep Shows, and without losing the memory of its prized history? Actually, Aradale is too costly to destroy and too costly to restore. In its disrepair it stands defiant on that high hill, speaking of mental illness that everywhere beyond its boundaries still refuses to go away.

The era of institutionalised long-term care for mentally ill patients is largely over. Before the turn of the century – around 1993, in fact, Aradale was closed and people, like my brother Robert, were eased back into the community, for compassionate reasons as well as economical ones. There are town doctors responsible for the care of the former inmates still psychologically ill, still being administered drugs, but now given injections that do not leave the patients as docile or stuporous as was the case in former times. Strait jackets and cells for solitary confinement, together with immersion in hot and cold baths are substituted by freedom in many cases, for them to go where they please.

Yet, such freedom can cause anxiety in communities, whenever and wherever mentally ill people lose control, causing harm to themselves and others. This has become apparent with many in our time through drug addiction and alcohol, amongst other causes. Great numbers of people enter hospitals everywhere because of mental illness, hospitals far more humane than places such as Aradale of old. Still, such hospitalization is a form of essential isolation like that of old for the patients' sake and for others in society.

All kinds of causes can be said to attribute to mental illness – an injury, an illness, biochemical imbalances in some cases, a childhood crisis... Such things that we all can suffer to a degree.

In the early days of Aradale and the J Ward for the criminally insane, it is safe to say that there were not a few who could have lived outside such institutions without being a danger to themselves or others. It seems the powers that existed in those days could have with good counsel prevented many from entering or remaining for any length of time in the aforementioned institutions. There was a haste to certify some as insane, it appears, but the authorities were victims of the times, just as the inmates were.

Were there any of yesteryear who could have said with R. Porter, "They called me mad, and I called them mad, and damn them, they outvoted me"? Or, like the Scottish novelist who wrote, "I think for my part one half of the nation is mad – and the other half not very sound."

Still, there is such a thing as mental illness, to such disturbance that everyone to a degree is a victim, even though it may not be always hard to define.

And many a rather well-balanced person knows albeit occasionally perhaps when madness or mental illness is coming on him or her. Think of Shakespeare's King Lear. As King Lear learns that two of his daughters are despising him and being cruelly inhospitable towards him, after he generously parcelled out for them territories of England and an inheritance, he becomes so enraged at their ingratitude that he says to his fool (court jester): "This heart shall break...or ere I'll weep. O fool! I shall go mad." It is a growing madness. Earlier he had exclaimed in fear that he may turn mad: "O! let me not be mad, not mad, sweet heaven! I would not be mad." Later, as madness overthrows him, he resigns: "I fear I am not in my perfect mind." He dies of a broken heart.

Yet, when we are even very young, are we bedevilled by madness or mental illness so that we are conscious victims of shame? I was six, going on seven, when I entered the Sutherland Homes and became alert to what appeared as a set proverb among the inmates there –

" 'Talking to yourself" is the first sign of madness."

When one or two inmates jibed me with the saying, it caused little shame insofar as I did not discontinue talking to myself. I merely continued with what was essentially audible daydreaming out of earshot of everybody. My desire to daydream in this way was such a fierce desire that it was not halted by any shame at thinking that the practice was madness.

What was madness? I was too young to understand there was any illness in what I was constantly indulging in, that certain something that by its nature found me often alone. Being alone did not trouble me.

Even at the age of 12, I must have been still showing "the first sign of madness." It was summer, I was staying with the Willis family on their large sheep farm at Meerlieu for what had become an annual summer holiday with them. Down by the shearing shed I was playing out a dream of being a doubles partner alongside the brilliant, strikingly handsome Lew Hoad, Australia's great tennis player, who in of that year of 1953 had won the Davis Cup for Australia, along with the other teenager Ken Rosewall. Tension was in the air with the American Tony Trabert crouching to return my serve. The crowd became hushed. Lew turned at the net and smiled back at me with confidence. Whoosh! Trabert stood stunned as the thunderbolt serve of mine fled past him. Suddenly, there appeared Bill, Willis's son, on his horse Tom, looking down and chuckling before he rode out of site. It is not possible to describe such shame that struck me and left me blushing. Indeed, for the rest of the holiday, whenever Bill looked my way, I felt ever so small.

As for the first actual sign of madness in history, it is of interest that Graeme Burgin, the aforementioned historian of Ararat, writes –

> "If we take the Bible as the definite early history of human race, it can probably be said that the problem goes right to the creation....(when) Cain attacked his brother Abel and murdered him. It could be said that this was caused by a jealous rage, surely a form of mental illness when taken to the extreme of murder."

Indeed, many on a murder trial have escaped judgement with impunity on the grounds that a fit of insanity overcame them. Cain received some form of unusual mercy but still had to suffer the consequences of his jealous rage.

There is much in what Christians believe to be God's word, a divinely-inspired history of mankind, to have even people who are not Christians to pay more than a passing interest in its accounts that reveal how the blazing wheel of fiery madness has been rolling down the long hill of history, and how we all without exception have been affected by what theologians call the Fall, even if there be varying degrees of mental illness. When that someone aforementioned said somewhat jokingly: "I think for my part one half of the nation is mad – and the other not very sound," it is felt that many a true word is spoken in jest.

We can afford to jest to some degree about mental abnormality, if it appears harmless, and I guess that such abnormality as I have written concerning myself was harmless to others perhaps but, in particular the self-consciousness of being an orphan and living what should have been formative and more normal years than in an institution for neglected children, was a vexing one in my thinking after I left the place. For years I pretended Cyril and Beryl Smith were my actual parents whenever I was cornered into covering up my past. As for what Sutherland's inmates deemed as "the first sign of madness" in talking out loud to myself, maybe the second sign of madness was playing the game of pretence with a surname that gave relief when cornered and showed "dis-ease" within me.

Yes, I loathed it even as a young man when 'Auntie Lil' spoke to strangers about me being an 'orphan' while I was on holidays with her and her husband at Preston, and while still living in the institution – imagining that I was meant to be looked on as an object of pity, even someone abnormal.

On leaving Sutherland I did not know enough about human nature to realise that it is rare for people to ask about one's early life. I imagined people would be asking about it far more often than I anticipated, and therefore I feared needlessly in that regard. When through certain circumstances people would ask about 'family', I felt compelled to keep up appearances to mislead them, never saying too much, so as to provoke curiosity. Yet it was rare for it to happen.

Well, I feared needlessly.

In coming out in the open about early years in the institution, I am tempted to be proud of the uniqueness of having lived in Sutherland, together with a unique family history. Yet I add this: life is a balance: the quest to remain humble as against the readiness to be proud.

My desire is to tip the scales in favour of humility, but before becoming a believer in Christ at 17 years of age, I scarcely knew what humility was. I found it by having the mind of Christ. I still like the King James Version of Philippians 2:5 –

> "Let this mind be in you, which was also in Christ Jesus."

By having the mind of Christ I can see upon reflection that when people discover about my past as a boy, it becomes an encouragement for them. To paraphrase Paul's words in his letter to the Philippian Christians –

> "Since I have encouragement from being united with Christ, since I have known the comfort of His love and known the fellowship of the Holy Spirit, since I have experienced divine tenderness and compassion, then I am able to make others' joy complete – others who are like-minded, who had the same love, and the same spirit and purpose."

Once it became more widely known about my early life, believers in Christ in particular could see how God surprisingly and wonderfully revealed

Himself when I was still living in the institution. While it was described as an institution for *neglected children*, it became the place where I learnt that I was one of God's *accepted children* in Christ. Believers were heartened to learn that the testimony of God's sovereign grace was clear to see at work in me all those years ago. The chapter in *The Silver Poplar* called "From Death to Life" was the key to the book. One pastor-friend praised my honesty. One friend wrote of God's care "when everything was against (me)." Others were so stirred upon reading the book that they gave it to loved ones in the hope that God's truth would speak to them too. Another friend said it was "a faith-inspiring work."

Imagine if I had remained silent about my early life. Everyone is to know rationally it was not my fault that I was as good as an orphan when I entered Sutherland as a six-year-old. That I became a neglected child – in a true sense a rejected child – was entirely out of my hands. Madness lends itself to the irrational, and to what can become a sickening occupation with self. Blame could be at the feet of those who early led to the neglect of me, but shame on my part was out of order. Thank God (in the true sense of it) that I came to learn that in being saved by grace, it is to be "Less of self and more of Thee."

When at 18 I attended my first Belgrave Heights Convention, a certain hymn arrested me (as mentioned previously) so that on my return to the institution I sang it over and over. I was blessed with a good memory for words of songs in those days and, without the aid of the Convention's hymn book, I knew the hymn's four verses with their telling phrase at the end of every sixth line of the stanzas.

You will recall, the hymn passes progressively from speaking of "All of self, and none of Thee" to finally "None of self, and all of Thee" –

> "All of self, and none of Thee,"
> "Some of self, and some of Thee,"
> "Less of self, and more of Thee,"

"None of self, and all of Thee."

I had been assigned to water daily the institution's sizeable summer pumpkin patch. As I walked around among the yellow trumpet flowers, and any number of small grey pumpkins appearing here and there hidden beneath the large sheltering leaves, with the morning sun having early risen, I sang well out of earshot the hymn that filled my heart with such joy that I felt that there was none of self and all of the Lord. The convention had set my soul on fire. Oh, how I loved the Lord!

Often I reflect on those early 'days of May,' when it seemed I had more joy then – that I thought on God with less distractions. Yet, in a few years after those early 'days of May,' I discovered through trials that there was more of self than I first realised. With God at work in me, joy did not leave me entirely as I trusted in Him, but each day was more searching while I learnt there was *much* of self when God left me stranded, so that in a sense there seemed to be *less* of Him in trials.

I saw that I was vulnerable to the way I think. People remark on the good memory I have. I attribute that to being melancholic. As Tim Le Haye has said: When having a melancholic temperament, it means harbouring "the great ability to suggest images to the screen of the imagination – probably in living colour with stereophonic sound." I survive on memories – much of life still sees me dwelling on memories. Many memories are beautiful, bringing untold joy. I mull on them – they age like good wine. However, they can be the devil of me so that they conjure up sadness at times.

The tendency to feel miserable at length, however, about perfectionism that could not be attained has been to a good measure overcome.

I know readers of *'The Silver Poplar'* appreciated the honesty and the openness of what was written.

If I am in any way insane, I want to be as insane as Christ! Christ was considered mad, or having a fit of madness, according to His own family at one stage – so Mark tells us. And yet, how could He do so much good, and even cure mad men? Mark in his gospel tells us at length how a certain demoniac was instantly healed by Jesus when no-one else could restrain the fellow. I love that story. It tells of the man no longer demon-possessed, sitting at Jesus' feet, "dressed and in his right mind." Even if one has not known the extremity of insanity that the unfortunate fellow knew, it is uplifting to think that Jesus is concerned that we are in our right mind.

Yes, even Paul the apostle of Christ was accused of being out of his mind, with Governor Festus shouting at the apostle as he spoke of the good news of salvation: "Your great learning is driving you insane." Festus knew enough to know that there are people whose great learning does drive them mad, but who has ever heard of an insane person such as Paul saying "I am not insane?" And "What I am saying is reasonable and true"?

Paul was convinced that he would witness for God in Rome – oceans away from where he spoke to Festus. Here is another thing that may suggest to some that Paul was definitely mad. How could he be convinced that he would testify for God in faraway Rome? Humanly speaking, anything could have happened to prevent him from reaching Rome, even though the succeeding governor of Jerusalem in Felix imperially allowed Paul to go to Rome to make an appeal to Caesar for his freedom and protection from his opponents the Jews.

In setting sail to Italy under the guard of a Roman centurion, the journey was fraught with danger. Things occurred that were unexpected, incidents that almost spelt the end of all lives on board on the boat, including the life of Paul. Against the advice of Paul, the captain of the ship exposed all on board to the dreaded "Northeaster." The ship became easy prey to that wild wind so that Luke, Paul's companion, said "We finally gave up all hope of being saved."

Neither sun nor stars appeared to them day after day as the storm raged.

Then unexpectedly an angel of God appeared to Paul who was the virtual commander of the ship with God's help. He faced the unexpected of the voyage – doubtless with some trepidation – but he had faith in God and gave wise counsel at critical times.

Even when the ship reached Malta, the soldiers aboard wanted to kill all the prisoners including Paul because, if the prisoners had escaped from their guard, they could expect to lose their lives under Rome's martial law. As it was, the centurion prevented the soldiers from executing their plan because he wanted Paul's life saved.

Paul's voyage to Rome reminds us that life is full of the unexpected – some things to our sadness, others to our joy.

Even before I became a believer in Christ, God was at work to achieve His good purpose. Even adverse circumstances were being shaped by God as a potter shaping clay. At one time I could have been killed, as *The Silver Poplar* discloses. It was an advantage for my good that as an orphan no-one was interested in adopting me – people were scared off because my mother was in the lunatic asylum of Aradale, and there were fears in the early years that I appeared to inherit her mental condition. I remained in Sutherland, long enough when the time came to be under the guardianship of the Smiths in order to get a good grounding in the things of God. While I became saved after they left the institution, I am sure that eternity will reveal the formidable part they played in planting the seed of God in my mind, ready in its time to germinate.

Then I was blessed to have the Smiths kindly take me in once I left Sutherland, for I had nowhere to live after the institution. Once I was living with them, I had constant Christian fellowship, not only with them but many other believers they knew.

My ministry could be said to have finished with a fizzle. The merge with the larger church at the end made a maelstrom that could have found me bitter and longing for a life that promised peace with little or no perturbance. Yet, despite the disenchantment Kerryn and I knew when robbed of a ministry, we remained firm believers, who rested in the knowledge that we had our fill of the goodness of God.

In the beginning He made me a teacher in order to train me to be in the end a preacher, in a life that has been laced by sweet lingering memories.

My admittance to Coburg Teacher's College went against expectation, for reasons previously stated.

Finally, acceptance by the Baptist Advisory Board was not exactly expected, but I trained at Whitley College for the ministry, and then began the journey with its unexpected twists and turns, together with its pleasant surprises too, enabling me to become God's *expected teacher and preacher! To Him be the glory!*

God in His grace blessed us with many promises for all kinds of circumstances, and I believe that He moved Dr Vose, who at the time was President of The Baptist Union of Australia, to reassure me concerning the kind of ministry I was to have down the years. The words he wrote are worth repeating, for they are still a great comfort to reflect on –

> "I was particularly glad that we had the opportunity to talk together during the School of Theology. It does seem to me that God has given you a significant pastoral teaching ministry, but this is perhaps one of the most difficult roles within the church, as so often it lacks the glamour of missionary or evangelistic service."

So the working of God and the words of Noel Vose were right. Absolutely!

Top: The 1959 group of Eltham High house captains and vice-captains. I am third from the left in the front row. Peter Brock stands behind me as vice-captain.
Bottom: First year at Coburg Teachers' College. In my group I am standing far end of the right in the back row.

Top: My late sister Joyce in her younger days with her beloved terrier "Penny."
Bottom: My first year as a rural school teacher at the tiny timber-milling town of Bulumwaal. The tallest girl was the victim of the kidnap that became the subject of two newspaper articles in the Bairnsdale Advertiser in 1962.

REMAND FOR MILL WORKER

A 34 year-old mill hand was remanded this morning to appear at Bairnsdale Court of Petty Sessions on August 23 on charges of child stealing, assault with a weapon, and being armed with felonious intent.

First Constable K. J. Machen and Constable W. J. Stewart arrested the man in bush near Bullumwaal yesterday after he had allegedly stopped a car and taken a girl with him at gun-point.

Mr. R. E. Lane, J.P., fixed bail at £200.

MAN ON BAIL FOUND DEAD

A 34-year-old man was found dead beside a car at Mount Taylor this morning by a pulpwood cutter.

The dead man was Alfred Markic, an Austrian mill hand, of Bulumwaal, who was due to appear at Bairnsdale Court of Petty Sessions today on a charge of child stealing, two charges of assault with a weapon and one of being armed with a weapon with felonious intent.

After receiving a telephone call from the pulpwood cutter, First Constable W. J. Stewart and Constable Norman Cox went to Mt. Taylor and found that Markic had been shot.

A discharged shotgun was hooked to the radio aerial on the car.

They believe Markic had been dead about two hours before they found him at 8 a.m. Markic was arrested last Sunday morning by First Constables K. J. Machen and W. J. Stewart in the bush near Bulumwaal, after he had allegedly taken a 13-year-old girl with him at gun-point.

Markic was on bail for £200.

Top: A newspaper article that told of the man's arrest.
Bottom: A following article told of the suicide of the man who kidnapped the girl of my Bulumwaal school.

Top: My foster brother Peter and I pictured at our twenty-first birthday celebration. ***Bottom:*** With my foster-brother Peter and foster-parents Beryl and Cyril at the twenty-first birthday party.

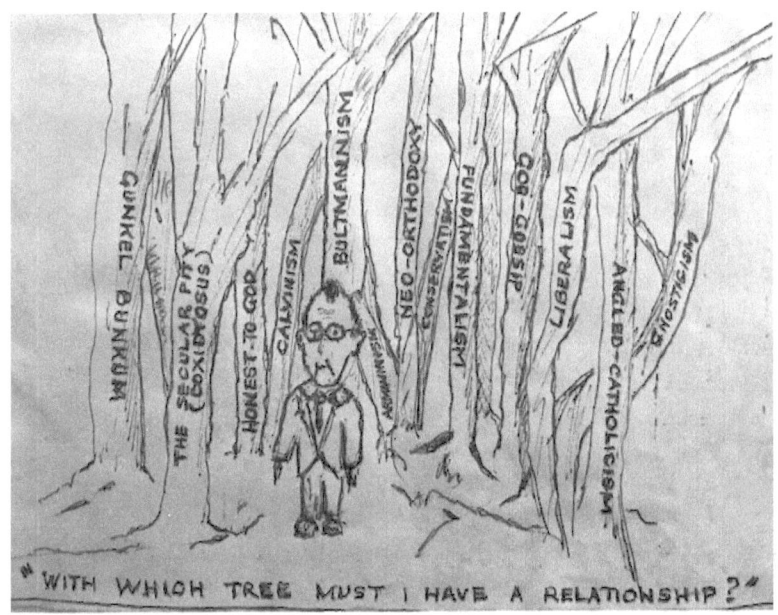

Top: A humorous spin in the shape of a cartoon I drew at Whitley Baptist College in response to Professor Watson's sometime statement "You can't have a relationship with a tree". Above is an esoteric joke that amused friends when we reflected on all the theological "trees" we came face-to-face with at Whitley. A mixture of the orthodox and unorthodox.

Bottom: The town of Ulverstone, Tasmania. One of numerous town railway crossings appears in the foreground. Behind is seen the Zenotaph, and the Baptist Church where I served as pastor for three years.

Top: My late brother Robert reading his Bible on the steps of a pub in Ararat.
Bottom: The entrance to Aradale, "the lunatic asylum" that sat imposingly on a hill overlooking the town of Ararat. My brother and mother spent some years there as patients.

Top: Part of the interior of the vast centre of Aradale, looking towards its entrance. ***Bottom:*** The Ha Ha Wall of Aradale that was designed to discourage Aradale's patients from escaping.

Top: My dear Grade Two teacher, Miss Luxford, pictured with me at her home in Greensborough. Always been a faithful follower of the Lord. ***Bottom:*** My son Stephen sums up cartoon-style much about my life in retirement, to the amusement of my family.

www.ingramcontent.com/pod-product-compliance
Lightning Source LLC
Chambersburg PA
CBHW020346170426
43200CB00005B/70